I0729571

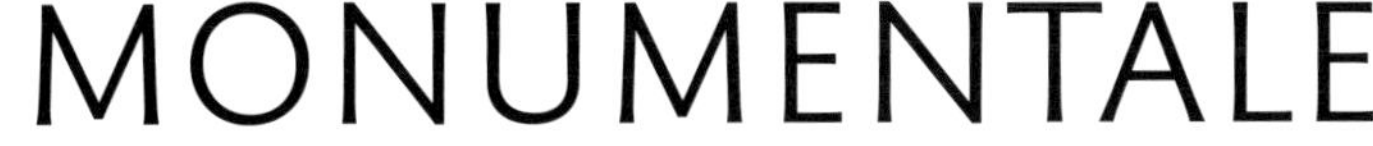

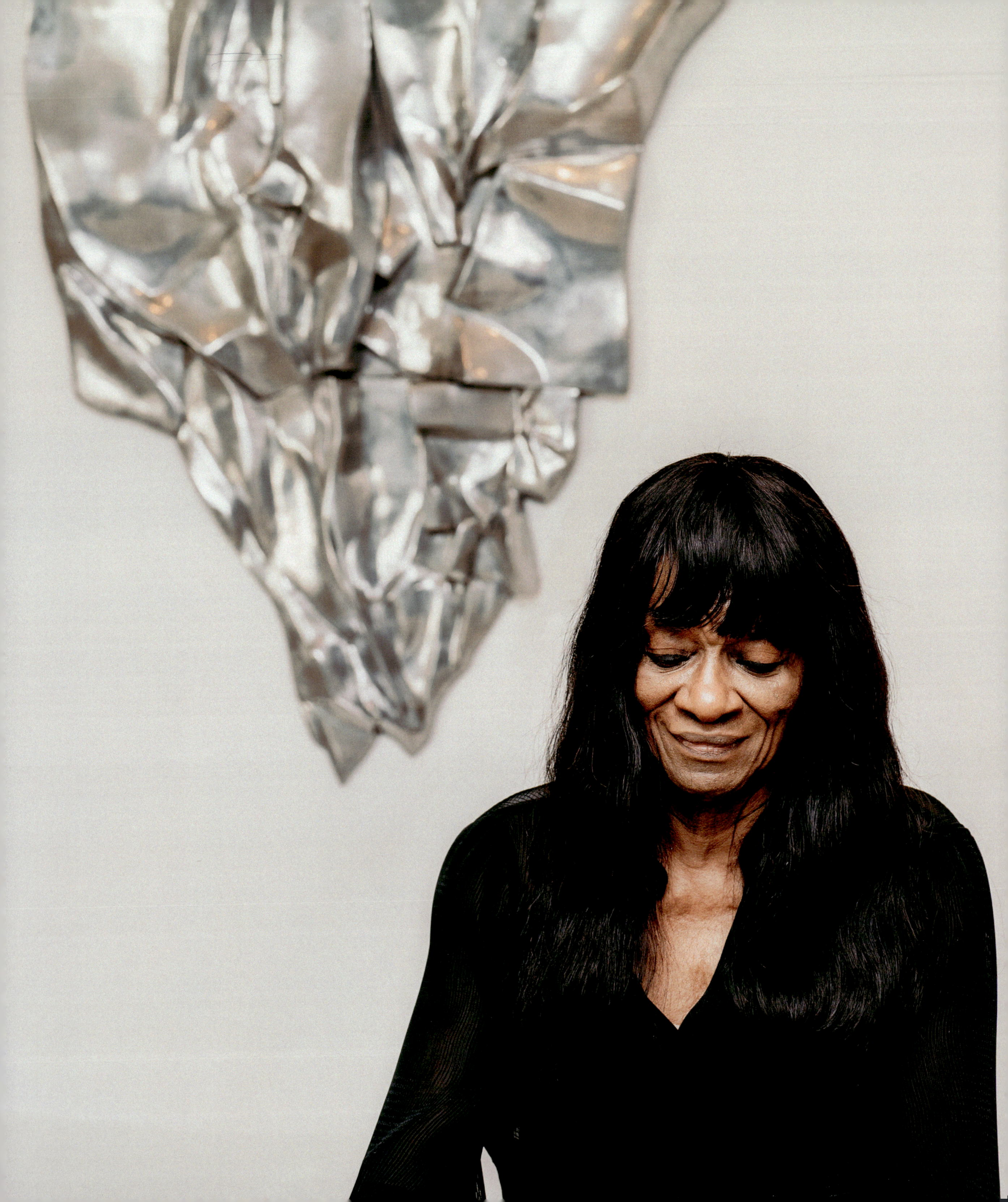

Barbara Chase-Riboud

MONUMENTALE

THE BRONZES

Edited by
Stephanie Weissberg

Contributions by Barbara Chase-Riboud, Christophe Cherix,
Erin Jenoa Gilbert, Reginald Jackson, Courtney J. Martin,
Akili Tommasino, and Stephanie Weissberg

Pulitzer Arts Foundation
In association with Princeton University Press
Princeton and Oxford

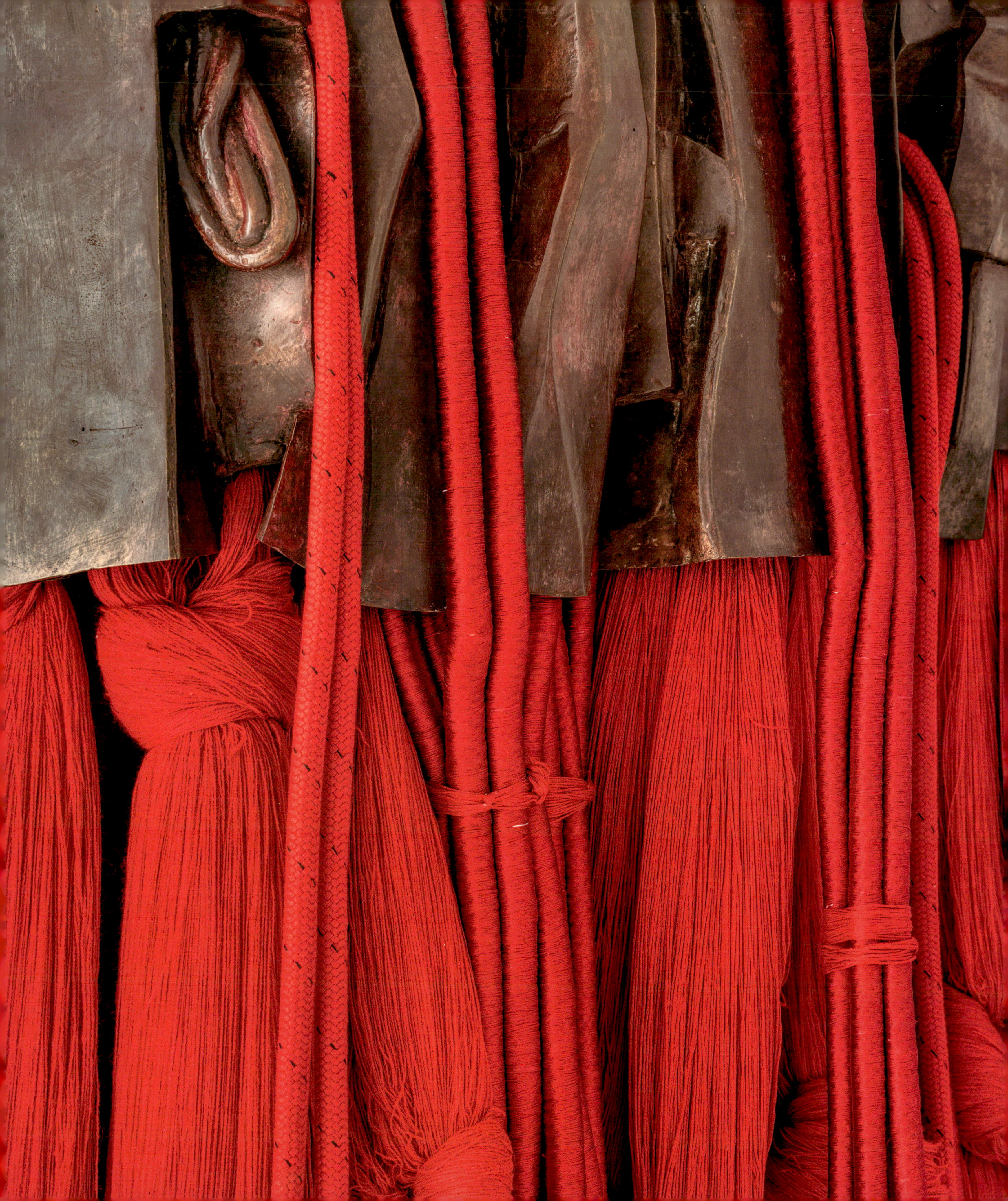

CONTENTS

DIRECTOR'S FOREWORD

With a staggering array of influences and a singular approach to material, Barbara Chase-Riboud is truly exceptional. Through her towering bronzes, intimate works on paper, and poetic reflections on memory and monument, this remarkable artist exhibits an unparalleled aptitude for form, process, and the written word. The retrospective exhibition *Barbara Chase-Riboud Monumentale: The Bronzes*, released in tandem with her lyrical memoir *I Always Knew*, offers unprecedented insight into the artist's trailblazing seven-decade career and extraordinary life. The Pulitzer Arts Foundation is honored to have had the opportunity to collaborate with Chase-Riboud on these groundbreaking projects. We are thrilled to be able to unite, for the first time since their creation, significant bodies of work, such as the monumental *Cleopatra* series. We are likewise delighted to present her sculptures and works on paper alongside her poetry and personal memoirs, which shed new light on the connections between her biography and her artwork. Chase-Riboud's architectural approach to her bronzes and her careful considerations of space are augmented by the installation in the Pulitzer's Tadao Ando–designed building, which seems uniquely suited to complement her work during this retrospective.

I extend my most gracious thanks to the artist for her infectious energy and warmth of spirit throughout our collaboration. I am also deeply grateful to Stephanie Weissberg, curator at the Pulitzer, for championing this one-of-a-kind project, and her thoughtful and steadfast commitment to this important undertaking. For their perceptive contributions to this publication, I would like to thank Christophe Cherix, the Robert Lehman Foundation Chief Curator of Drawings and Prints at the Museum of Modern Art; Courtney J. Martin, Paul Mellon Director at the Yale Center for British Art; Akili Tommasino, associate curator of modern and contemporary art at the Metropolitan Museum of Art; and

Stephanie Weissberg. Their insightful analyses highlight Chase-Riboud's groundbreaking contributions to the field, and offer an unprecedented glimpse into the experiences and touchstones that have informed her practice. Likewise, the oral history conducted by Erin Jenoa Gilbert and the artist's manifesto co-authored by Reginald Jackson offer readers an opportunity to learn from this incomparable artist in her own words. I give special thanks to Ryan Polich, of Marquand Books, for his brilliant design of this catalogue, as well as Donna Wingate of Artist and Publisher Services, Michelle Komie of Princeton University Press, the Pulitzer's former curatorial assistant Katherine B. Harnish, and editor Susan Higman Larsen. Their astute editorial work was critical to the success of this publication.

Barbara Chase-Riboud Monumentale: The Bronzes was made possible by generous loans from more than a dozen cultural institutions and private collections. I offer my profound gratitude to Beth Rudin DeWoody; Thelma Golden, director and chief curator of The Studio Museum in Harlem; Nigel and Ayodele Hart; Stella Jones, Stella Jones Gallery; Glenn D. Lowry, David Rockefeller Director of the Museum of Modern Art; Sean O'Harrow, executive director of the Kemper Museum of Contemporary Art; Komal Shah and Gaurav Garg; Gardy St. Fleur; Sasha Suda, George D. Widener Director and CEO of the Philadelphia Museum of Art; Stephanie Wiles, The Henry J. Heinz II Director of the Yale University Art Gallery; and those lenders who wish to remain anonymous. This exhibition was also made possible by the contributions of so many others, who supported us in numerous ways. For their continuous assistance across so many aspects of the show, I extend my warmest gratitude to Marilyn Paed-Rayray and again to Erin Jenoa Gilbert.

The multifarious talents of the Pulitzer staff have ensured the success of *Barbara Chase-Riboud Monumentale: The Bronzes* at all stages. I would like to express my most sincere appreciation to Kristin Fleischmann Brewer, deputy director of public engagement; Natalie M. Foster, registrar; Steve Gibbs, lead preparator; Charlie Hoppe, visitor associate; Brittny Koskela, assistant registrar and publications manager; Danielle Kronmiller, curatorial administrative assistant; Tamara H. Schenkenberg, curator; Shane Simmons, director of exhibition design and installation; and Heather Alexis Smith, curatorial associate, along with our dedicated colleagues in the Marketing and Communications, Public Engagement, and Visitor Experience departments. Finally, I offer my deepest gratitude to Board Chair Emily Rauh Pulitzer and to all members of the Pulitzer's Board of Directors. Their support and enthusiasm is a steadfast beacon every step of the way.

Cara Starke
Executive Director, Pulitzer Arts Foundation

"I BUILD MY MONUMENT"

Courtney J. Martin

For many years, predating my own entry to Yale University as a graduate student in the early aughts, I was captivated by the lore of Barbara Chase-Riboud's school days. Despite the thinness of the (art) history of her long and accomplished (across a number of fields) artistic career, the stories that I heard about her time there rose to the level of myth. She seemed to have emerged from nowhere specific to successfully conquer that overdetermined place (Yale) before bursting out to captivate the world. When I returned to New Haven to take up the directorship of the Yale Center for British Art, she gave me a copy of her Cleopatra-inspired melologue, *Portrait of a Nude Woman as Cleopatra* (1987). While reading it I was reminded of all that she represented to me and the ways in which her reimaging found the Egyptian queen ready to actively construct a life rather than passively existing. "I build my monument," ends the first verse, as if Cleopatra's ancient journey can only be fully understood in architectural allusion. Perhaps we should expect no less from Chase-Riboud, whose own journey to the present began with the pursuit of building.

When Barbara Chase arrived in New Haven in the fall of 1958 to study architecture, she was among a handful of women on the urban campus. Though women had been a part of the School of Fine Arts since 1869, when two daughters of a professor were admitted into its first class—thus making the university's graduate and professional schools coeducational —the first female undergraduates did not matriculate until 1969, a full twenty years after the first woman graduated with an architecture degree in 1949. The years 1869, 1949, and 1969 plot points on a graph to suggest one aspect of the singularity of Chase-Riboud's experiences at Yale between 1958 and 1960. The other aspect, of course, is race.

She entered as a burgeoning architect, following the thwarted trajectory of her father, who had hoped to join the profession but had been denied access to education, and mentors who, perhaps, mistook her

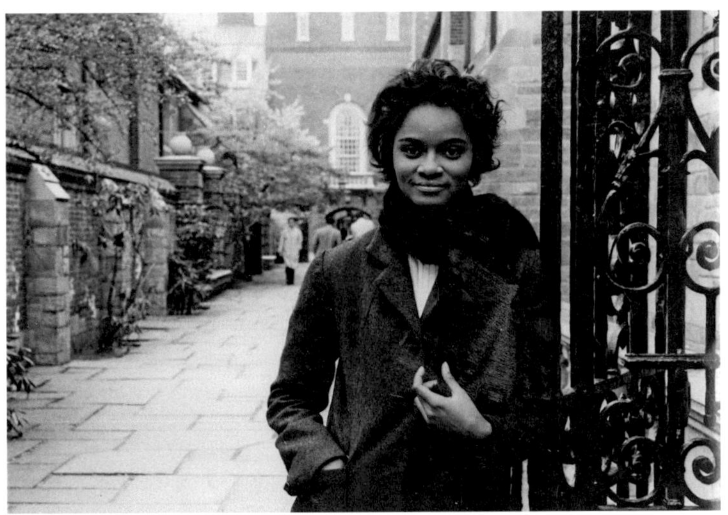

Barbara Chase-Riboud as a student at Yale University, 1960

facility in drafting, proportion, and scale to be indicative of a future architect. Whatever the reason, by her second year, she had, for herself and to herself, transitioned from the pursuit of designing buildings to making structures, avowedly declaring herself not generically an artist but specifically a sculptor.

As she changed, so did the program. In 1959, her second year, the School of Art and Architecture emerged from the School of Fine Arts as a professional school in its own right. Throughout the years, she has noted the influence of a number of eminent professors that speaks to the ways in which her heterogeneity would have been acknowledged, encouraged, and, if not fully nurtured, then at least modeled at Yale. These include Josef Albers, the Bauhaus and Black Mountain College theorist-painter who brought design to the fore and on par with painting and sculpture; Philip Johnson, a practicing architect and the founder of the Museum of Modern Art's Department of Architecture, who established the museum, writ large, as a place of conceptual exploration for the built environment; the architect Louis Kahn, whose drawings of places and spaces demonstrate his equal access to the technical and the artistic; and Paul Rand, the famed commercial artist whose dominance in American consumer visuality transported to generations of graphic design students the ability to work in and between the fields of art and design. Even the school's dean, Gibson Danes (they both arrived in 1958), was an art historian, trained initially in an art school.

The absence of women from this list reflects the patriarchal administrative structure of both the school and the field of architecture at the time, but Chase-Riboud had a close friend in fellow student Sheila Hicks, the textile artist. Another peer, Eva Hesse (Yale College 1959), engaged with the same teachers and critics, and would, like Chase-Riboud, define the contours and expanses of post-Minimalism as a direct material and conceptual restructuring of three-dimensional art-making. Situated among this trio and against the backdrop of their training at Yale, sculpture is materially experimental, large and radical in form.

Chase-Riboud's time at Yale came just a few years after the reopening of Kahn's first major commission, the concrete, glass, and steel addition to the Yale University Art Gallery. The semitransparent building included studio and exhibition spaces that seemed to invite students, like Chase-Riboud, to undertake the fluidity of the overlap between the disciplines. Seen in this light, her shift from one discipline to another while at the university is less a replacement of one for another and more a refinement of her craft by deftly using the variety of resources available to and provided for her. Almost immediately she put the intricate knowledge of structure and materials required of an architect to good use as a sculptor, frequently of large-scale works. Upon graduation in the spring of 1960, she had already produced her first public commission.

My office in the final Louis Kahn structure has a large, rectilinear window from which I can look out and across to the buildings in which Chase-Riboud once took classes, viewed art, and began to build the life that she would someday inhabit. This exhibition and its catalogue will go some way toward making those successes known and furthering an exploration of her incomparable practice.

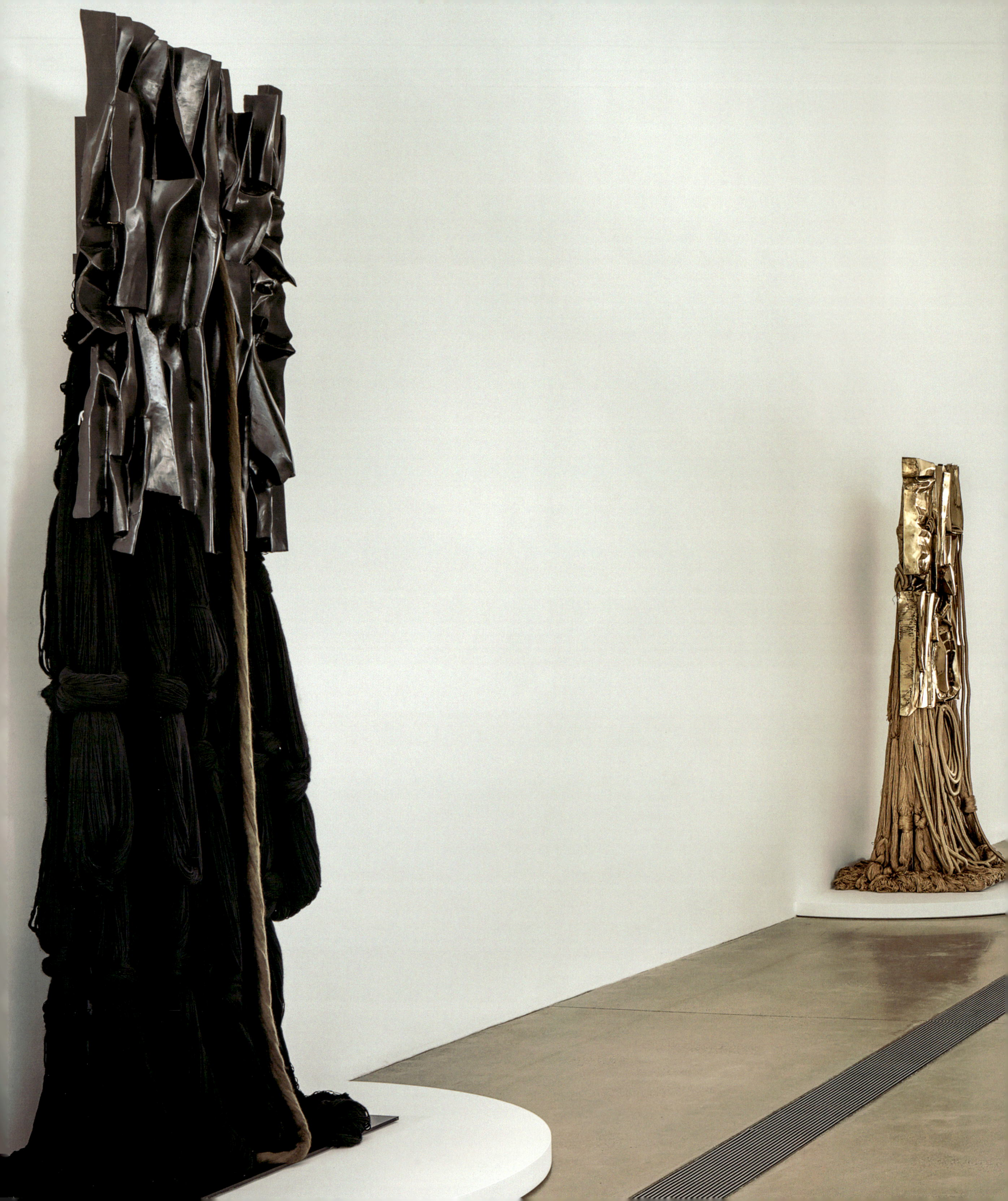

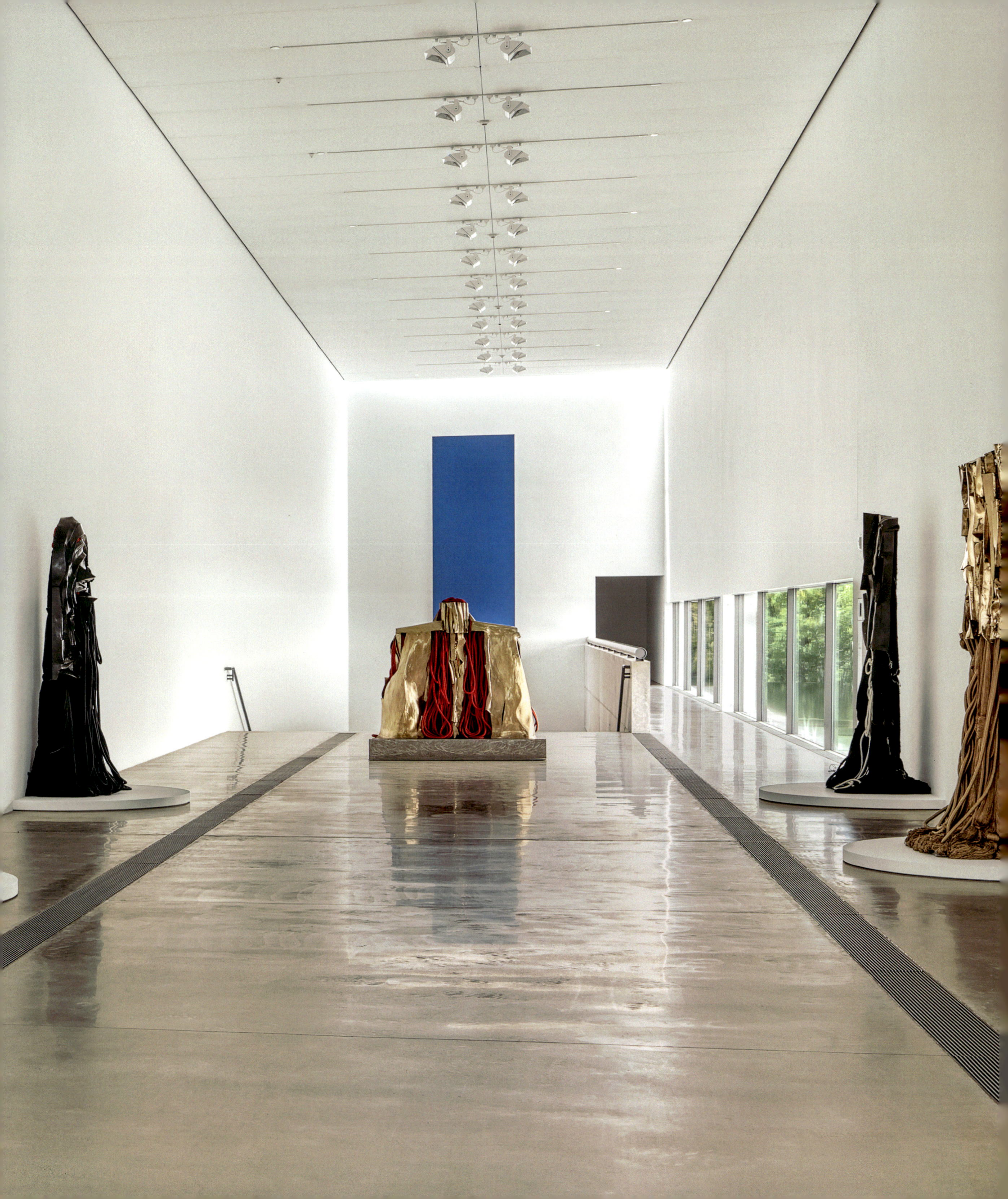

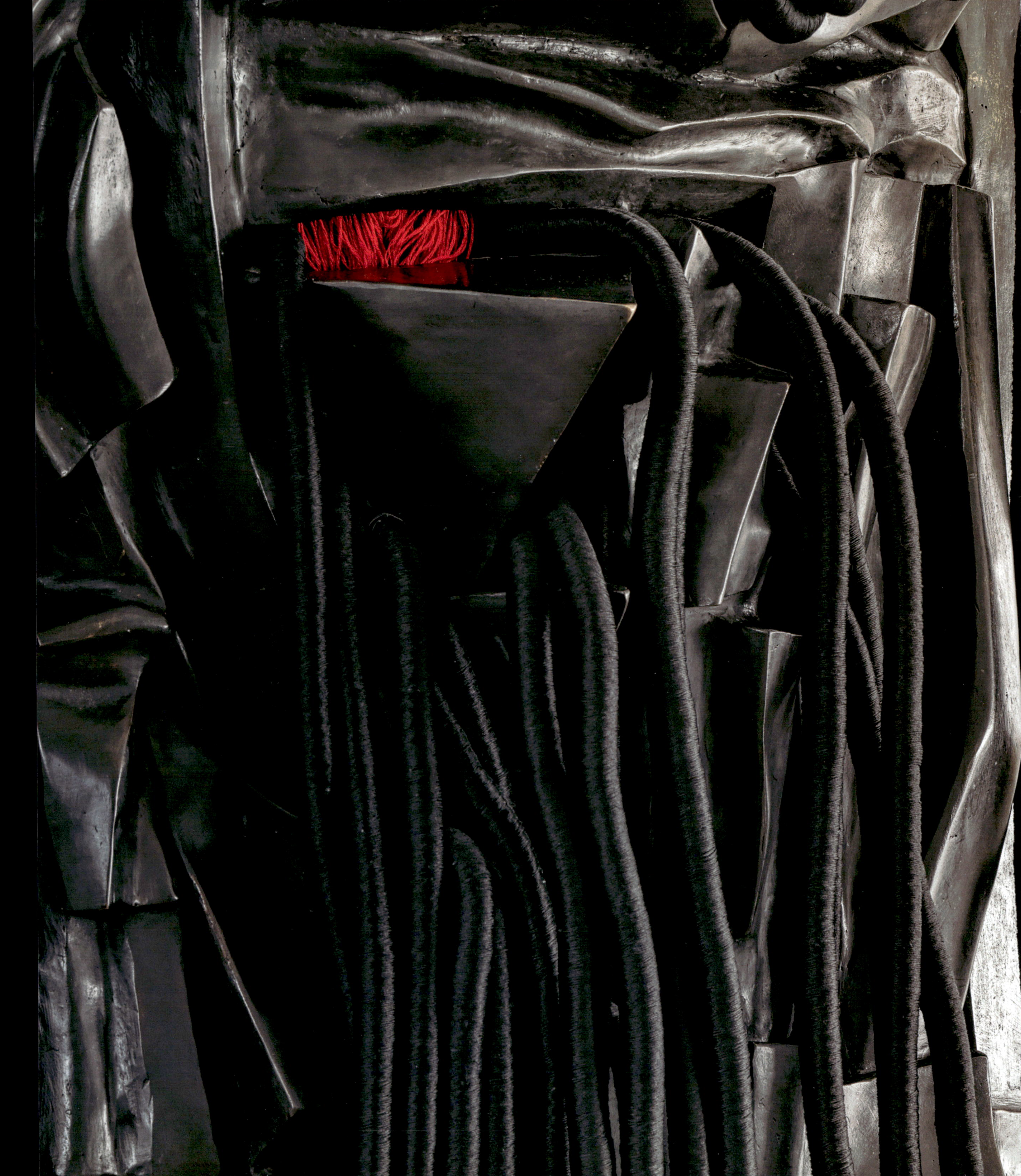

INDELIBLE

Stephanie Weissberg

In many ways, Barbara Chase-Riboud is peerless. Working in Paris since the early 1960s, the American sculptor established a visual style that offered a dramatic departure from the predominant movements of the time. In a number of mediums, particularly bronze, she developed a hybrid style, embracing and innovating centuries-old techniques that had long fallen out of favor. While her mostly white male counterparts pursued the machine-made aesthetics of Minimalism, she paved her own way with a series of historic firsts, gaining recognition early in her career in both academic and professional spheres. Her ambition and talents were not limited to her artistic practice, however; by the early 1970s, she had embarked on a literary career that would attain equal creative importance and match the recognition she received for her work in sculpture. *Barbara Chase-Riboud Monumentale: The Bronzes* examines her remarkable six-plus-decade career and brings her contributions to the field of sculpture—material innovation, stylistic originality, and the discourse of memory and monuments—into focus.

Since the beginning of her mature practice in the late 1960s, Chase-Riboud has pushed bronze, her signature material, to its limits. Using lost-wax casting, a process dating to the Bronze Age, she forms metal into ultra-thin sheets with complex pleats, undercuts, and folds that could not be achieved with any other method. The artist has built on the legacy developed by abstract sculptors making monumental work in bronze, including Constantin Brancusi and Barbara Hepworth, by introducing fiber, a contrasting yet complementary material, into her artworks. This innovation has allowed Chase-Riboud to create the illusion that bronze, a medium associated with heft, permanence, and memorialization, is levitating atop bases of silk and wool. She is drawn to the fibers for their inherent, natural strength; countering perceptions

Barbara Chase-Riboud, *Malcolm X #19*, 2017 (detail). Bronze with black patina, silk, wool, polished cotton, and synthetic fibers with steel support. 89¼ × 44 × 27 inches (226.7 × 111.8 × 68.6 cm)

that they are fragile and ephemeral materials associated with the labor of women, she positions them as indelible.

Chase-Riboud's unique perspective has been formed through her remarkable voyages and education, which few women—and even fewer women of color—from her generation achieved. An avid world traveler, the artist has developed a visual language that is fundamentally global and transhistorical. She synthesizes an array of materials, forms, and techniques drawn from the modernist avant-garde in Paris, the Italian Baroque, Chinese and West African bronzes, and ancient Egyptian statuary. The result is a singular visual vocabulary that reflects her interest in light and surface, monumentality, and the tension that comes from harnessing opposing forces. Her approach to form is also situated with an attention to architecture and space, cultivated while she was a student in the graduate architecture program at Yale University.

Chase-Riboud's engagement with monuments is a key aspect of her practice, and for much of her career, including in her most well-known bodies of work, she has memorialized important yet under-recognized or misunderstood historical figures, often women and people of African descent. Each of her sculptures has a carefully considered relationship to its context. She often describes her bronzes as "steles," slabs or pillars, often with relief carvings, embedded in the wall of a tomb or memorial site. By employing abstract visual language while simultane-ously overturning conventional associations of metal and fiber, Chase-Riboud complicates centuries-old aesthetic traditions of Western monuments as indestructible markers of European-Anglo male influence. With few peers working at her scale and ambition, she has offered a diverse and global chronicle of human achievement while helping to pave the way for a younger generation of artists to redefine abstraction and memory in sculpture.

Beginnings

Barbara Chase-Riboud was born in 1939 in Philadelphia. Her mother was a British Canadian immigrant who became a medical technician in histology. Her father had ambitions of studying architecture at the University of Pennsylvania, but after being denied admission because of his race, he pursued a career as a contractor. After showing promise from a very young age in both academic and arts courses, Chase-Riboud was accepted to the elite, private Philadelphia High School for Girls, where she would be in the first integrated class. In 1952 she enrolled in the Tyler School of Fine Arts at Temple University, where she received classical training in bronze casting, wood and stone carving, engraving, and draftsmanship. At the end of her first year, her professors decided she should pursue sculpture as her attention to form was remarkable. Chase-Riboud later reflected on the decision, conceding, "Color, for me, didn't exist."[1] In addition to teaching the fundamentals, Boris Blai, the program chair, and Raphael Sabatini, the head of sculpture, both of whom spent their formative years in Europe, promoted travel and stressed the fine arts within a liberal arts context with the former, arguing, "It is the principle of the school that students . . . are individuals who must contribute to the life and development of society at large."[2]

After graduating, Chase-Riboud followed the advice of Blai and Sabatini to broaden her focus beyond the United States and pursue a

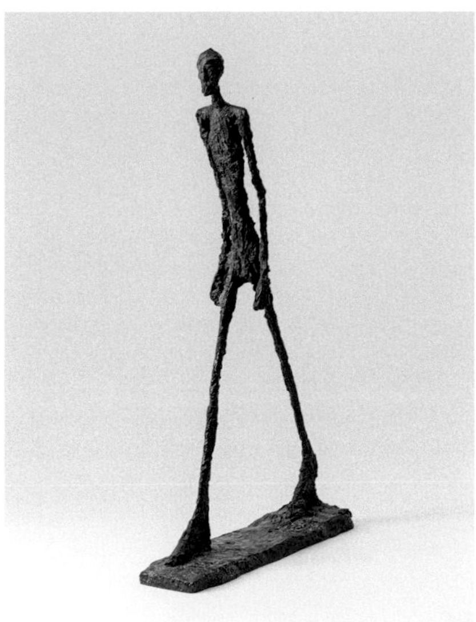

Fig. 1 Alberto Giacometti (1901–1966), *L'Homme qui marche II*, 1960. Bronze, cast 4/6, 74½ × 11½ × 43¾ inches (188.5 × 29.1 × 111.2 cm); inscription: "Susse Fondeur Paris." Fondation Beyeler, Riehen/Basel, Beyeler Collection

more international stage. She accepted a John Hay Whitney Fellowship at the American Academy in Rome, where she was the first female black resident. Her journey began in 1957 when she sailed across the Atlantic. During this voyage she began writing to her mother, a practice she would continue over the next fifty years. These letters, recently released under the title *I Always Knew*, act as a kind of memoir. They trace Chase-Riboud's incremental development from a young student to an internationally recognized sculptor and writer, and offer an intimate glimpse into her unfiltered thoughts on her art, personal life, and the historical events and figures that would shape the zeitgeist of the times.

During her year-long fellowship at the Academy, Chase-Riboud, who was working on a fixed budget, produced mostly small-scale figurative works of cast bronze modeled in clay. After earning money as an extra in the film *Ben-Hur*, the artist was able to finance her largest bronze to date. *Adam and Eve* (1958), a seven-and-a-half-foot sculpture, depicts two figures at the border between figuration and abstraction, huddled together under the sloping Tree of Knowledge. Like much of her work from the period, the slender elongated forms and rough-hewn surfaces share a resemblance with the work of Alberto Giacometti (fig. 1). While the scale of *Adam and Eve* was unprecedented for Chase-Riboud, it was not the most significant breakthrough she would make during her time in Rome.

Her most important development came through collaboration with workers at a local foundry, who showed her how to use lost-wax casting to produce deep undercuts in bronze.[3] As Chase-Riboud later reflected, "I knew the only way to do serious undercutting was to do it in wax and not to do a mold which would amputate the forms . . . then I was on my way."[4] The technique of sculpting and heating the wax introduces great unpredictability into the process, a factor Chase-Riboud embraced rather than resisted. Unlike other casting methods, lost-wax casting does not allow for the serial production of many sculptures from a single mold. In contrast to the widespread popularity of seriality among her Minimalist and Pop art contemporaries, Chase-Riboud used each of her singular sculptures as an opportunity to experiment with new forms and techniques.

One of the earliest works she produced with this new method was *The Last Supper* (1958; fig. 2). The work represents the early formations of two building blocks that would become foundational to her career—both the lost-wax casting technique and a growing sphere of international influences. The modestly scaled bronze includes thirteen forms arranged lengthwise across a horizontal plane. Here, Judas is represented with the letter "X" and Christ with a cross, while the figure in the place of Philip the Apostle takes the form of a Kota reliquary figure (*mbulu ngulu*). Such figures were created as guardians for the dead by the people of present-day Gabon. It would be a number of years before Chase-Riboud traveled to Senegal and Algiers, where she would be exposed to a diverse array of African art and critical dialogues that would deeply inform her practice. At this early stage in her career, however, the citation may reflect the influence of such modernists as Pablo Picasso, Henri Matisse, and Paul Klee, who co-opted iconography from African visual culture, including Kota reliquaries, as a base for the language of Cubism and Expressionism in the early part of the twentieth century.

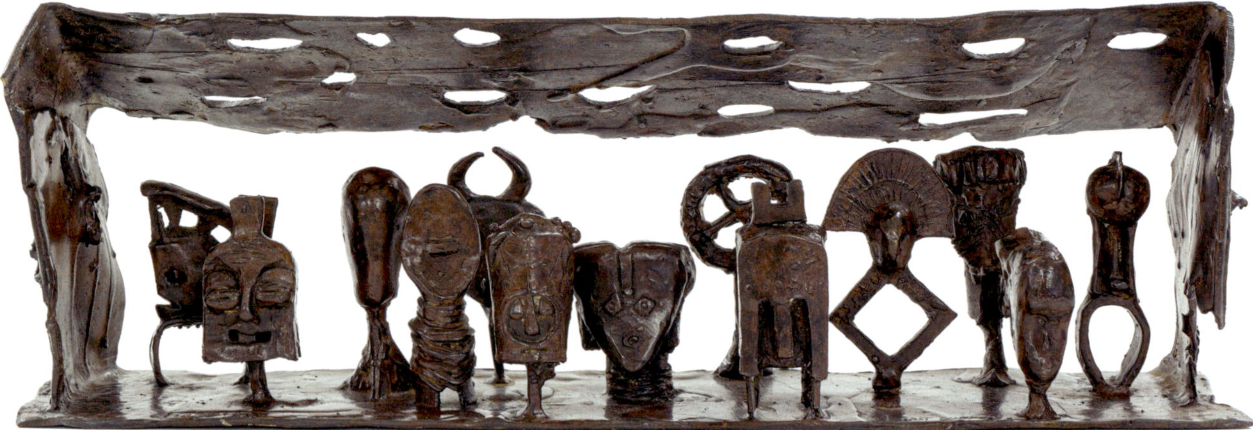

While in Rome, Chase-Riboud also drew inspiration from the Baroque art and architecture that surrounded her. In particular, she was inspired by Gian Lorenzo Bernini's expressive and elaborate rendering of bronze, making it appear "as flexible as wax."[5] She has since reflected on the impact of witnessing *The Ecstasy of Saint Teresa* (1647–52), his iconic work in white marble and bronze, in which he "used drapery as abstraction and its surface modeling is a prominent fact in supporting the work's emotional power" (fig. 3). Notably, Bernini's saint seems to float in midair, encompassed by radiating rays of gilded bronze light and positioned in careful consideration of the surrounding niche to create a unified composition. While the influence of Bernini is less apparent during this period, Chase-Riboud would spend much of her career harnessing the emotive power of bronze through her expert handling of abstraction, surface, and space.

Of equal or greater importance to Chase-Riboud's exposure to the Baroque was her direct experience with ancient Egyptian art and architecture. Several months into her fellowship, the artist took a month-long trip to Egypt, traveling up the Nile to visit Alexandria, Cairo, and Khartoum. Describing the significance of this encounter, Chase-Riboud reflected,

> It was the first time I realized there was such a thing as non-European art. For someone exposed only to the Greco Roman tradition, it was a revelation. I suddenly saw how insular the Western world was vis-à-vis the nonwhite, non-Christian world. The blast of Egyptian culture was irresistible. The sheer magnificence of it. The elegance and perfection, the timeliness, the depth. After that, Greek and Roman art looked like pastry to me. Though I didn't know it at the time, my own transformation was part of the historical transformation of the blacks that began in the '60's.[6]

Chase-Riboud's trip to Egypt came six years before Malcolm X's highly publicized 1964 sojourn to Cairo and later sub-Saharan Africa, which further fueled the already burgeoning movement to reclaim Egypt from

Fig. 2 Barbara Chase-Riboud, *The Last Supper*, 1958. Bronze, 9 × 26⅜ × 5⅞ inches (23 × 67 × 15 cm). Private collection

Fig. 3 Gian Lorenzo Bernini (1598–1680), *The Ecstasy of Saint Teresa*, 1647–52. Cornaro Chapel, Santa Maria della Vittoria, Rome

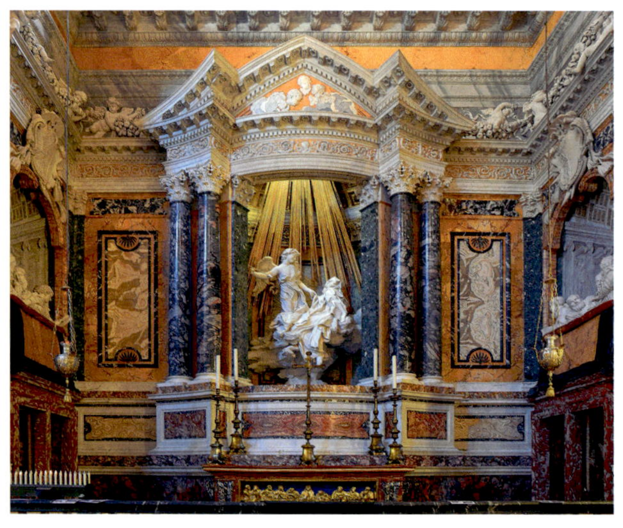

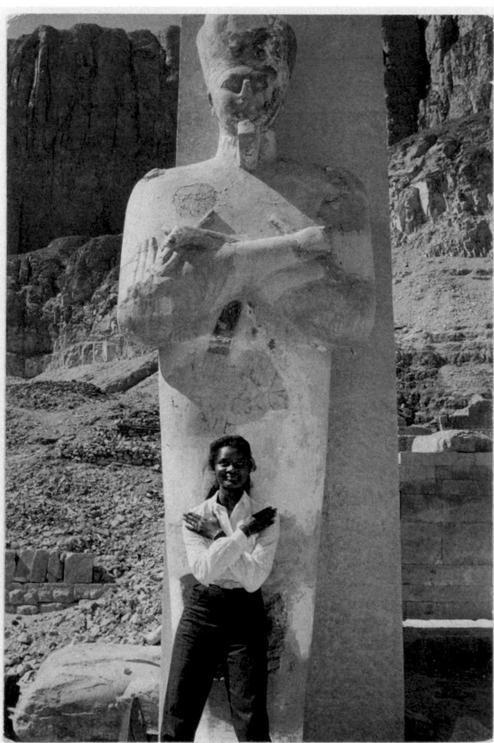

Fig. 4 Barbara Chase-Riboud in the Valley of Kings, Egypt, 1957

the historical narrative of European classicism and acknowledge its true lineage as an African civilization. A photograph taken by the Swiss photographer René Burri shows the young Chase-Riboud dwarfed against the lower portion of a pharaonic statue (fig. 4). Throughout her career, references to ancient Egypt have run deep in Chase-Riboud's work, both formally in her formidable, vertical forms with strong frontal presentations and conceptually in linkages to the architectural and political legacy of the great civilization.

Chase-Riboud's time in Rome proved to be hugely influential for her technical and intellectual development as an artist. Her early trajectory was so impressive, in fact, that while still in Italy she was recruited to attend Yale University's School of Design and Architecture (now the Yale School of Architecture). She began coursework in 1958 and made history by becoming the first African American graduate of the program in 1960. She enrolled initially with a focus on architecture, studying with Louis Kahn and Philip Johnson, among others. Through these courses, she furthered her training in draftsmanship and developed a greater appreciation for the relationship between form and space. After her first year in the program, she transitioned from architecture to visual art in the Department of Design under the tutelage of the department chair Josef Albers, who reinforced professionalism, technical discipline, and rigorous thinking.[7] Though Albers placed great emphasis on color, Chase-Riboud devoted the lion's share of her attention to form. For her thesis submission, she produced a public fountain made from cast steel (fig. 5).[8] With this ambitious abstract sculpture of monumental scale, she signaled many of the core facets she would continue to pursue as her career progressed.

Shortly after graduating in August of 1960, Chase-Riboud moved to London with her then-fiancé, the noted architect James Stirling. She would later pay tribute to him and acknowledge the importance of his architectural vision on her thinking with her poem "For Sir James Stirling (1929–1991)." In this concrete poem, she makes literary reference to global architectural forms such as pyramids, cathedrals, and skyscrapers,

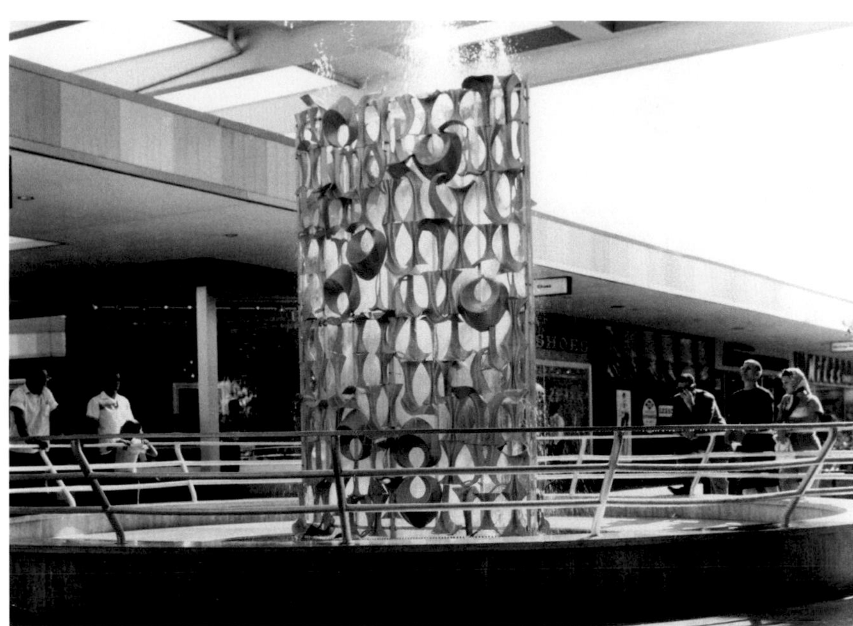

Fig. 5 Barbara Chase-Riboud, *Wheaton Plaza Fountain*, 1960. Aluminum and water, 192 × 98 × 11 inches (487.7 × 248.9 × 27.9 cm). Wheaton, MD. No longer extant

while underlining her interest in space by arranging the words graphically. By the fall of 1960, she had broken off the engagement and relocated to Paris, where she would marry the photojournalist Marc Riboud in 1961. There she started to develop her style independent of academia for the first time. Without the funds to work at the scale she had realized in an institutional context, by 1962 she turned to found materials as a source of inspiration. Spurred by a chance encounter with a large collection of animal remains at a local taxidermist, she created bronzes from cast bones. Her works from this period are figurative and reminiscent of those by such Surrealists as Giacometti and Germaine Richier, which provided inspiration for her early work. Sculptures like *Le Couple* (The Couple) (1963; fig. 6) combine expressive abstraction with the verticality and stability of ancient Egyptian statuary.

By 1962 Chase-Riboud had established a relationship with Bronzalumax foundry in Paris, where over the next several years she began working on a new series of sculptures made from sand-cast aluminum.[9] In contrast to the lost-wax process, sand casting relies on an intermediary model that can be reused to create multiples. A number of the works she produced with this method came to be known as her *Time Womb* series, the first of which were finished in 1967. These aluminum forms are a significant departure from her previous bone sculptures. With more pared-down geometric forms and a highly burnished finish, they indicate an attention to surface and its interaction with light. The *Time Womb* works also represent the first sculptures in which the artist employed textiles. She integrated both loosely gathered strands and tightly woven cords of silk, which were dyed to match the aluminum. The fibers were either suspended below, rested on, or nestled within her cast-aluminum forms. While the artist does not directly link these works to feminism or motherhood, it is hard to ignore the circumstances of her own personal experience of birthing her two sons in 1964 and 1967, as well as the burgeoning second-wave feminist movement that gave rise to global networks of women artists who developed iconographies to describe the political, personal, and biological realities of their lived experiences.

In 1966 Chase-Riboud began a related but distinctly separate series of drawings titled *Le Lit* (The Bed) that depict two figures in a bed; the female figure appears to be pregnant with a gently sloping belly. The figures in the first drawing are elongated like the forms in her early bone sculptures, though they are rendered in a more realist manner (p. 35). As the series progresses, however, they become more abstract and eventually dissolve into geometric forms that resemble the rippling, pleated sheets of metal that she had recently begun producing with sand-cast aluminum (p. 54). Reminiscent of the undulating folds of Bernini's bronze and marble sculptures, the contours in these drawings signal an important leap for the artist in her corresponding sculptural practice. Her poem of the same title, published in 1974, synthesizes a passion for form and surface with the vivid eroticism that the artist has maintained as a central theme in her literary work, with phrases such as "Blue-veined as Carrara marble" and "Contours still raging like burnt-out onion skin" (p. 55). Soon after producing her *Le Lit* drawings, Chase-Riboud would depart from aluminum, which offered more limited detail and dexterity, in favor of bronze. Once again she would return to lost-wax casting, which allowed her to produce forms even more twisted and furled than

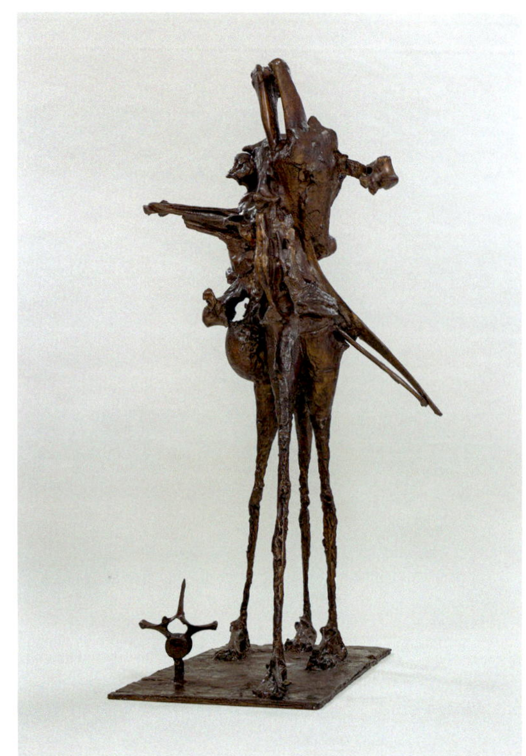

Fig. 6 Barbara Chase-Riboud, *Le Couple*, 1963. Bronze on painted steel base, 48⅜ × 27½ × 27 inches (123 × 70 × 68.5 cm). Private collection

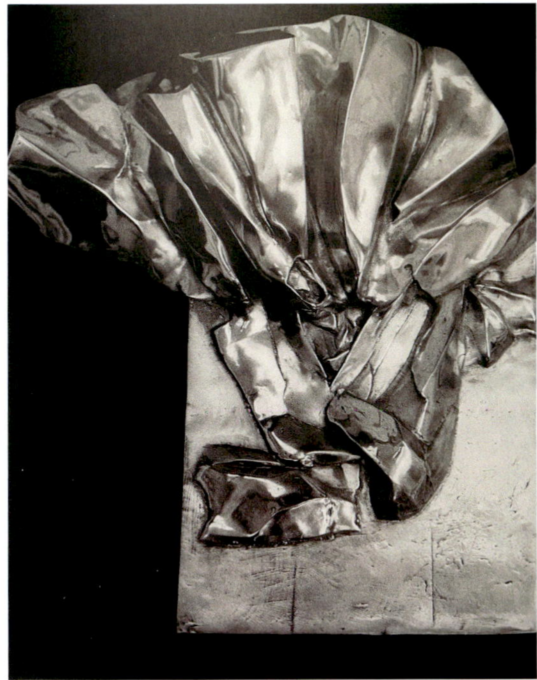

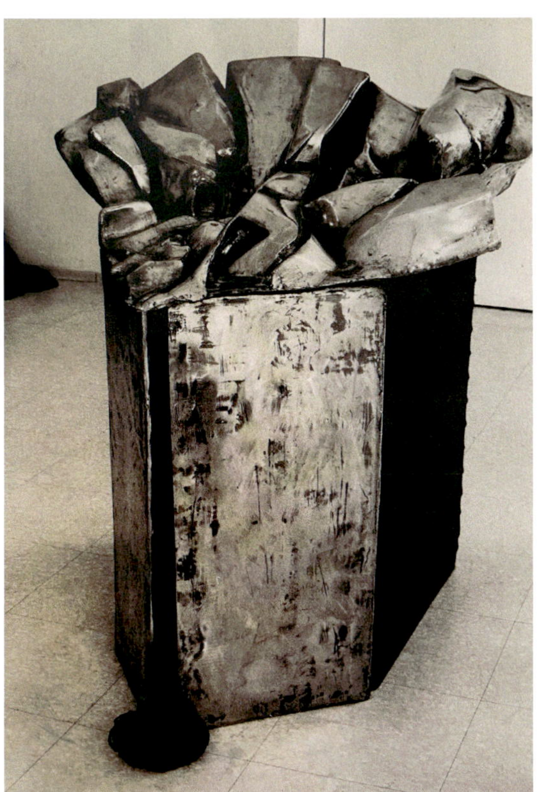

Fig. 7 Barbara Chase-Riboud, *Malcolm X #1*, 1969. Polished bronze, 16 × 29½ × 29½ inches (40.6 × 74.9 × 74.9 cm). Private collection, Germany

Fig. 8 Barbara Chase-Riboud, *Malcolm X #4*, 1969. Polished bronze and wool, 47½ × 43¼ × 43¼ inches (120.7 × 109.9 × 109.9 cm). Private collection, Germany

she had rendered in charcoal on paper with her *Le Lit* series. Once she set off in this direction, she would pursue abstraction to more ambitious and monumental ends than ever before. The *Le Lit* drawings are, therefore, an important series in their own right as well as a significant record of the evolution of her process.

All That Rises

In 1969 Chase-Riboud finished four sculptures that would crystallize many of the formal hallmarks of her mature career. Her *Malcolm X* series, which was named for the iconic civil rights leader only after the completion of the initial four works, represents the first instance in which Chase-Riboud memorialized a historical figure through the dedication of her work. The artist had been devastated by the assassination of Malcolm X four years prior, writing to her mother that she was "very upset over the death."[10] Two important trips to Africa in 1966 and 1969 had also exposed her to the growing discourse of Pan-Africanism, which reinforced her desire to pay tribute to the late champion of the movement.

In the first of these two trips, Chase-Riboud represented the United States with several of her bone sculptures in the inaugural World Festival of Negro Arts (now FESMAN) in Dakar, Senegal. The festival marked an important moment for Chase-Riboud personally as her first trip to Africa and for the development of Pan-Africanism as the first state-sponsored festival of African and African-diasporic arts represented on a global stage. According to the artist, "At the first festival at Dakar which was historic and which was unrepeatable, Malcolm was the presence. The whole festival was imprinted with his presence, with his philosophy, with his urging. . . . We were all there . . . to pay tribute to Malcolm."[11]

The first two *Malcolm* sculptures Chase-Riboud produced (figs. 7 and 8) were floor works with forms that share a close relationship with the pleated metal of her cast-aluminum sculptures from the same period, such as *Time Womb Jacqueline* (p. 58). She made a significant leap with the next two *Malcolms*, working at five times the scale and raising the forms off the floor.[12] She also added nuance to her approach to color and light by introducing a black bronze patina for the first time with *Malcolm X #2* (fig. 9). In contrast to her brilliantly polished aluminum and gold bronze works, the flat dark surface absorbed light, resulting in a more somber monolithic tone. With *Malcolm X #3* (fig. 10), the final edition to the series she produced that year, she further explored the material's edge with deeper pleats and contours than she had realized in any previous work. Rather than a construction rendered from a single, unified piece of wax, this sculpture seems to draw more from the language of Cubism, bringing together many fractured geometric forms into a towering work of unprecedented monumentality for the artist.

As she neared the completion of her bronzes in July 1969, Chase-Riboud traveled to Algiers for the Pan-African Cultural Festival, where delegations from more than thirty nations presented art, performances, and lectures. Organized in the wake of Algeria gaining independence from the French in 1962, the program was deeply anti-colonial, anti-imperialist, and anti-capitalist. Chase-Riboud later reflected, "Because the French and the Algerians were so politicized, they sort of gave a

    INDELIBLE

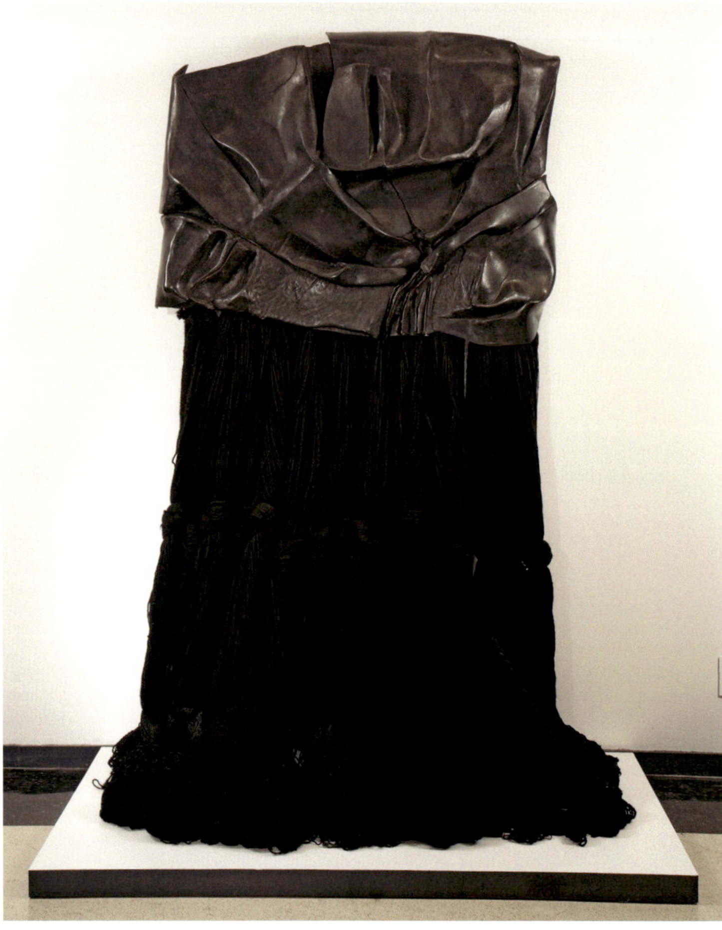

Fig. 9 Barbara Chase-Riboud, *Malcolm X #2*, 1969. Bronze and wool, 92 × 42½ × 24 inches (233.7 × 107.5 × 61 cm). Purchase 1971 Anonymous Gift Fund 71.143. Collection of The Newark Museum of Art

Fig. 10 Barbara Chase-Riboud, *Malcolm X #3*, 1969. Polished cast bronze with spun artificial silk and mercerized Egyptian cotton, 102½ x 37 x 32 inches (260.4 × 94 × 81.3 cm). Philadelphia Museum of Art: 125th Anniversary Acquisition. Purchased with funds contributed by Regina and Ragan A. Henry, and with funds raised in honor of the 125th Anniversary of the Museum and in celebration of African American art, 2001-92-1

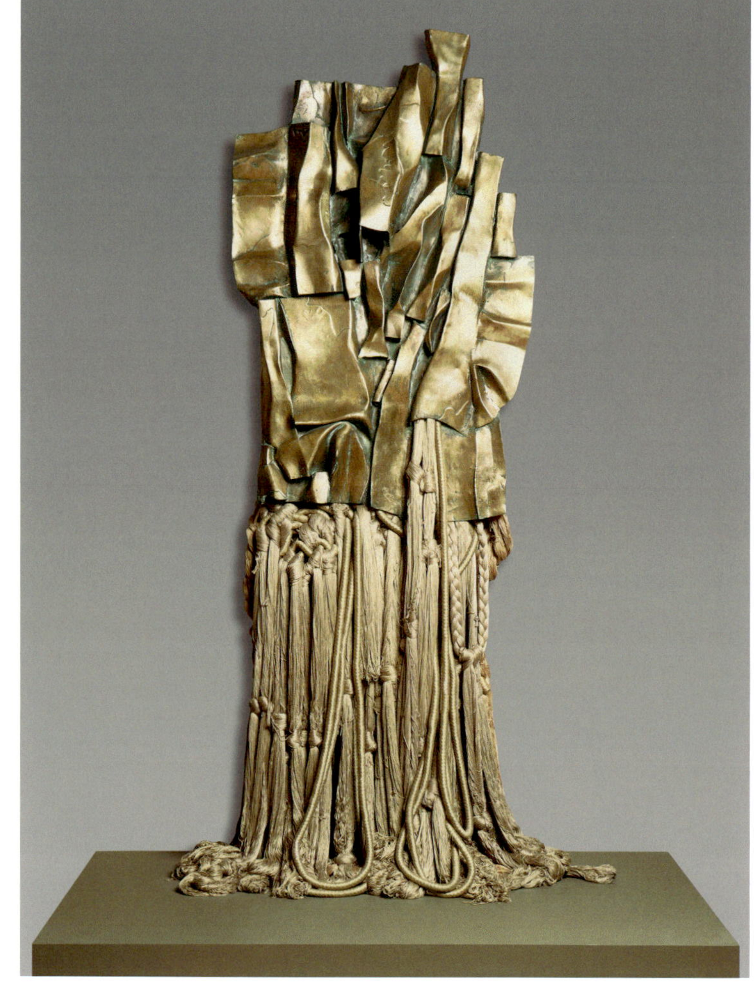

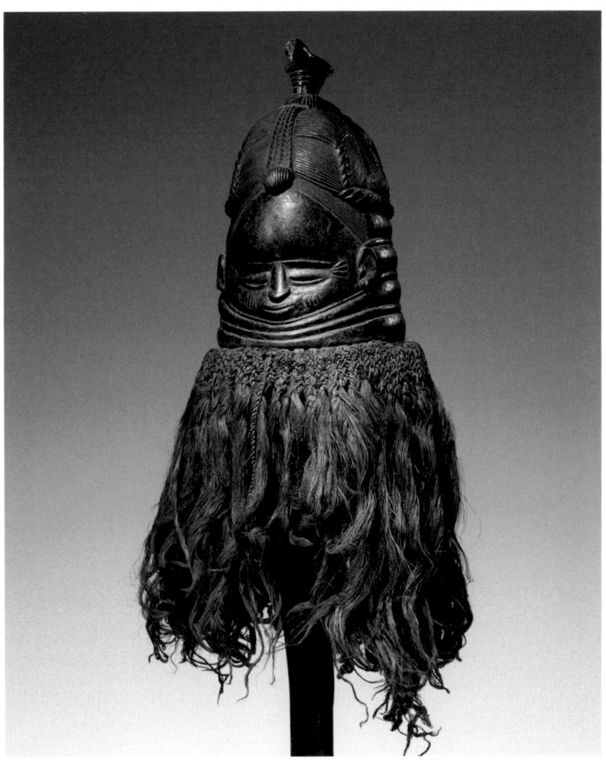

Fig. 11 Mende, Sierra Leone, Sande mask, second quarter of 20th century. Wood and raffia, 13 × 8 × 8 inches (33 × 20.3 × 20.3 cm). Minneapolis Institute of Art, The Christina N. and Swan J. Turnblad Memorial Fund, 72.69.1

lesson to the Americans about how to politicize anything."[13] While there she wrote to her mother that she had arrived at an "underlying theme for a new series of sculptures."[14] After returning to Paris, she designed fiber elements that she would integrate into all but her first *Malcolm*. Each of the skirts would be dyed to match the corresponding bronze, continuing the artist's preference for monochromatic compositions. The late-stage addition would prove to be monumentally important for the development of her creative vision, allowing her to free herself "from the tyranny of the base" by obscuring it with a skirt of wool and silk.

While the artist has not offered a single point of inspiration for the textile skirts that would become synonymous with her visual style, a number of associations have been posited. Frequently cited are the strands of raffia that adorn carved wood ceremonial masks made in West and Central Africa (fig. 11). Though this is not a comparison the artist herself emphasizes, Chase-Riboud would have certainly encountered such masks and seen them in use during masquerades on her trips to Dakar and Algiers. Notably, the raffia, sometimes plaited and dyed and sometimes left raw, serves to disguise the identity of the performer donning the mask, allowing for a transcendent spiritual experience. Chase-Riboud similarly felt that the combination of fiber and bronze created a kind of "transfiguration" in her work. She reflected, "this phenomenon had revelatory importance to the sculpture and what I was trying to do. The combination of these elements took abstraction in a new and entirely original direction. The transformation of the materiality of the two opposing elements had produced a third entity neither hard nor soft, black nor white, male nor female, totally visual nor totally literary."[15]

While she exclusively worked with silk and wool rather than raffia, it was important to the artist to engage with natural materials that "exist independent of human will and manipulation." She describes being attracted to these "primal, eternal" fibers for their great strength and cites silk's historical use in Japanese and Chinese armor. Rather than employing elaborate weaving techniques, she used "my hands, my touch, my arms" to gather, twist, and knot the silk and wool into formations that allowed the fibers to behave naturally, thinking more in terms of movement and flow than a predetermined design.[16]

For the artist, placing textile and bronze in proximity had an enormous impact, allowing her to fully realize what would become a long-standing interest in achieving balance and tension by harnessing opposing forces. She attained this feat not only through the combination of hard bronze and soft fiber but by pairing geometric and organic forms and juxtaposing moments of tightly controlled order with spontaneity. While the presence of contrasting elements is a significant aspect of Chase-Riboud's practice, what is perhaps more notable given the time period during which the works were produced is her interest in turning the associations of her material signifiers on their heads. While a few of her contemporaries, including Eva Hesse and Robert Morris, combined fiber and metal, none did so in a way that so directly challenged Western notions of material hierarchies. Chase-Riboud's work offers an alternative value system to that which esteems bronze, a material associated with memorializing the historical achievements of a male-dominated society, over textiles, which were viewed as a craft-based medium rooted in female and non-Western domestic arts.

Chase-Riboud does not shy away from relating this series to the history of monuments and memorials; in fact, they were first exhibited as *Monuments to Malcolm X* at Bertha Schaefer Gallery in 1970. She later began referring to the works as steles, making linkages to ancient funerary objects used to commemorate the dead (fig. 12). She explained, "I started the steles because there had to be some reckoning with [Malcolm X's] presence on Earth. And the Egyptians had a tradition of these memorial funeral steles dedicated to a person. . . . As soon as I decided that they were going to be dedicated to him, not as portraits and not as gravestones but as memorials, they became themselves and they became an abstraction of what he stood for."[17] Formal similarities do exist between the ancient carved stone steles and Chase-Riboud's *Malcolms*, including an elongated vertical axis and a shallow depth. Like their ancient counterparts, Chase-Riboud's *Malcolms* were intended to function within an architectural surround that would frame and contextualize them. A notable aspect of Chase-Riboud's memorial sculptures, which would grow into a very significant thread of her career, is their seriality. Within a single year Chase-Riboud would finish four sculptures she dedicated to Malcolm X, and over her career she would eventually add sixteen more.

While seriality was becoming predominant in the second half of the 1960s as Minimalism dominated the American art world, Chase-Riboud's work has little in common with her contemporaries in her home country. She has described herself as in direct opposition to the industrial, highly ordered, and emotionally removed aesthetic of Minimalism, embracing instead a very physical process rooted in automatism, improvisation, the Baroque, and maximalism. "Although I feel isolated from the current trends in American art, this is not true of the current trends in American music. The fascination with African and Oriental music which began in the early sixties with John Cage and John Coltrane, to name only two, founded a strong underground movement in avant-garde music. The dense complex and primary music of Steve Reich, Terry Riley, and Alice Coltrane are much closer to what I'm after."[18]

In 1972 Chase-Riboud built further in this direction with her most monumental work to date, *Confessions for Myself* (fig. 13). At ten feet, the black bronze and wool sculpture towers over human scale. The form strikes an aggressive and domineering stance, with jagged horizontal and vertical strips of bronze that converge in an impenetrable core. With an overwhelmingly dark color palette and the presence of a central void, the work shares commonalities with the metal and canvas sculptures of Chase-Riboud's contemporary Lee Bontecou (fig. 14). Chase-Riboud and Bontecou both spent time in Rome in 1958, where they were inspired by ancient ruins and Baroque architecture. Both artists also harness abstraction and relief to create works that draw the viewer in through a magnetic and elusive sense of interiority. *Confessions for Myself* has been linked to Chase-Riboud's thirteen-part poem *Anna*, published in

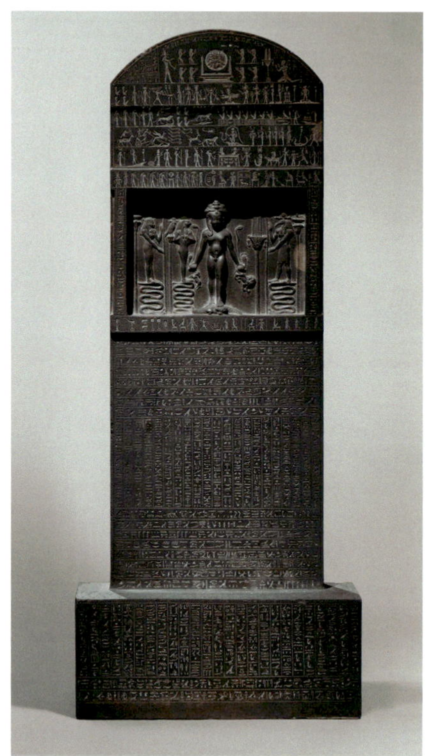

Fig. 12 Egyptian, Magical Stela (Cippus of Horus), 360–343 BCE. Meta-Greywacke, 32⅞ × 13³⁄₁₆ × 2¹³⁄₁₆ inches (83.5 × 33.5 × 7.2 cm). Metropolitan Museum of Art, New York, Fletcher Fund, 1950, 50.85

Fig. 13 Barbara Chase-Riboud, *Confessions for Myself*, 1972. Black patinated bronze and wool, 120 × 40 × 12 inches (304.8 × 101.6 × 30.5 cm). University of California, Berkeley Art Museum and Pacific Film Archive. Purchased with funds from the H.W. Anderson Charitable Foundation

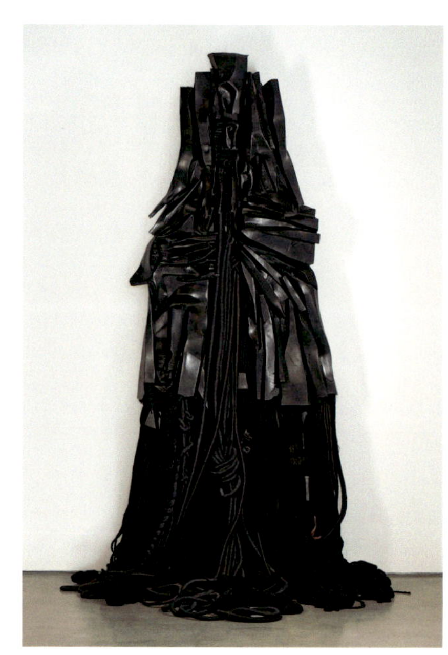

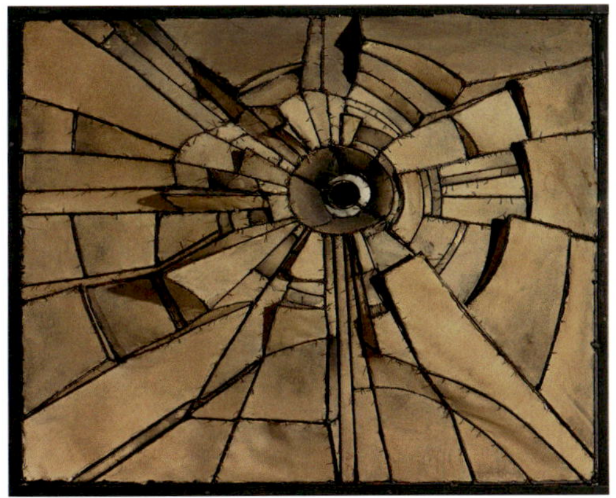

Fig. 14 Lee Bontecou (1931–2022), Untitled, 1961. Welded steel, canvas, wire, and soot, 24 × 29 × 7 inches (61 × 73.7 × 17.8 cm). Collection of the Kunstmuseum Den Haag

Fig. 15 Barbara Chase-Riboud, *Zanzibar/Black*, 1974–75. Bronze with black patina, silk, and wool over a steel armature, 82 × 30 × 27 inches (208.3 × 76.2 × 68.6 cm). Smithsonian American Art Museum, Museum purchase through the Luisita L. and Franz H. Denghausen Endowment, 2018.2

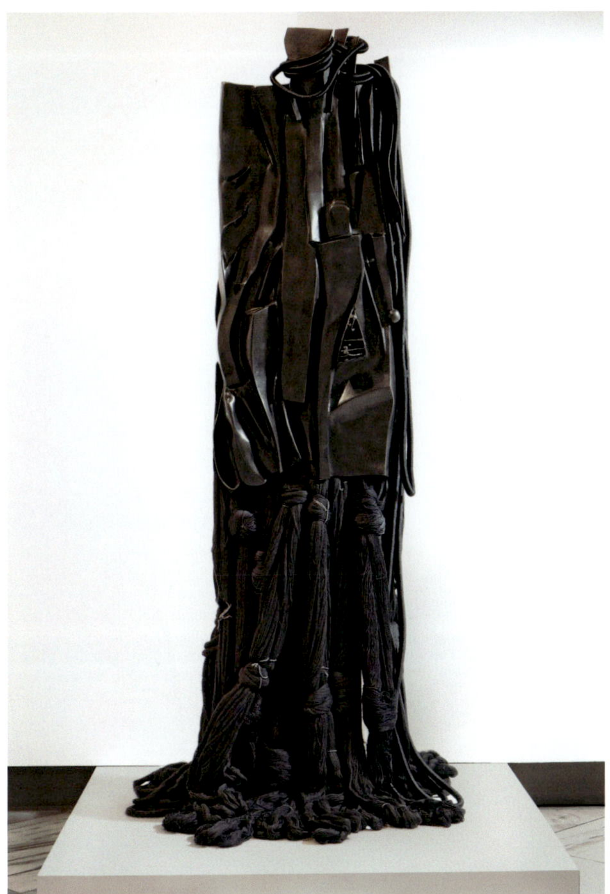

1974, which traces the legacy of the artist's great-grandmother and her ancestors who were forcibly transported by European merchants to North America from Africa as slaves. Like the sculpture, the writing is captivating and disarmingly intimate while barbed with a somber and unsettling tone.

At the same time she was producing *Confessions for Myself*, Chase-Riboud was furthering many of the techniques she put to use in her *Malcolms* with her *Zanzibar* series, titled for the East African archipelago that was the center of the Indian Ocean slave trade with the Middle East beginning in the seventeenth century. The series shares the title of her 1969–70 epic poem about the transatlantic slave trade, "Why Did We Leave Zanzibar?" (p. 72). In these black and gold bronzes, Chase-Riboud further elaborates the forms she developed with her *Malcolms* and *Confessions for Myself*, fashioning long, thin strips of bronze to which she added greater dimensionality and volume. In addition to the large-scale *Zanzibars*, she also produced a number of much smaller related works that she called the *Zanzibar Tables*. She used these more modestly scaled versions to explore casting and fiber techniques. In *Zanzibar Table Black #2* (p. 74), for instance, she integrates silk, linen, and synthetic fiber. The artist loops and ties the cords around each other and feeds them through holes in the bronze—techniques she would later repeat in several works, including her large-scale *Zanzibar/Black* (fig. 15). Through her *Zanzibar* series, along with the *Malcolms* and *Confessions for Myself*, Chase-Riboud established what would become a career-long commitment to addressing themes of reflection, time, and memory. Furthermore, she crystalized a consistent visual vocabulary using her signature mediums of bronze and fiber.

From Memphis and Peking

Just as Chase-Riboud arrived at a consistent formal language, she entered a new phase of radical experimentation, turning to previously unexplored material applications and conceptual references. In 1973 she completed the first of her *Cleopatra* sculptures, a series of seven works that would stretch almost thirty years. The most representational sculpture the artist had produced in more than a decade, *Le Manteau (The Cape),* or *Cleopatra's Cape* (p. 83), would eventually become part of a constellation of sculptures representing personal effects belonging to the queen of Ptolemaic Egypt. Chase-Riboud uses the works in the series to synthesize references to ancient Egypt with another region that had a significant impact on her artistic vision. In 1965, seven years after her trip to Egypt, Chase-Riboud traveled to China, India, and Cambodia. There she described "entering into a love affair that would last through forty years," rooted in a fascination with "Buddhist theology, Chinese philosophy, and Mao's little red book." She noted, "most of all I would be mesmerized by five centuries of Chinese art which would shimmer and gleam in my unconscious and which I would eventually use subversively to shape my own art."[19] Though the idea for the *Cleopatra* sculptures did not come to Chase-Riboud until more than half a decade after her initial visit, the series, like much of the work she would produce in the following years, was deeply influenced by the inspiration she found there.

The specific spark for the Cleopatra work came after her husband, Marc Riboud, relayed a description of jade burial suits from the Han

Dynasty he encountered while on assignment in China. The ceremonial suits, which were produced exclusively for the aristocracy, are constructed of thousands of small jade plaques woven together with wire or silk (fig. 16). Chase-Riboud adopted the same approach for her *Cape*, although she used bronze instead of jade. In order to translate the iridescent quality of the stone to her chosen medium, she introduced scrap iron in the final stage of casting, a technique that produced unpredictable results and left each plaque with a unique surface. Relying on the Surrealist technique of automatism, she created seven abstract designs that are repeated across the surfaces of the plaques.

These techniques were completely new for the artist, though they do share continuity with her practice to date on a few fundamental levels. Much like her earlier sculptures in which Chase-Riboud approximated the complex folds of drapery through large sheets of bronze, she expressed an interest in transforming metal into fiber with the *Cleopatra* works. Importantly, she employed a much more literal approach with the later series in which she wove together plaques of bronze to create an actual cape. Chase-Riboud also continued her pursuit of manipulating the effects of light with *Cape*, though she achieved it by producing a faceted, iridescent surface rather than through polish and contour. When considered as a whole, the series also signals a novel approach to the artist's continued interest in space and memorialization. Each of the sculptures references domestic architecture and the trappings of royalty, namely *Cleopatra's Door*, *Chair*, *Bed*, *Dress*, and *Marriage Contract*. When situated in the same space, they stage an intimate portrait of one of the most powerful women in history by imagining the objects that surrounded her in daily life (pp. 80–81). With material and formal references to ancient Egyptian and imperial Chinese mortuary rituals, the *Cleopatra* series represented a new level of direct engagement with memorialization that Chase-Riboud had not previously broached in her work. In 1987, fifteen years after beginning the sculptural series, Chase-Riboud penned a collection of poetry on the same subject titled *Portrait of a Nude Woman as Cleopatra*. Written from the perspective of Cleopatra, the poems explore the queen's torrid and tragic relationship with Marc Antony. Once again, geography, history, materiality, and commemoration are present in verses such as "In the turquoise-veined granite of the Hammamet, I build my monument."

Though this collection of poems was written years later, Chase-Riboud was exploring other cross-cultural and transhistorical connections in her writing about the time she began her *Cleopatra* sculptures. The year after she completed *Cleopatra's Cape*, the artist published her first collection of poetry, *From Memphis and Peking* (1974). As the title suggests, the book contains writings that reflect on the two cities with ancient roots that left significant impacts on Chase-Riboud's artistic psyche. Her book of poetry deftly weaves personal reflection with mythological and literary references to mesmerizing effect. The publication marked an important turning point in Chase-Riboud's career as the scope of her professional creative output grew beyond the realm of

Fig. 16 Jade suit, unearthed from Tomb 2, Dayun Mountain, Xuyi, Jiangsu, China. Western Han period (206 BCE–9 CE). Jade and gold, 68 × 33 inches (175 × 84 cm). Nanjing Museum

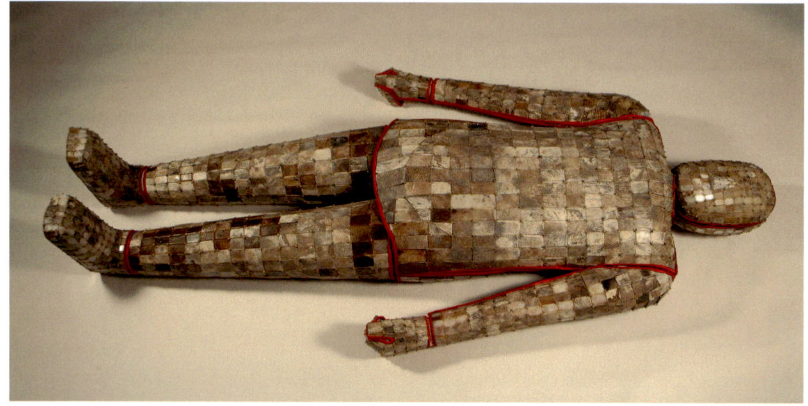

the visual. From that point on, she would toggle between writing and sculpture, working exclusively in one medium at a time.

The following decade marked very significant touchstones in her personal and professional lives. After a divorce from Riboud in 1980, she described a new level of freedom and agency as she moved from a supporting role in the shadow of her husband's creative endeavors to a more fully realized and independent expression of her artistic and literary vision.[20] During this transition, she published her breakthrough novel of historical fiction, *Sally Hemings*, in 1980, which unexpectedly became the center of a maelstrom for exposing the intimate relationship between Hemings and Thomas Jefferson, who legally owned Hemings as his slave and fathered six of her children. Chase-Riboud's attention was primarily turned to writing during this period, though she did produce a small number of sculptures, largely continuing her *Zanzibar* series.

Like the *Cleopatra* series, the next two major bodies of work Chase-Riboud created, *Tantra* and *La Musica*, built on core aspects of her early work while also departing in significant ways from the style for which she has become best known. The artist describes using the *Zanzibar* works as a bridge to her *Tantra* series, which she began in 1984. She experimented with the "same kind of folding and melting and fusion, with very thin slices of wax, even thinner than I was used to doing."[21] In fact, the first three sculptures in the *Tantra* series share the same central inverted triangular shape, which is quite similar to the form of *Malcolm I* as well as works from her *Time Womb* series. Chase-Riboud was drawn to the triangle as a form used to symbolize nature and creation within tantric philosophy. While the reference to Indian metaphysical traditions is distinct from the citations embedded in the first half of Chase-Riboud's career, the series continues her ongoing interest in developing poetic tension through the use of contrasting forces.

Much like the *Tantra* series, Chase-Riboud's *La Musica* sculptures take an abstract principle as their point of departure. The series, which Chase-Riboud began in 1990 and has continued to the present day, makes oblique references to the forms of musical instruments and the bodies that play them. Recurring triangular geometries evoke crooked arms supporting the neck of string instruments, while bronze that terminates in coiled curls act as reminders of treble clefs or violin scrolls. The *La Musica* sculptures possess a fluidity and lightness that stand apart from much of Chase-Riboud's work. These sculptures are rendered with more delicate forms that rely on the interplay of bronze and fiber to draw the focus between positive and negative space. Unlike earlier works in which Chase-Riboud braids or tightly wraps silk into cords, here she uses unwoven skeins of silk. She describes this process as more similar to working with clay than fiber, as the strands of silk can be easily molded to reflect the influence of the hand. The results are more abstract and less controlled than her previous work with fiber.[22]

Africa Rising

As Chase-Riboud continued to produce works exploring realms of the metaphysical and experiential through abstraction, she simultaneously began a new line of inquiry, leading her in an entirely different direction. Returning to one of the cornerstones of her practice, the artist created a number of works that, in her own words, "crossed swords with public history."[23] While these sculptures and drawings are not from a single series, many share a focus on making visible the overlooked, suppressed, and ignored histories that stem from the institution of slavery. While Chase-Riboud had previously addressed the subject of slavery in series such as *Zanzibar*, the late 1980s marked a turning point during which she began to develop not just abstract monumental sculptures but public monuments in a more literal sense. These works were designed at an architectural scale, often representational, and consistently aimed at explicit correctives of the historical record.

Chase-Riboud's unflinching confrontation with this taboo and painful subject is evident not only in her sculptural work but also in her literary career. In 1989 she published her novel *Echo of Lions*, which tells the story of the 1839 revolt staged by kidnapped Mende people from Sierra Leone who were being transported as slaves aboard the Spanish ship *La Amistad*. The book details the following Supreme Court case, United States v. Schooner Amistad, which declared the Africans free. Two years after the release of her novel, Chase-Riboud conceived of her *Middle Passage Monument* to "honor the 11 million victims and the 30 million deportees of the African diaspora." Presented to the Clinton Administration as the first and, at the time, only monument to commemorate "this tremendous miscarriage of justice and humanity," the proposal is the artist's first large-scale sculpture imagined for the public realm.[24] The unrealized work was intended to soar to roughly one hundred feet. Scale models show two pillars connecting a central beam, bound with a length of chain. The form resembles a raised drawbridge or open gate signaling the traversal from one continent to another, one state of being to another.

The same year that Chase-Riboud submitted her proposal for the *Middle Passage Monument*, a literal unearthing of history would lead to her most ambitious work to date. In May of 1991, construction of the Ted Weiss Federal Building in Lower Manhattan led to the discovery and excavation of a forgotten pre-Revolutionary African cemetery. The six-acre plot is possibly the only preserved eighteenth-century urban African cemetery in the United States and offers unprecedented insight into the little-studied lives of Africans living in New York during the late 1700s. After the cemetery was designated a National Historic Landmark, the city mounted a call for proposals for a monument to commemorate the hugely significant site. In 1995 Chase-Riboud won a commission to create *Africa Rising*, an eighteen-foot bronze sculpture dedicated to the memory of "the African Burial Site and the transport of Africans to this land, their bondage and struggle for freedom" (fig. 17). The work depicts Sarah Baartman, a Khoisan woman from South Africa who was brought to Paris under false pretenses by a member of the British military in 1810 and put on public display as a curiosity. Her captors placed great emphasis on her physical features as representations of the erotic exoticism and savagery Anglo and European cultures assigned to African peoples.

Chase-Riboud's expressive rendering of Baartman blends references to heroic figures throughout history with stylistic influences that nod to her classical European training. Though Baartman's history is a tragic one, Chase-Riboud renders her as a triumphant symbol, invoking the winged goddess of victory depicted in the Nike of Samothrace (fig. 18). Like the Hellenistic cult image, *Africa Rising* depicts a valiant female figure atop

Fig. 17 Barbara Chase-Riboud, *Africa Rising*, 1998. Bronze, 185 × 102 × 52 inches (469.9 × 259.1 × 132.1 cm). Ted Weiss Federal Building, New York, NY. Commissioned through the Art in Architecture Program. Fine Arts Collection, US General Services Administration

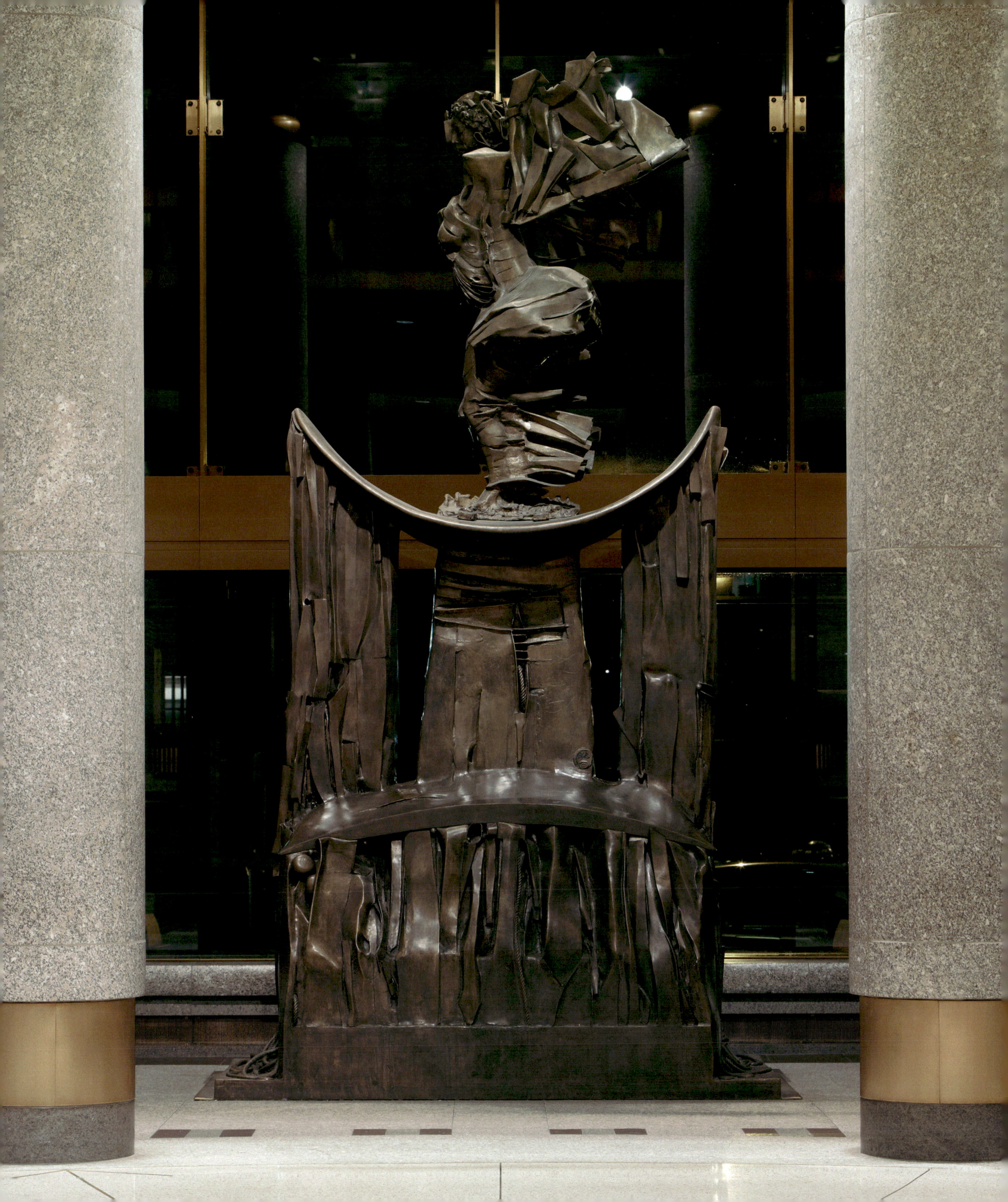

the prow of a ship, in this case with the addition of a colossal base that resembles the artist's *Middle Passage Monument.*

In addition to the Nike and her ship, Chase-Riboud was informed by another monument intended to mark oceanic voyage—Frédéric-Auguste Bartholdi's 1869 proposed colossal lighthouse for the newly opened Suez Canal, *Egypt Carrying the Light to Asia*, which would eventually be reimagined as the Statue of Liberty. The neoclassical beacon was likely a point of reference not only for its personification of the struggle for freedom but also for its stylistic rendering of flowing, windswept drapery. Like their precursor the Nike of Samothrace, both Bartholdi's proposed and realized monuments use inflexible material to create the illusion of lightness and movement. Working at a highly ambitious scale, Chase-Riboud deftly fashioned a network of finely attenuated sheets of bronze into a length of fabric carried aloft by gusts of ocean air.

While Chase-Riboud looked heavily to the Hellenic for inspiration, she also turned to more modern influences, including that of the Futurist sculptor and painter Umberto Boccioni. With an interest in conveying movement through space and time, she uses fragmentation and abstraction to show materials in relation to the forces that act upon them. Unlike Boccioni's *Unique Forms of Continuity in Space* (1913, cast 1950; fig. 19) in which the movement derives from a lunging, forward stride, Chase-Riboud's Baartman stands with feet planted firmly against a headwind. Her wings—a loose network of folded and pleated bronze— soar behind her torso, conveying a defiant spirit in the face of overwhelming oppression.

While working to realize *Africa Rising*, Chase-Riboud further investigated the themes of monument and memory with her *Monument Drawings* series. She created the portfolio of twenty-four works on paper, each dedicated to a historic figure, over just a few months between 1996 and 1997. The foundation for each of the drawings is an etching that serves as a leitmotif. The form resembles a column of wrapped cords, of the kind she employs in her bronze and fiber sculpture, flanked by two rugged blocks of stone. This central component always stretches horizontally across the paper, though it appears alternately at the top and bottom of the composition and is sometimes rotated 180 degrees. Opposite the column, the etching also depicts a single cord stretched into an organic line. To complete the *Monument Drawings*, Chase-Riboud built on the etchings with charcoal and pen, working quickly and in most cases only dedicating the drawings once they are completed.

A number of the drawings relate directly to the histories she explored in her sculptural monuments from the period. *The Foley Square Monument, New York* (1996), for instance, is named for the square in Lower Manhattan where the African burial site was discovered. The drawing depicts stairs leading down toward blackness, calling to mind a subterranean tomb. *Middle Passage Monument, Washington* (1997) bears significant similarities to her sculptural proposal of the same title with a post-and-lintel structure bound in cord. Many others represent a departure from the focus on accounts of slavery, memorializing figures of personal significance to the artist, "the invisible people that pass through history, making history, but never being noted as such," as she put it.[25] Literary heroes, such as the Russian poet Anna Akhmatova,

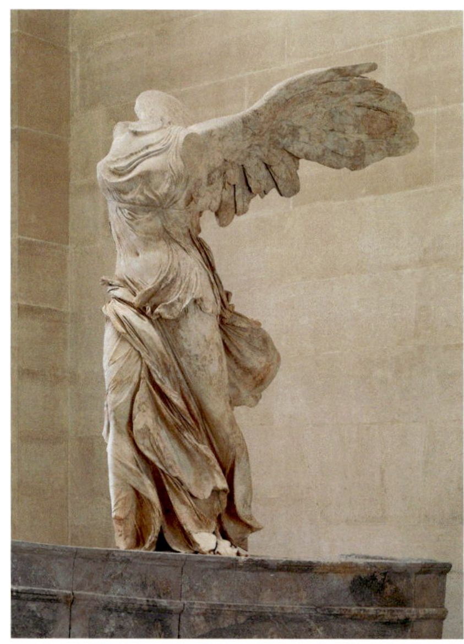

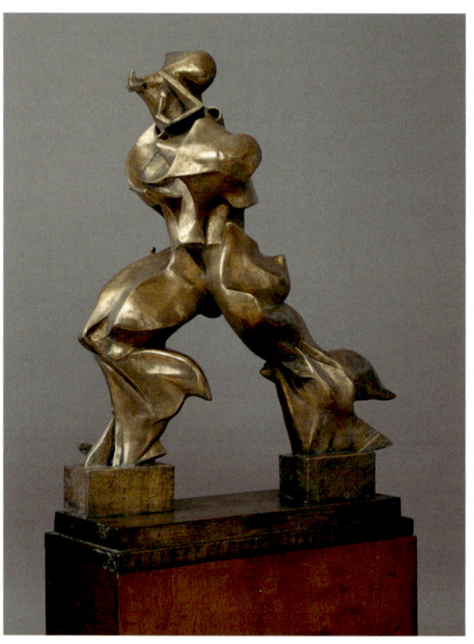

Fig. 18 *Nike (Winged Victory) of Samothrace*, c. 190 BCE. Marble, 10¾ feet high (3.28 m). Louvre, Paris

Fig. 19 Umberto Boccioni (1882–1916), *Unique Forms of Continuity in Space*, 1913, cast 1950. Bronze, 47¾ × 35 × 15¾ inches (121.3 × 88.9 × 40 cm). The Metropolitan Museum of Art, New York, Bequest of Lydia Winston Malbin, 1989 (1990.38.3)

appear alongside artistic influences, such as Man Ray, and world leaders, such as the founder of the Zulu Empire, Shaka Zulu (p. 101).

Her masterful draftsmanship can be observed in her careful line work, which the artist uses to balance light and dark, delineate texture, and suggest form. Her architectural training is also evident here as she renders built environments in multiple styles with elevations sometimes embedded into larger drawings that integrate perspective, as in *Zola's Monument, Paris* (p. 100). In addition to her line work, Chase-Riboud also added automatic writing to many of the drawings. She characterizes this Surrealist technique as a kind of poetry that is "untranslatable because it's in a language that no one understands except me."[26] The *Monument Drawings*, therefore, represent an important bridge between her literary and visual minds. They also share connections to her bronze and fiber sculptures as an exploration of the synergy between hard and soft, rigid and flowing. Perhaps the most important and fully developed series of drawings Chase-Riboud produced, they represent her most direct examination of memory and monument in the works using her signature abstraction and materiality.

Returns

The completion of the *Monument Drawings* in 1997 and installation of *Africa Rising* the following year closed a chapter for Chase-Riboud. In subsequent years, she revisited many of the series she developed prior to her work with public monuments, integrating new techniques and approaches to innovate her practice. Notably, in 2003 she returned to her iconic *Malcolm* series, adding another sixteen to her original four over the following decade and a half. While Chase-Riboud employs the same fundamental components—a frontal vertical composition with bronze resting above a skirt of silk and wool—she uses the formula as a starting point to iterate countless combinations.

In comparison to the first four *Malcolms* she produced in 1969, the later versions are more dimensional and elaborately worked, often with narrow strips of bronze fashioned into pleats, cuts, rips, and curved planes. Chase-Riboud reintroduces techniques she developed in other series, such as tightly wound tendrils in *Malcolm X #16* (p. 134), resembling the treble-like forms in her *La Musica* series, and incised grids, as in *Malcolm X #5*, of the kind that first appeared in her iconic 1972 *Confessions for Myself*. Additionally, rather than treating the bronze and textiles as two separate elements that meet along a single horizon, she broadened her vocabulary to include a wider array of interactions. Wrapped wool and silk, for instance, are often pushed through holes in the bronze where the textile drapes, coils, and pools, creating added layers of textural complexity against the sheen of the adjacent metal. Pops of white and red wool against matte black bronze in *Malcolm X #13* and *#19* (pp. 133, 140), introduce color contrast not represented in the earlier monochrome works in the series. As the largest body of work the artist has produced to date, it has become a kind of index for the impressive range of expression she is capable of producing within a single theme.

More recently, the artist has returned to some of her earliest sand-cast aluminum works for inspiration. While the mold is destroyed during lost-wax casting, it survives in the sand-casting process, allowing

Chase-Riboud to revisit decades-old forms to new and inventive ends. Her 2021 black bronze *Standing Black Woman of Venice* (p. 142) was cast from the mold used for her 1969–72 *Bathers*. While *Bathers* is presented either directly on the floor or horizontally on the wall, Chase-Riboud reoriented the new work vertically. Compared to the *Malcolms*, its surface is much less baroque—a single plane marked by creases and wrinkles rather than a series of deep undercuts and folds. Though its low relief makes the work less receptive to light, especially when rendered in black bronze, Chase-Riboud polished the dark surface to a high luminosity, making it almost as reflective as the aluminum sculptures she produced early in her career. Significantly, she also eliminated fiber from this composition, resulting in a more austere and monolithic aesthetic than much of her previous work. The elemental form harkens back to her longtime passion for the sublime order of ancient Egyptian statuary, while the title makes reference to Giacometti's 1956 *Woman of Venice* series, modifying it to acknowledge the descendants of Africa's great civilizations.

In recent years, Chase-Riboud has continued to iterate on one of her most prolific series, *La Musica*. Beginning in the 2000s, she expanded its focus beyond the principles of music by introducing historical references that memorialize figures of great personal import. Her 2007 work *Mao's Organ* resembles the form of the instrument for which it is named with an uncharacteristically wide composition topped with a narrow neck (p. 124).[27] Working with gold bronze and red silk, Chase-Riboud makes reference to the colors most closely associated with the Communist leader Chairman Mao—a figure that has fascinated her since her 1965 sojourn to China. Her most ambitious addition to the series, a red bronze and silk sculpture titled *La Musica Red Parkway, Josephine* (2007; p. 119), is dedicated to the St. Louis–born jazz singer, dancer, and civil rights activist who became one of the most influential entertainers in Paris beginning in the 1920s. Notably, Josephine Baker and Chase-Riboud share a number of biographical details as African American expatriates and renegades who have left lasting impressions on their chosen fields. In *La Musica Red Parkway, Josephine*, Chase-Riboud uses abstraction to visualize the physical embodiment of the acoustic while also celebrating the impact of Baker's singular contributions to the twentieth-century musical landscape.

From her earliest experiments in bronze to her most recent sculptures, Chase-Riboud's work has acted as an important bridge between her modernist forebears and younger generations of artists. She has created space for a significantly broadened definition of sculpture and asked important questions about who and what deserves to be remembered and monumentalized. Though Chase-Riboud has drawn on a broad range of global influences, her work has remained singular. Her originality is due in part to the enormous difficulty of her working methods, which are labor intensive and not easily reproduced. Beyond her technical achievements, the artist also brings to bear a truly remarkable set of personal experiences amassed over eight decades of moving through the world as a deeply inquisitive, ambitious, and trailblazing individual. She has integrated these experiences with her technical skills to put forth a remarkable body of sculpture, drawings, fictional writing, and poetry that together redefines what it means to be monumental.

Notes

1. Interview with the artist, April 2021. Her limited palette can be observed in the artist's c. 1954 woodcut *Reba*. The print was acquired by the Museum of Modern Art in 1955, making her the youngest artist to have a work enter the museum's collection at the time.

2. Cited in Boris Blai, Stella Elkins Tyler School of Fine Arts of Temple University Bulletin, 1945: https://bulletin.temple.edu /undergraduate/tyler/#:~:text=%22It %20is%20the%20principle%20of ,developments%20of%20society%20at %20large.%22.

3. Often referred to as direct casting, the lost-wax method allows artists to achieve great detail by sculpting a model in the highly malleable medium of wax. Rather than creating an intermediary plaster mold from the original model, plaster investment is built up directly around the wax. The mold is turned upside down, melting the wax through a hole in the investment. After this, the bronze is poured into the resulting hollow space.

4. Interview with the artist, April 2021.

5. Rudolf Wittkower described Bernini as having made marble "as flexible as wax"; quoted in Peter Selz, "Barbara Chase-Riboud's Sculpture," *Callaloo* 32, no. 3 (Summer 2009): 872.

6. Selz, "Barbara Chase-Riboud's Sculpture," 862.

7. Peter Selz and Anthony F. Janson, *Barbara Chase-Riboud: Sculptor* (New York: Harry N. Abrams, 1999), 21.

8. The thesis committee at Yale rejected Chase-Riboud's proposal, on the grounds that it was produced outside Yale supervision. Instead, she submitted etchings of Arthur Rimbaud's *A Season in Hell*.

9. The sand-casting process involves encasing a mold in compact sand. Once the sand is compacted, the mold is removed. Carved channels in the sand then allow molten bronze to be poured into the negative space remaining to create the final form. Because the sand is not completely fixed, unlike the plaster investment in the lost-wax casting method, the technique does not allow for the kind of high relief forms with deep undercuts Chase-Riboud had previously achieved with her signature method.

10. Barbara Chase-Riboud, *I Always Knew* (Princeton, NJ: Princeton University Press, 2022), 149–50.

11. Barbara Chase-Riboud, Ilyasah Shabazz, and Erin Gilbert, "Artist Conversation," in *Saint Heron*, https://www.saintheron.com, 2021.

12. The first four *Malcolm* steles are not numbered in the order in which they were produced. Chase-Riboud finished them in the following order: *Malcolm #1*, *Malcolm #4*, *Malcolm #2*, *Malcolm #3*.

13. Barbara Chase-Riboud, oral history interview by Erin Jenoa Gilbert, Archives of American Art, Smithsonian Institution, Washington, DC, June 7–11, 2019.

14. Chase-Riboud, *I Always Knew*, 240–41.

15. Barbara Chase-Riboud, "The *Malcolm* Steles and the Silenced X," in *Barbara Chase-Riboud and the Malcolm X Steles*, ed. Carlos Basualdo (New Haven and London: Yale University Press, 2013), 83–84.

16. Interview with the artist, May 2021.

17. Chase-Riboud, Shabazz, and Gilbert, "Artist Conversation," 12–13.

18. Selz and Janson, *Barbara Chase-Riboud: Sculptor*, 59.

19. Chase-Riboud, *I Always Knew*, 145.

20. Chase-Riboud, oral history interview.

21. Interview with the artist, May 2021.

22. Barbara Chase-Riboud and Suzette Spencer, "On Her Own Terms: An Interview with Barbara Chase-Riboud," *Callaloo* 32, no. 3 (Summer 2009): 748.

23. Barbara Chase-Riboud, "Slavery as a Problem in Public History or Sally Hemings and the 'One Drop Rule' of Public History," *Callaloo* 32, no. 3 (Summer 2009): 826.

24. Chase-Riboud imagined that her *Middle Passage Monument* would be produced serially and could be made available for any city that had the interest and resources.

25. Chase-Riboud, oral history interview.

26. Chase-Riboud, oral history interview.

27. Notably, the form also closely resembles the base of *Africa Rising*.

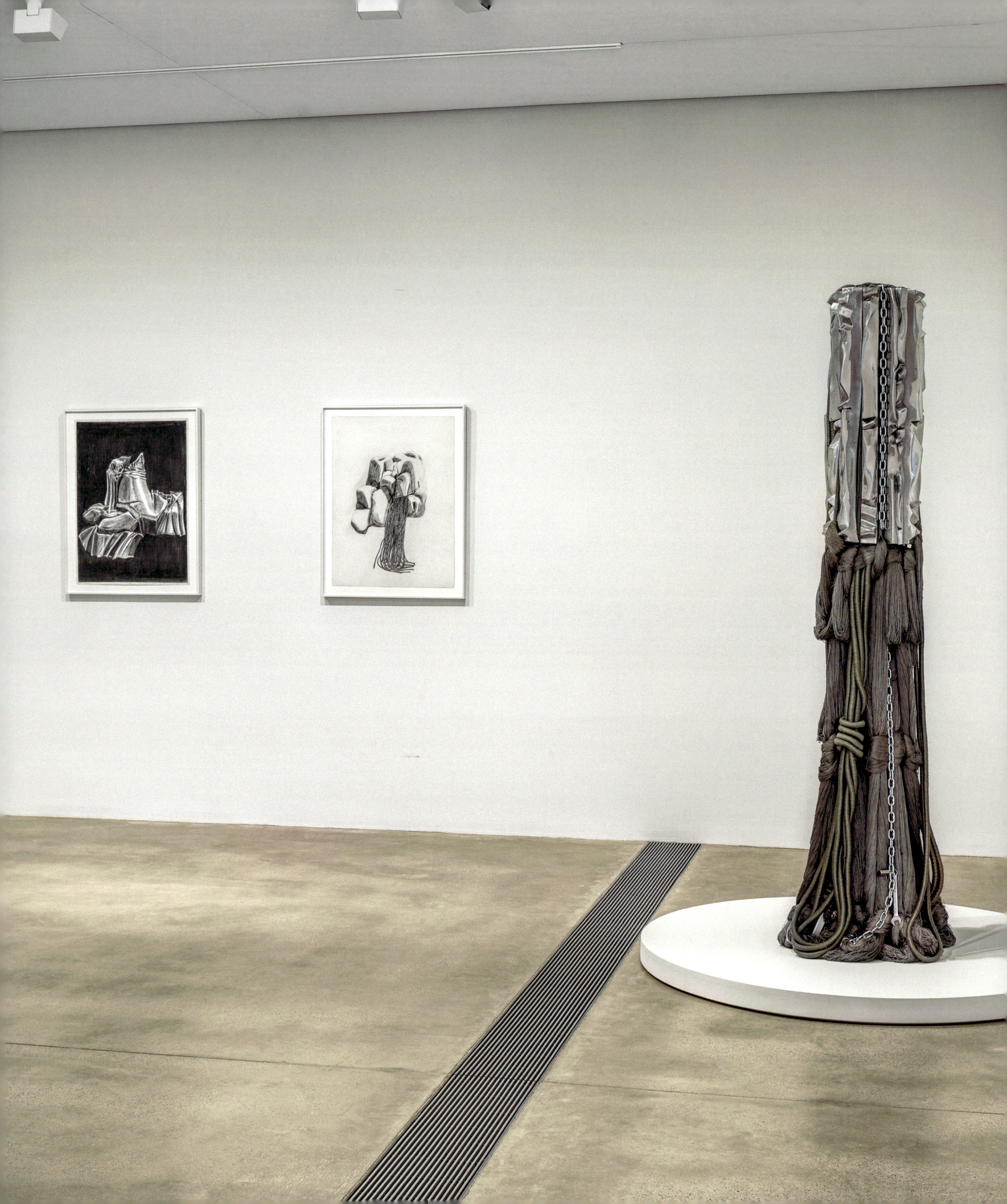

DRAWING THROUGH TIME

Christophe Cherix

In 2021, the Giacometti Institute in Paris paired the work of Alberto Giacometti and Barbara Chase-Riboud in an outstanding exhibition. The two sculptors of different generations and nationalities had each moved to Paris early in their careers—in 1922 and 1961, respectively. Despite that span of forty years, the French capital provided equally fertile ground for their works to blossom. Chase-Riboud recalled her first visit to the sculptor's studio in 1962, a year after she settled in Paris:

> It was the most rundown, decrepit habitation I had ever seen— made of wood planks and an iron roof, crumbling stairs and no windows except a skylight. It was tiny, no more than five meters by five meters. Everything was covered in plaster—the walls, the floors, the ceiling and the first [time] I saw him, he himself was a walking Egyptian mummy, entirely white, covered in white plaster from his shoes to the Afro curly hair on his head: his clothes, his hands, his feet and his cigarette which dangled from his lips from which a long curl of white smoke escaped.[1]

According to Chase-Riboud, as she entered his studio, Giacometti's body had dissolved into whiteness, and was practically reduced to a wisp of smoke. Chase-Riboud's recollections offer remarkable insight into her connection with the Swiss sculptor. The artist she discovered might not have been the one she had anticipated to see. Rather than the great heir of Surrealism, she found a man completely absorbed by his work whose studio practice seemed to reflect the influence of long-vanished culture, particularly Egyptian art. Chase-Riboud had shared a similar fascination for ancient worlds since her time spent in Rome, in 1957 and 1958, as a fellow at the American Academy. She traveled from there to Egypt during the same period, opening her eyes much beyond the Eurocentric narrative of the first part of the twentieth century.

One of Chase-Riboud's earliest works—*Reba*, a circa 1954 woodcut known in a unique copy, produced a couple of years before her trip to Europe—was also her first work to enter a public institution (fig. 1). William Lieberman, then curator of prints at the Museum of Modern Art (MoMA), acquired it in 1955 for the museum's study collection. He must have known very little about Chase-Riboud at the time, but he certainly knew that she was young, as the proof was purchased from an exhibition held at New York's Carnegie Hall for the winners of a National Scholastic Art Contest. The magazine *Seventeen* sponsored the show and dedicated part of its January issue to the topic, asking art students to illustrate stories written by aspiring writers.[2] While Chase-Riboud might have been the youngest artist to enter MoMA's collection at the time,[3] it is unlikely that the woodcut was acquired on the merits of her age. *Reba*, an intriguing print, revolves around concepts that would become hallmarks of the artist's ongoing work: a focus on materiality and texture, revealed by the direct impression of an inked piece of wood in the background of the composition, and a particular attention to the relationship between a body and space—the latter in the print being defined by the placement of the figure's hands and feet

Despite early recognition with *Reba*, Chase-Riboud did not elect printmaking as her primary medium going forward. Aside from contributing woodcuts to the yearbook of the Tyler School of Fine Arts,[4] the first art school she attended, the only other print project she undertook in the following years was a volume of engravings illustrating Arthur Rimbaud's *A Season in Hell*, made in order to complete her MFA at Yale University in 1960.[5] While sculpture became the artist's medium of choice, drawing played a more consistent role throughout her practice than printmaking.

The relationship between drawing and sculpture in the postwar era is fascinating. In the 1960s, distinctions between mediums became increasingly blurred. Artists began using each medium predominantly for its own sake, rather than, as was often the case for drawing, to lay the ground for another work. Like many of her American peers born in the late 1930s—Nancy Graves and Eva Hesse, both also trained at Yale, come to mind—Chase-Riboud is no exception. In her early years, it was rare for her drawings to relate directly to her sculptures, and, when given the opportunity to show her drawings, Chase-Riboud always treated them as equal to her three-dimensional work or showed them on their own.[6]

Chase-Riboud's first exhibition in Paris took place in 1966 at Le Cadran Solaire.[7] The show brought together small bronzes rooted in Surrealism with a number of charcoal drawings, both figurative and semiabstract (figs. 2 and 3). Some of these drawings belong to a small group of works on paper from 1966 depicting a woman and a man on a bed—their naked bodies in inverted positions, the woman facing up and the man facing down. The scene feels both familiar and uncanny, in part because of the contrast between the white mattress and the darkness surrounding the couple, but also due to the featureless quality of the figures. While the woman appears pregnant—the artist would give birth to her second son the following year—the internal structure of the

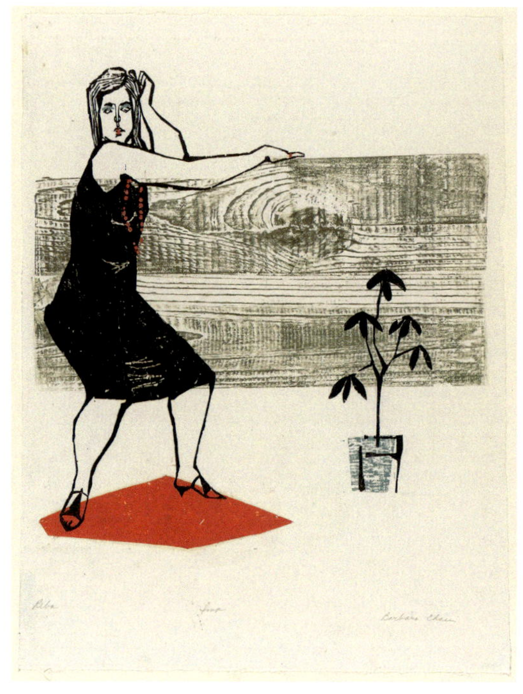

Fig. 1 Barbara Chase-Riboud, *Reba*, c. 1954. Woodcut, 17³⁄₁₆ × 16¹⁄₁₆ inches (43.7 × 40.8 cm); sheet: 23⁷⁄₁₆ × 17⅜ inches (59.5 × 44.1 cm). The Museum of Modern Art, New York. Given anonymously, 1955

two bodies appears to be more carefully defined than their external attributes. A web of lines, connecting the figures' genitals to their heads and their limbs to each other, is further reinforced by blended charcoal areas evoking the flow of energies and fluids.

In an interview printed in the catalogue for the Paris exhibition, the artist expressed her interest in the internal makeup of bodies: "I like bones. They are beautiful, but above all, solid sure, neutral, neither male or female. It is the beginning of everything, and it's also what's left at the end."[8] In these drawings of couples, the inversion of their bodies and the focus on internal anatomy serve to unify the composition into an organized whole, itself defined by a network of relationships. It might appear surprising for an artist whose signature sculptures emphasize verticality that these drawings should take on a theme so intrinsically horizontal. But the view from above and the stern geometry of the bare mattress, as it both exposes and compresses the bodies contained within, dramatically tilts the composition vertically. The crushing of the space around the figures reveals their inner energy and recalls Chase-Riboud's visit to Giacometti's Montparnasse studio, during which the body of the Swiss artist was reduced to a wisp of smoke.

In many respects, 1966 was a pivotal year for Chase-Riboud. In addition to displaying her art publicly in Paris, the artist traveled to Dakar, Senegal, in April as the US representative to the first World Festival of Negro Arts. She had traveled to northeast Africa ten years earlier as a young expatriate, but until then had never encountered the rich West African cultural tradition that would become a key influence in the development of her sculpture. At this occasion, Chase-Riboud also had the opportunity to interact with members of the artistic African diaspora from around the world. Could it be the moment when the sculptor was able to free herself from the Surrealist circles she encountered during her arrival in Paris? In any case, Chase-Riboud seems to begin embracing a broader horizon—geographically, historically, and politically—allowing her later sculpture to undergo a radical transformation.

Such a shift can be observed in the group of works on paper shown at Le Cadran Solaire. It is tempting—even if these drawings have never been characterized as such—to think of them as a series. Some works are figurative, while others are almost abstract, but all feel closely related to one another. The webs of lines running through the bodies in the more figurative works seem to take on a life of their own in the less representational drawings. The white mattress is gone, absorbed into the sheets' black margins. One of the drawings depicts a freestanding assembly of bones, as if the limbs of the couple had been rearranged to create an entirely new entity (fig. 3). These experimental works appear to lead to another set of drawings, sometimes referred to in the artist's inventory as "black drawings," in which a semiabstract structure floats in a black environment (pp. 54, 56–57). While anthropomorphic associations are still present, the artist's focus seems to have shifted from the whole body to its anatomical details, evoking bone articulations and cartilage growth.

In relation to earlier works, the "black drawings" are freed from figuration while maintaining a clear link to the human body. They portray aggregates of matter liberated from gravity, and close inspection reveals that the shapes they contain are united by networks of thin charcoal

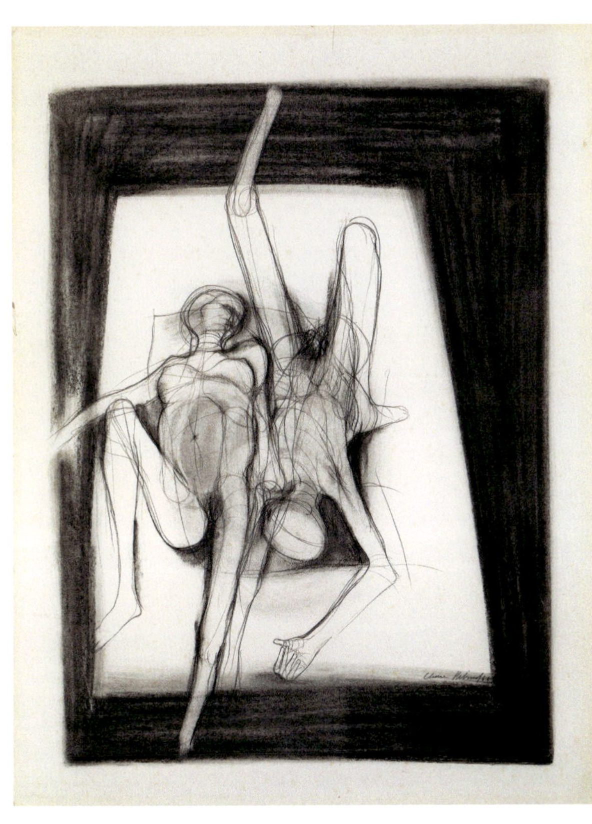

Fig. 2 Barbara Chase-Riboud, *Le Lit*, 1966. Charcoal, charcoal pencil, and ink with engraving and aquatint on paper, 31½ × 23⅞ inches (80 × 60.6 cm)

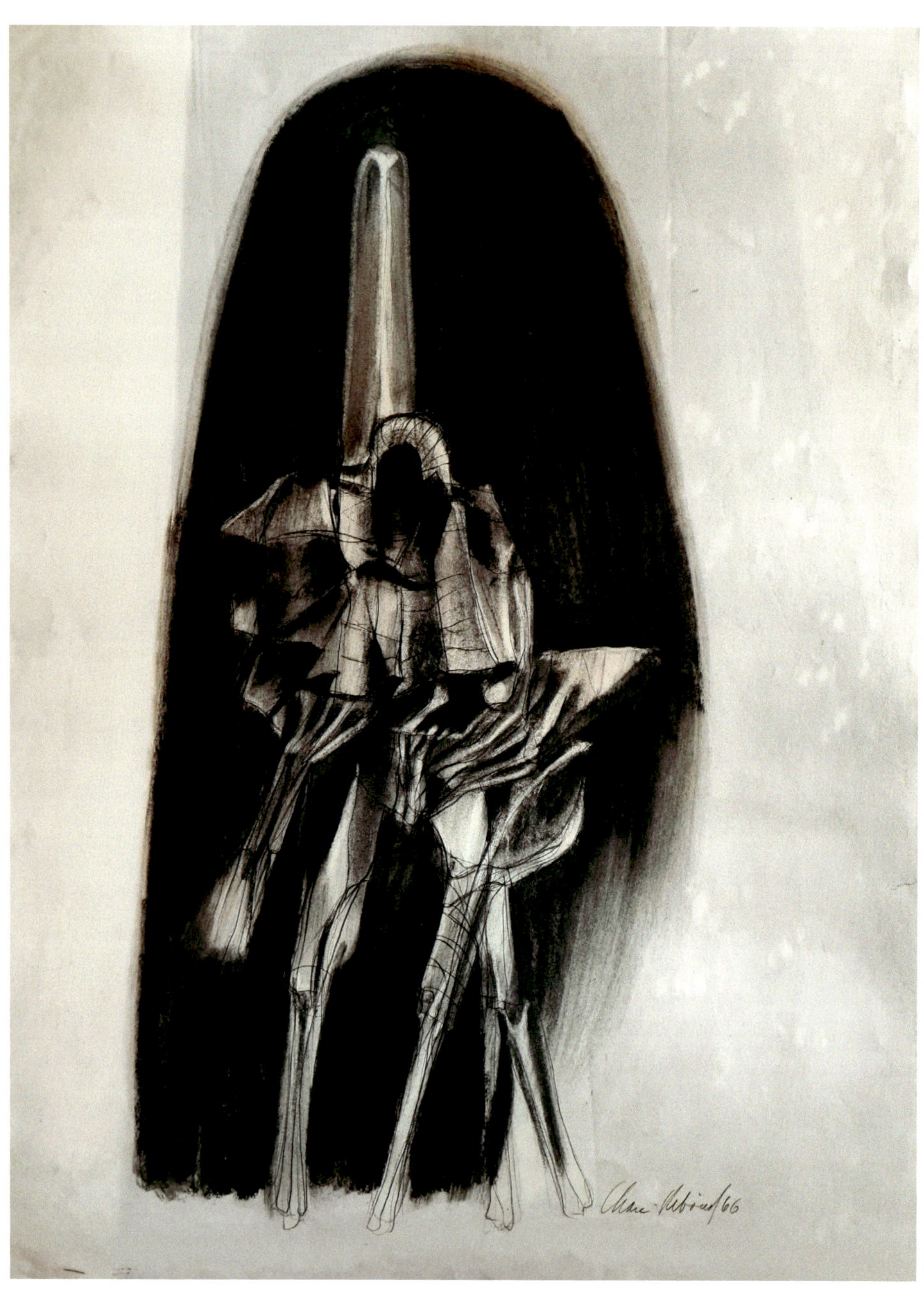

Fig. 3 Barbara Chase-Riboud, *Le Couple*,
1966. Charcoal and charcoal pencil
on Arches paper, 29⅞ × 22¹³⁄₁₆ inches
(76 × 58 cm). Private collection

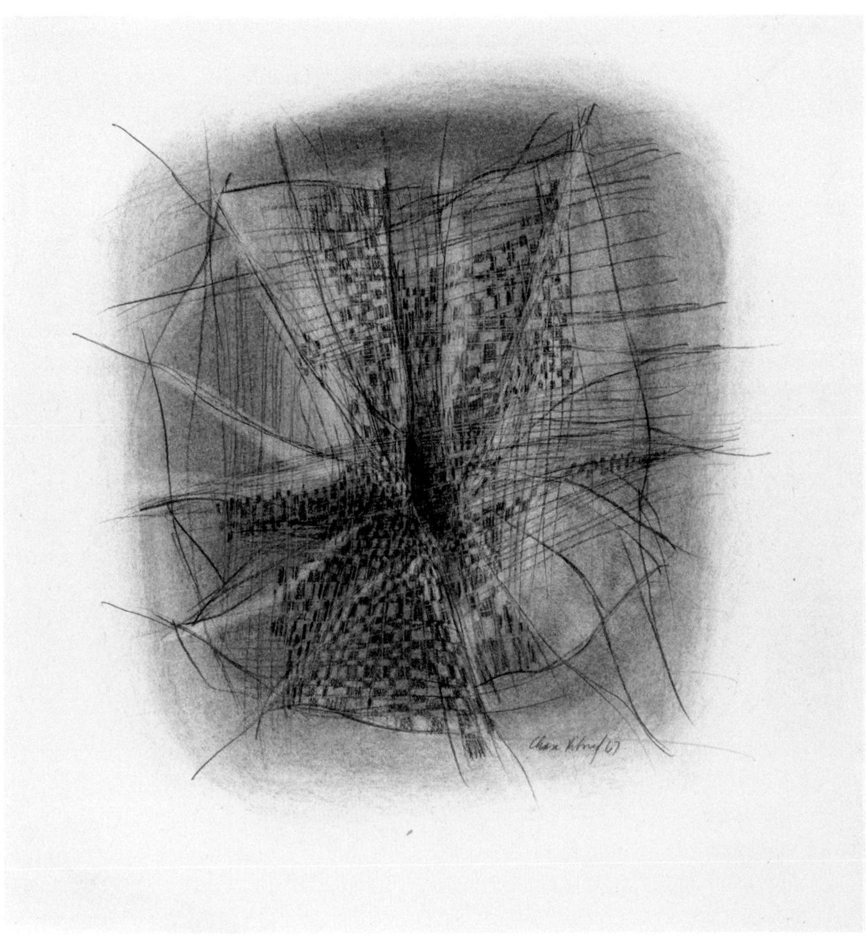

Fig. 4 Barbara Chase-Riboud, Untitled, 1967. Pencil and charcoal on paper, 11⅛ × 10¼ inches (28 × 26 cm)

lines, often applied on top of blended charcoal areas. The spiderweb associations they suggest—both literal and figurative—is further emphasized in an untitled drawing executed a few months later, in 1967 (fig. 4). It reveals a distinctive spiderweb structure encrusted within a checkerboard pattern. Through these works on paper made over a short period of time, Chase-Riboud establishes a pictorial language in which near invisible lines serve to structure and amalgamate the fractured surfaces. And it is precisely this new language that would be applied to her sculptures in the years to come.

The sculptures made by Chase-Riboud in the late 1960s and early 1970s share, beyond their monumental verticality, the fact that they often combine different materials, predominantly bronze and ropes made of wool, silk, and other fibers. The bronze element is usually obtained through lost-wax casting, a technique that dates back to ancient Egypt. In conversation with the art critic Eleanor Munro in 2000, the artist reminisced about these works:

> In the early pieces, I had used bronze in a fluid, liquid way, while the wool was static. So there was a paradoxical transfer of power from the bronze to the silk or wool. It really looked as if the wool was holding up the bronze. The fiber became a column that literally seemed to hold up the bronze. So the wool became the strong element—let's call it, for argument's sake, the male element. And the bronze became the soft, or female, element. I liked the impossibility, the contradiction of that. It pleased me no end.[9]

Chase-Riboud's description points toward something larger than what it initially suggests. The binaries that her sculptures aim to reconcile—male and female or black and white—and the transfer of power that allows for such an operation are inherent to her practice. This is true not only over time, from her earliest to her current work, but also across mediums. On a formal level, the "black drawings" from 1966, which derived from the literal fusion of a male and female body, anticipate the way in which Chase-Riboud tends to bestow particular elements with the opposite of their usual function. In these works on paper, for instance, surfaces are not delineated through pencil lines. As with the sculptures, in which flexible ropes appear to support weighty bronze components, the lines in Chase-Riboud's drawings come later in the composition, not to outline but to hold surfaces together. The transfer of power in the sculptures, in which wool or silk becomes the dominant force, therefore, first took place in the drawings, in which line was given the stronger role. In many ways, Chase-Riboud's drawings lead to her sculptures, but not in the conventional sense, in which drawings might,

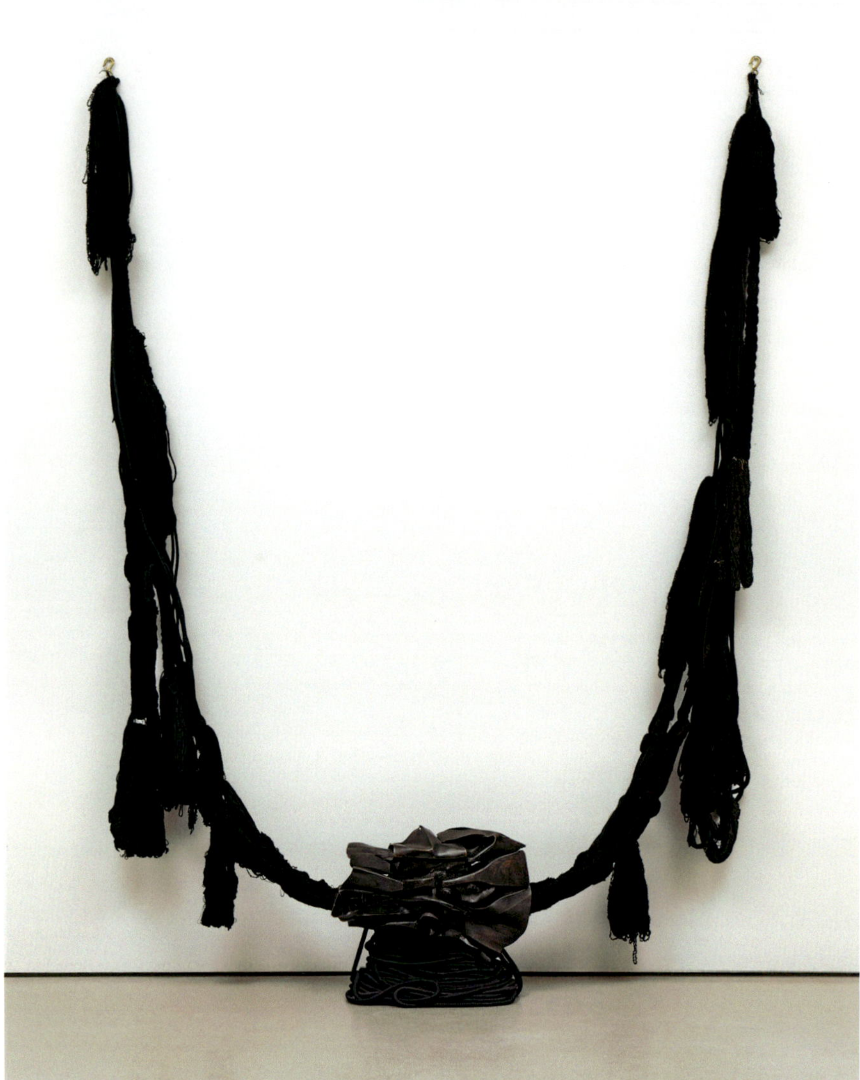

for example, be used to sketch out various volumes. They rather antici-pate the strategies operating in the sculptures.

And it is perhaps a passage from her poem "The Albino," written in relation to one of her breakthrough sculptures from 1972 (fig. 5), which most clearly evokes the tensions present in her early drawings, and their ultimate resolution in her three-dimensional work:

> *I am as male as I am female*
> *I am as white as I am black*
> *There is no difference*
> *Between She and He*
> *Between You and Me*
> *You are as female as you are male*
> *You are as black as you are white*
> *Together we are*
> *One*
> *Yet together*
> *We are not*
> *One*

Notes

1. Quoted by Emilie Bouvard in "Making-of,"
in *Alberto Giacometti, Barbara Chase-Riboud:
Standing Women of Venice, Standing Black
Women of Venice* (Paris: Fondation
Giacometti-Institut, 2021), 69.

2. The exhibition title was *It's All Yours*.
The woodcut *Reba* is not reproduced in
the January 1955 issue of *Seventeen*, but a
semiabstract composition by the artist is
pictured (p. 77). The print takes its title
from an eponymous short story, written by
Dorrit Weill and published in the magazine,
about a teenage girl's infatuation with a young
baseball player who is not ready to date.
Chase-Riboud commented in a recent
interview, "it was supposed to illustrate the
story. And the story was about a girl named
Reba, who was not colored: she was white.
And so the woodcut is the woodcut of a
young, white figure." Transcript of Barbara
Chase-Riboud, oral history interview by Erin
Jenoa Gilbert, Archives of American Art,
Smithsonian Institution, Washington, DC,
June 7–11, 2019. It is noteworthy to mention
that Chase-Riboud is given the age nineteen
in the interview while she was in fact fifteen,
and that Richard Hunt—another important
sculptor to be—illustrated another short story
in the same issue (p. 63).

3. During the 1970s, the director of MoMA's
Department of Photography, Edward
Steichen, acquired works by the American
photographer Stephen Shore when the artist
was fourteen years old.

4. Chase-Riboud, oral history interview.

5. See the excellent "Chronology" in *Barbara
Chase-Riboud—Malcolm X: Complete* (New
York: Michael Rosenfeld Gallery, 2017), 79.

6. See, for example, the exhibitions *Barbara
Chase-Riboud: Dessins et sculptures: Couples
mythologiques*, at Le Cadran Solaire in Paris
in 1966, and *Barbara Chase-Riboud: The
Monument Drawings* (Wilmington, NC:
St. John's Museum of Art, 1998), which
traveled the following year to the Metropoli-
tan Museum of Art, New York, and in 2000–
2001 to the African American Museum,
Philadelphia; Diggs Gallery of Winston-Salem
State University, NC; and the Walters Art
Museum, Baltimore.

7. The following year the same gallery
mounted the first exhibition of another
singular draftsman and sculptor, Pierre
Klossowski.

8. The quote, first published in French in the
Cadran Solaire catalogue, was translated into
English in *Alberto Giacometti, Barbara
Chase-Riboud*, 42.

9. Eleanor Munro, *Originals: American Women
Artists* (New York: Da Capo Press, 2000), 374.

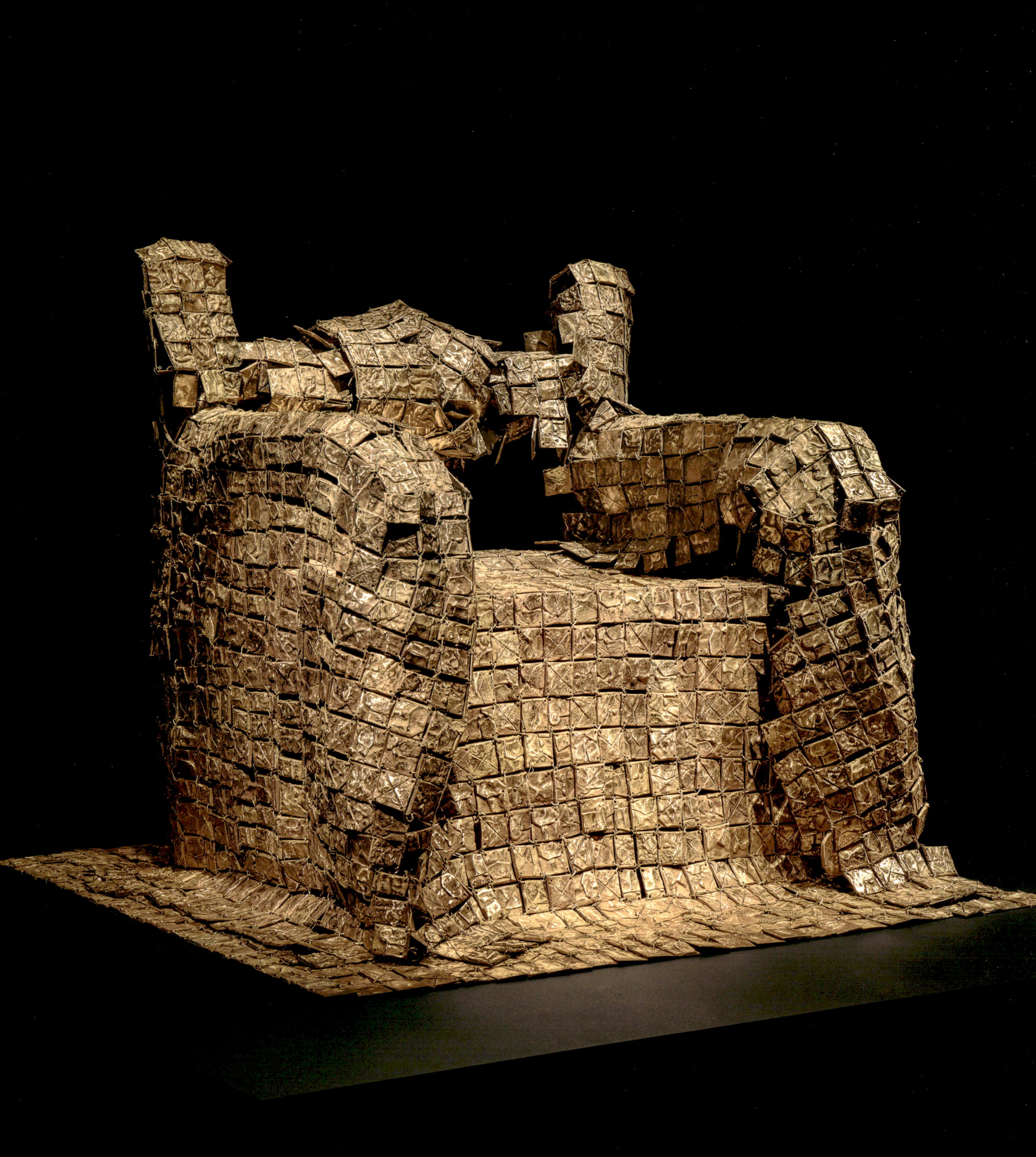

THE CLEOPATRA SCULPTURES

Akili Tommasino

Cleopatra VII Philopator, the queen of Egypt from 51 to 30 BCE, has been an enduring source of inspiration for the prolific visual and literary artist Barbara Chase-Riboud. Her work on the ruler, the last in the Ptolemaic line, includes an award-winning book of poems, *Portrait of a Nude Woman as Cleopatra* (1987); three mixed-media wall reliefs, each entitled *Cleopatra's Marriage Contract* (1973, 2000, and 2000); and five monumental, freestanding bronze sculptures—*Le Manteau (The Cape),* or *Cleopatra's Cape* 1973), *Cleopatra's Door* (1984), *Cleopatra's Chair* (1994), *Cleopatra's Bed* (1997), and *Cleopatra's Wedding Dress* (2003).[1] Situating these works within the artist's practice, this essay explores what the *Cleopatra* sculptures reveal about Chase-Riboud's working method and discusses their place in and contribution to the history of art.

Chase-Riboud's sculptural language disrupts expectations. Hard bronze, fragmented, linked, and draped against wood, is cast as supple fabric, while silk rope appears to be load-bearing. In the *Cleopatra* series, the juxtaposition of hard and soft materials mirrors the subject's place in a metaphorical limbo between Africa and Europe, and power and powerlessness, as her fortunes rise and fall. In 30 BCE, Cleopatra died ignominiously, if defiantly, poisoning herself after the defeat of her troops and the suicide of her husband Mark Antony. Octavian, the future Caesar Augustus, permitted the interment of her body with Antony in a crypt still to be discovered. With the *Cleopatra* series, Chase-Riboud has created a powerful monument for the legendary queen, who has no physical memorial. The artist has stated, "The genesis of my interest in Cleopatra is based on my fascination with POWER as wielded by women throughout the ages. The concept of women ruling the earth and shaping society in immutable ways continues to be a revolutionary idea even though it has been a fact for eons. The exceptional woman—a woman of

Barbara Chase-Riboud, *Cleopatra's Chair,* 1994. Multicolored cast-bronze plaques over oak, 39⅜ × 49⅝ × 43¼ inches (100 × 126 × 110 cm)

legendary status—is the essence of what Cleopatra is. She is an icon for modern women."[2]

The first sculpture in the series is *Cleopatra's Cape*, its shimmering shawl resembling a patchwork quilt of 3,500 bronze and copper squares (p. 83). The six-foot sculpture appears to sheath an invisible body. With this work, Chase-Riboud debuted a mode of working inspired by an ancient Chinese example. In 1972, Marc Riboud, her husband at the time, had written to her from China about seeing the recently excavated jade burial suits of Prince Liu Sheng and Princess Dou Wan.[3] Interred side by side, the Han Dynasty rulers must have reminded Chase-Riboud of Antony and Cleopatra, who likewise share a tomb. The form-fitting jade suits resemble suits of armor. Are they meant to preserve physical remains or gird souls for battles in the afterlife? Even before her *Cleopatra* series, Chase-Riboud had used armor as a motif. For the opening of Pierre Cardin's fashion house in 1962, she had designed an abstract suit of armor (fig. 1). *Cleopatra's Cape* conveys the dual properties of armor— protection and opulence—and forecasts its function as gear for eternity.[4]

That Chase-Riboud's sculptural cloak for an Egyptian queen is inspired by burial suits for ancient Chinese royalty reflects the syncretic notion of non-Western art that she developed through her experience of African and Asian cultures.[5] Her 1958 trip to Egypt and 1965 trip to China and Mongolia radically revised her perspective on Western art. Of her formative trip to Egypt, the artist recounts, "The blast of Egyptian culture was irresistible. The sheer magnificence of it. The elegance and perfection, the timelessness, the depth. After that, Greek and Roman art looked like pastry to me. . . . From an artistic point of view the trip was historic for me."[6] She later noted, "The Greco-Roman heritage was only part of a vast reservoir. There were other ways as important for me, as valid intellectually, deeper, and as beautiful. I could turn to the non-Western arts for ideas without feeling like I was working with folklore."[7] As the curator and art theorist Marta Kuzma observes, "Chase-Riboud attributes her 'radicalization' to these experiences wherein she was introduced to Black and Brown communities living in alternative economic and political systems. It was also from these experiences that Chase-Riboud adopted the perspective that art was not to mirror political reality but rather to abstract from it."[8] Chase-Riboud refers to her renowned, wholly abstract *Malcolm X* sculptures as "memorials in the Egyptian and Chinese tradition to an historical icon whose life radiated far beyond the politics of the temporal."[9] She similarly unites these non-Western aesthetics in her *Cleopatra* sculptures.

Cleopatra's Cape debuted in a presentation that included *Time Womb* (1971), a wall relief; *Bathers* (1972), a gridded floor work; *Le Lit* (1972), a compressed boxlike assemblage; *Zanzibar* (1972), a skirted assemblage; and *All That Rises Must Converge* (1973), a vertical column of bronze atop a skirt of silk. The formal heterogeneity of this group demonstrates Chase-Riboud's method of developing multiple series at a time and anticipates the sporadic emergence of the subse-quent sculptures in the *Cleopatra* series, all of which incorporate enchained bronze plaques draped over wooden structures that have been padded in some cases and embellished with braided silk. Personal effects the scale of architectural structures, the sculptures point to episodes in Cleopatra's life.

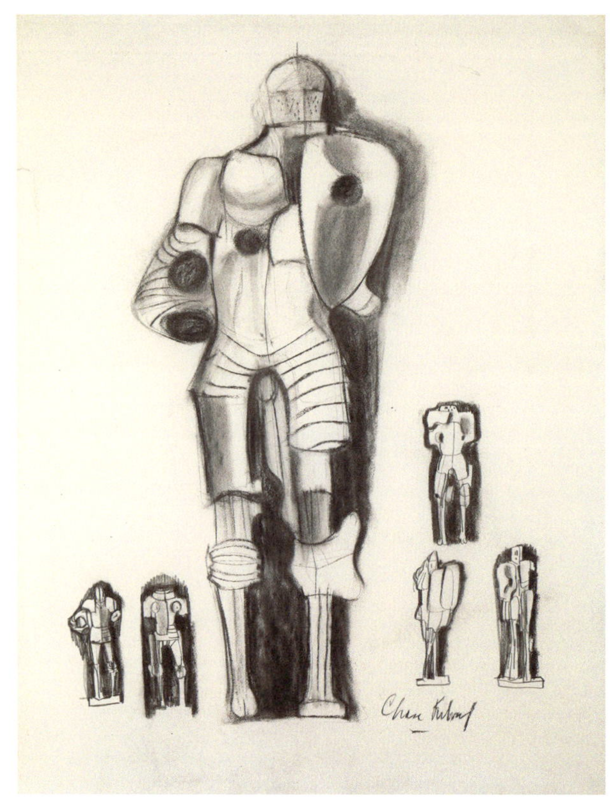

Fig. 1 Barbara Chase-Riboud, preparatory drawing for Pierre Cardin commission, c. 1962. Private collection

Cleopatra's Door, the second work in the series, consists of an eleven-foot-high oak frame draped with a sheet of patinated bronze tiles. Unlike the false doors of ancient Egyptian tombs, *Cleopatra's Door* is a perpetually open portal. The juxtaposition of organic and processed materials and the transformation of the appearance of hard bronze to malleable fabric underscore formal tensions between the solid and the void. This work also reflects the artist's enduring interest in architecture and the basic form of her monument drawings.

Cleopatra's Chair is a majestic, throne-like sculpture rendered in her signature stamped-bronze tesserae. It is the simultaneously opulent and austere descendant of a sculpture by another exceptional black woman who lived and worked in Rome a century before Chase-Riboud settled in Europe. Of Ojibwe and African American descent, Edmonia Lewis sculpted *The Death of Cleopatra* in 1876 (fig. 2). Unlike Lewis's dramatic depiction, which shows the queen in the throes of death, *Cleopatra's Chair* is conspicuously absent of its sitter. Paradoxically, it is both her throne and her deathbed.

Cleopatra's Bed (fig. 3) enshrines the other site of the tragic queen's power. Strands of a silk mattress are glimpsed through gaps in the quilt of bronze squares that covers the slablike form, while a thick braid of silk cord snakes onto the floor behind the bedpost. The Greek philosopher Plutarch reported that after her suicide, "when they opened the doors, they found Cleopatra stark dead, laid upon a bed of gold, attired and arranged in royal robes."[10]

Unlike the previous four sculptures in the series, which are placed directly on the floor, *Cleopatra's Wedding Dress* stands on a wooden base. Evoking the shape of a kimono, it is the most anthropomorphic of the *Cleopatra* sculptures. It is the triumphal conclusion to the series; the intricate and painstaking task of twisting wire to conjoin bronze plaques is now too onerous for the artist. *Cleopatra's Wedding Dress* possesses the "magical presence" Chase-Riboud ascribes to her seemingly gravity-defying sculptures that conceal their structure.[11] Along with three versions of *Cleopatra's Marriage Contract*, her "narrative paper sculptures," it reminds us that Cleopatra was eternally coupled with her husband Antony in death.[12]

The Cleopatra sculptures are as indebted to the jade burial suits and her reception of Egyptian aesthetics as they are to the compositional logic of the modernist grid. As she says, "My memories and impressions of Egypt were varnished with Bauhaus discipline."[13] Chase-Riboud's elegantly modular sculptures reanimate ancient forms to constitute something new. On innovation, the artist has said, "It's not a question of technique; it's a question of invention. The originality has a lot to do with the technique, but is not a function of the technique."[14] Chase-Riboud's mode of working combines highly skilled labor and the magic of chance. In a November 1973 interview with Friedrich W. Heckmanns, she

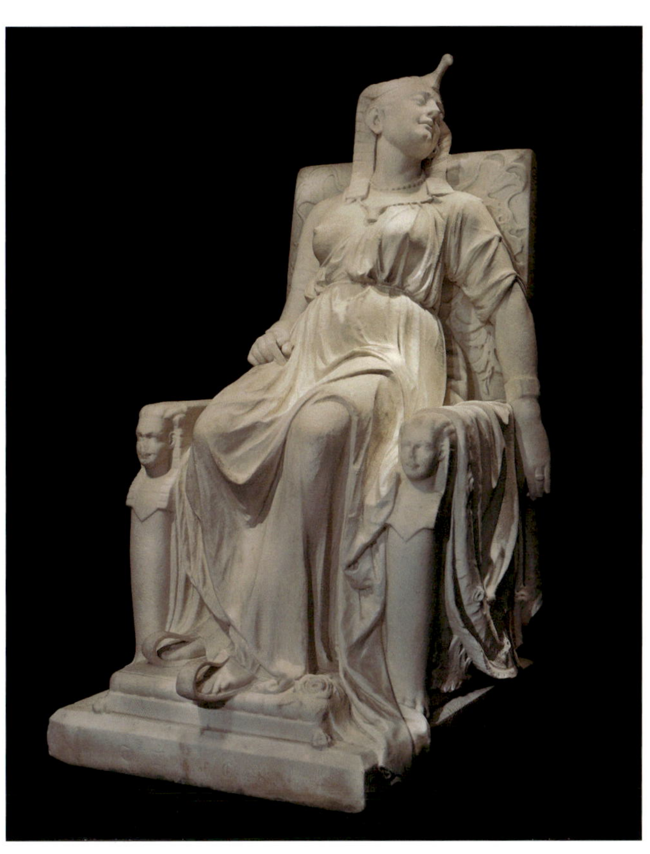

Fig. 2 Edmonia Lewis (1844–1907), *The Death of Cleopatra*, 1876. Marble, 63 × 31¼ × 46 inches (160.0 × 79.4 × 116.8 cm). Smithsonian American Art Museum, Gift of the Historical Society of Forest Park, Illinois, 1994.17

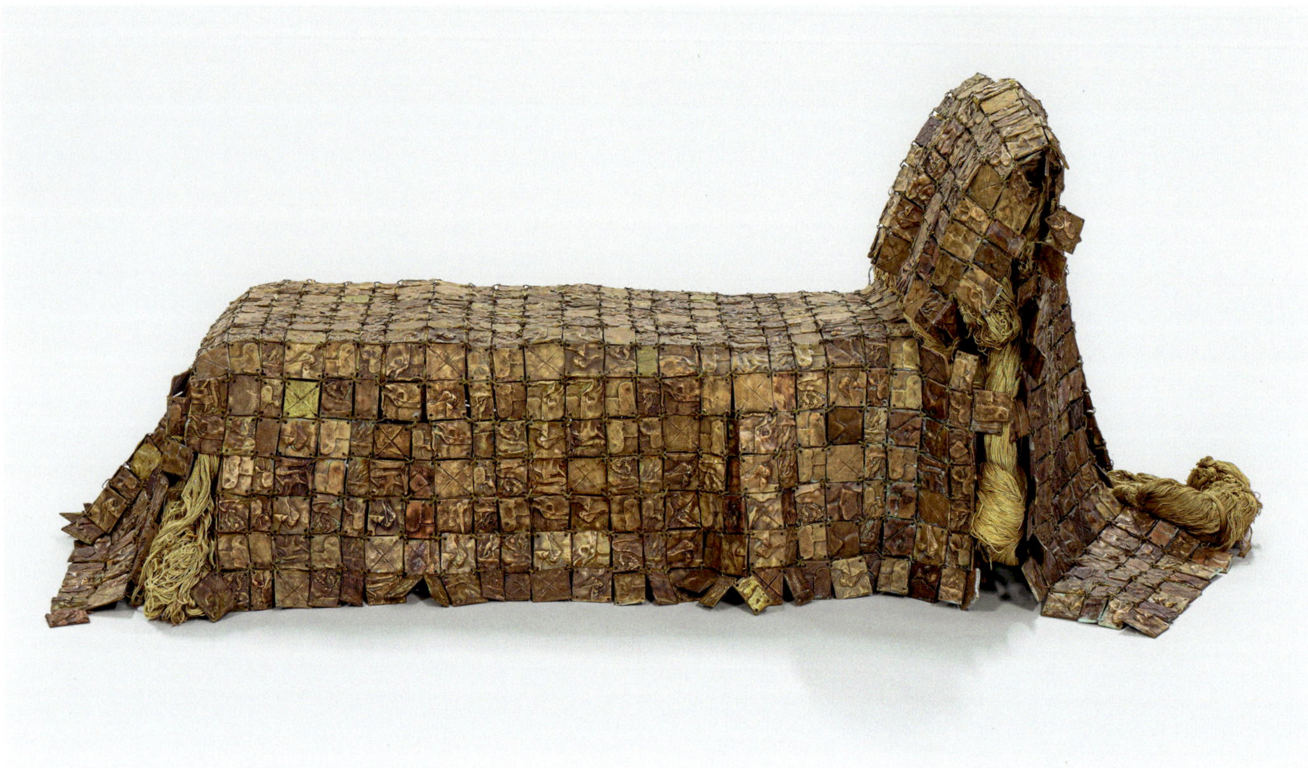

describes the innovative and proprietary process of fabricating the multicolored bronze plates for *Cleopatra's Cape*, which debuted in a German gallery exhibition.

> "The Cape" and "The Nursery" are the most recent sculptures completed just before this exhibition. They obviously show new tendencies of plastic realization. First, they are perhaps more "magical," more "mystical." Above all, however, the production technique for "The Cape" is almost alchemical. A process of color change of the bronze occurs at the moment of pouring into the mold through the addition of certain minerals. I reckon with this unlimited color change. I only work with that foundry in Paris, and they want to keep to themselves how they do it, i.e., how the iridescent colors are brought about, each tile has a different color, none is the same as the other and even the foundryman can't control the color, which varies from violet, blue, gray to green and gold. This uncontrolled, almost random process has a certain poetic quality. Furthermore, the metal, which hitherto had only been shaped and modeled, is now shattered, fragmented into small parts and then brought together again, by carefully selecting them for their coloration—so they are reunited under a certain control.[15]

The stamping, selection, and sequencing of similar-sized, bronze plaques evoke the modernist grid and compositional modularity, while the unruly alchemical process of the forge manifests as a chance operation.

These structural concepts have roots and reflections in language. Moreover, Chase-Riboud's sculpture must be understood within the

Fig. 3 Barbara Chase-Riboud, *Cleopatra's Bed*, 1997. Multicolored plates, steel structure, and mattress, 23⅝ × 47¼ × 23⅝ inches (60 × 120 × 60 cm). Private collection

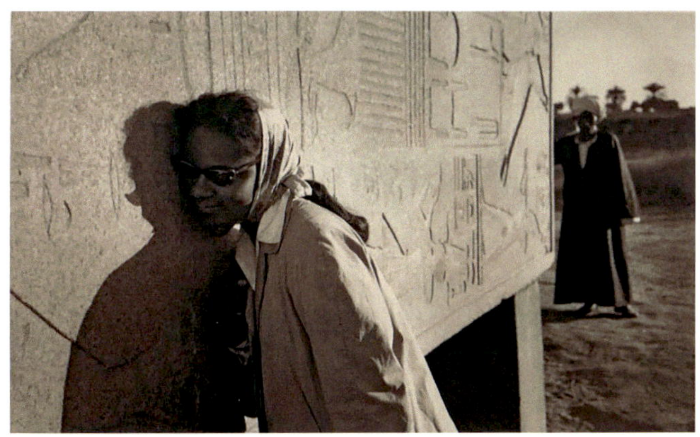

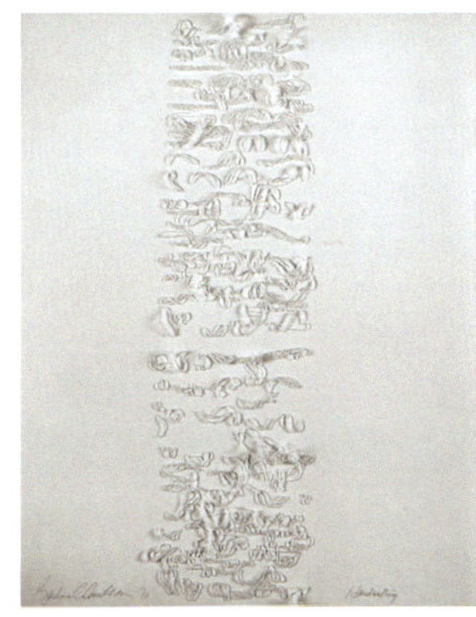

Fig. 4 Barbara Chase-Riboud in Karnak, Egypt, c. January–March 1958

Fig. 5 Barbara Chase-Riboud, *Handwriting*, 1976. Synthetic silk and paper, 25½ × 19¾ inches (64.8 × 50.2 cm). Private collection

greater context of her literary and visual production. The evidence that tactility and language go hand in hand for the artist is abundant throughout her oeuvre.[16] A photo from her formative trip to Egypt in 1958 shows her in a chic scarf, bespectacled, and smiling as she presses her ear against a massive granite block of carved hieroglyphs at the Karnak temples, as though the ancient reliefs were whispering a message to her that she elicits through touch, like braille (fig. 4). The verbal, the optical, and the haptic are linked in her parallel creative streams. *Handwriting* (1976) features rows of irregular loops of white yarn woven into paper to form a justified column of threaded "text" (fig. 5). Establishing an alphabet of thirteen unique engraved plaque designs for her *Cleopatra* works, Chase-Riboud sequences sculptural units in a manner akin to the linguistic syntax of the Egyptian cartouche or Chinese calligraphy block. The language established in 1973 with *Cleopatra's Cape* is one she returns to periodically, like a second language: sporadically, but with the precision and force of a native speaker. Shown with diverse bodies of work but never yet all together, the sculptures are distinct expressions of a shared formal language.

Chase-Riboud's *Cleopatra* sculptures occupy a unique position on the representational spectrum for an artist best known for wholly abstract forms. Though the cape, door, chair, bed, and wedding dress are not figurative sculptures, they are sculptures made for a vanished figure. Absent the subject, these objects evade the contemporary debates about Cleopatra's racial identity and appearance. They also avoid polemics concerning an imperative for black artists to make explicitly politically expressive work, as well as the political labor of figuration.[17] Peter Selz asserts that Chase-Riboud built the imposing structures *for* Cleopatra.[18] Many artistic depictions of the queen focus on the climactic moment of her death (by snake bite, according to the most sensational account). Reminiscent of the ancient Egyptian practice of burying the dead with deluxe versions of quotidian objects, Chase-Riboud's structures support vital concepts and activities: protection, rest, sex, marriage, sovereignty. Moreover, as most of the sculptures are installed directly on the floor, without pedestals (a Minimalist strategy), they appear to be more tangible and less part of the removed realm of art. Individually, the *Cleopatra* sculptures are monumental versions of mundane furnishings and accoutrements. Collectively, however, as the site for potential action or commemoration, they embody the form of abstraction contained in ritual.[19] Though the complete *Cleopatra* series has not been shown together, hypothetically assembled the sculptures might resemble the set for an eternal drama.[20] From the garments to the furniture one can conjure new and remembered emotive and phenomenological narratives.

Chase-Riboud has devoted four decades to the story of Cleopatra, revealing concepts layered throughout her artistic practice. The fusion of ancient Egyptian history and ancient Chinese funerary sculpture with the modernist grid and chance operations in the foundry reflects Chase-Riboud's eclecticism, dialogue with different cultures and temporalities, and technical innovation. Its syntactic compositional logic affirms the inseparability of language and sculpture for the artist. Its material metaphors that invert or hold oppositional forces and textures in tension reflect the dialectical nature of her aesthetic. Most of all, the *Cleopatra* sculptures evince the artist's transformation of mundane structures into spatiotemporal abstractions emblematic of the indomitable power of women.

Notes

1. *Portrait of a Nude Woman as Cleopatra* (1987), a collection of fifty-seven sonnets, was awarded the prestigious Carl Sandburg Poetry Prize in 1988. In 1994, Barbara Chase-Riboud would publish another book of Egyptian-themed poems, *Roman égyptien*.

2. Barbara Chase-Riboud, http://chaseriboud .free.fr/Poet2004.htm, accessed April 5, 2022.

3. Peter Selz and Anthony F. Janson, *Barbara Chase-Riboud: Sculptor* (New York: Harry N. Abrams, 1999), 49.

4. *Cleopatra's Cape* was highlighted in Joseph Manca, Patrick Bade, and Sarah Costello, *1000 Sculptures of Genius* (New York: Parkstone Press, 2007), 993.

5. Chase-Riboud also linked Egypt and China in the title of her 1974 book of poems, *From Memphis and Peking*.

6. Gregory N. Daugherty, "Barbara Chase-Riboud's Multimedia Receptions of Cleopatra," *New Voices in Classical Reception Studies* 8 (2013): 49.

7. Eleanor Munro, *Originals: American Woman Artists* (New York: Simon and Schuster, 1979), 373.

8. Marta Kuzma, "Nous savons son nom / We Know Her Name," in *Alberto Giacometti, Barbara Chase-Riboud: Standing Women of Venice, Standing Black Woman of Venice* (Paris: Fondation Giacometti-Institut, 2021), 26–27.

9. Barbara Chase-Riboud, "Taken to Its Extreme: The Malcolm X Steles," in *Barbara Chase-Riboud—Malcolm X: Complete* (New York: Michael Rosenfeld Gallery, 2017), 23.

10. Selz and Janson, *Barbara Chase-Riboud: Sculptor*, 50.

11. Munro, *Originals*, 373.

12. In *Cleopatra's Marriage Contract* (1973) and the subsequent works in this series, sculpture and writing explicitly come together. They combine drawings, handwriting, and sculptural elements such as wax pendants on Corten steel. I acknowledge that further analysis isn't possible without access to these works to read their dense texts, which prompt comparisons to Surrealist automatic writing. Gregory N. Daugherty calls these works ironic, as the legal status of Antony and Cleopatra's marriage was questionable; Daugherty, "Barbara Chase-Riboud's Multimedia Receptions of Cleopatra," 52.

13. Munro, *Originals*, 372.

14. Chase-Riboud, "Taken to Its Extreme," 13.

15. Barbara Chase-Riboud, interview with Friedrich W. Heckmanns, in *Chase-Riboud: Calderara* (Krefeld: Galerie und Edition Merian, 1973), unpaginated, 2 (my translation).

16. This is also reflected in the shared titles of some works across mediums.

17. This is also the case for Chase-Riboud's *Monuments* drawings, in which she privileges architecture and omits the figure.

18. Selz and Janson, *Barbara Chase-Riboud: Sculptor*, 50.

19. Many have noted the commemorative impulse throughout Chase-Riboud's work, from her *Malcolm X* series to her *Monument* drawings, and her historical novels that resurrect the memory of hidden figures to public monuments like *Africa Rising* (1997).

20. Picking up the polyphonic narrative potential of Chase-Riboud's work, the composer Leslie Savoy Burrs created in 2008 a jazz opera based on her book of poetry *Portrait of a Nude Woman as Cleopatra*.

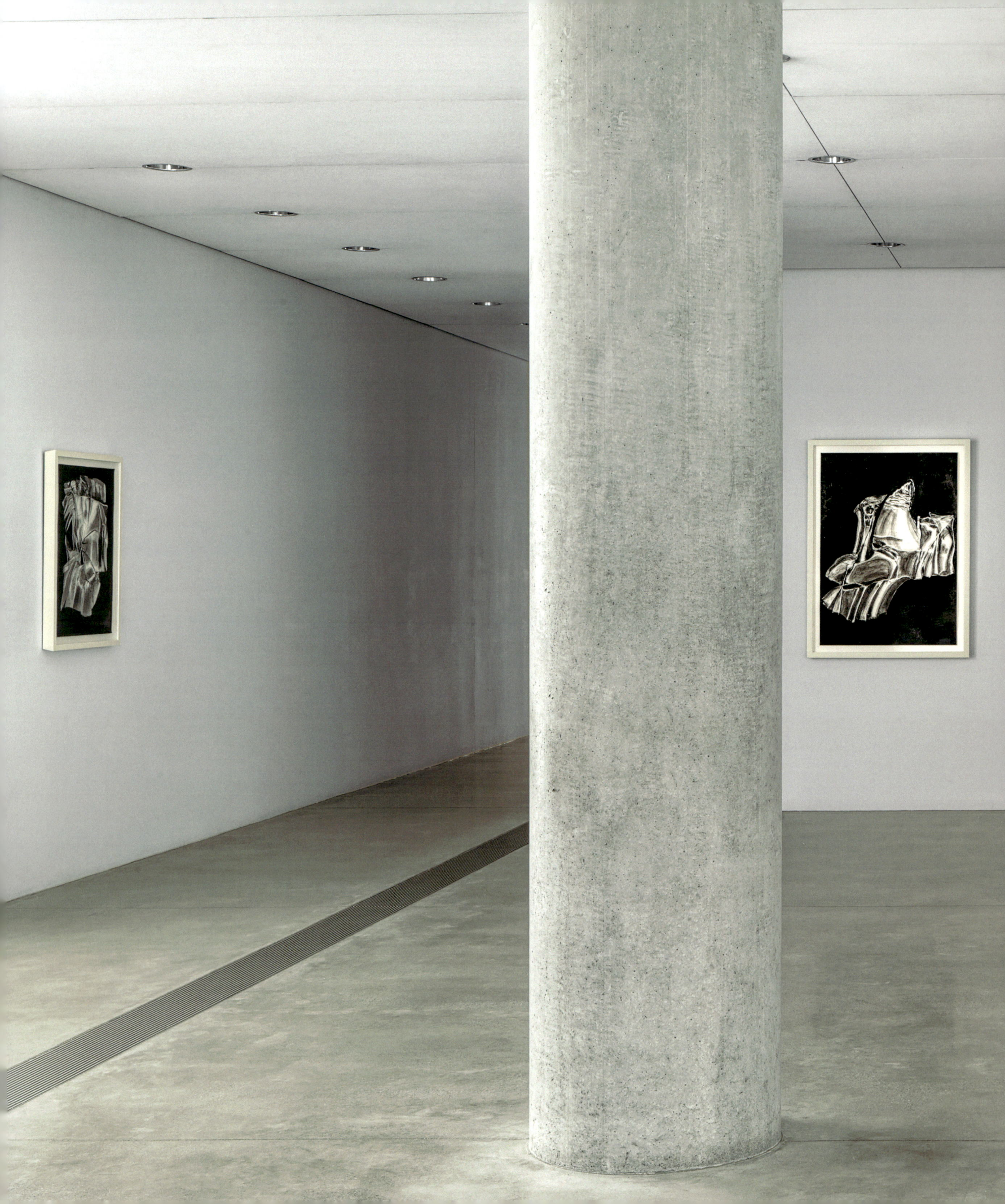

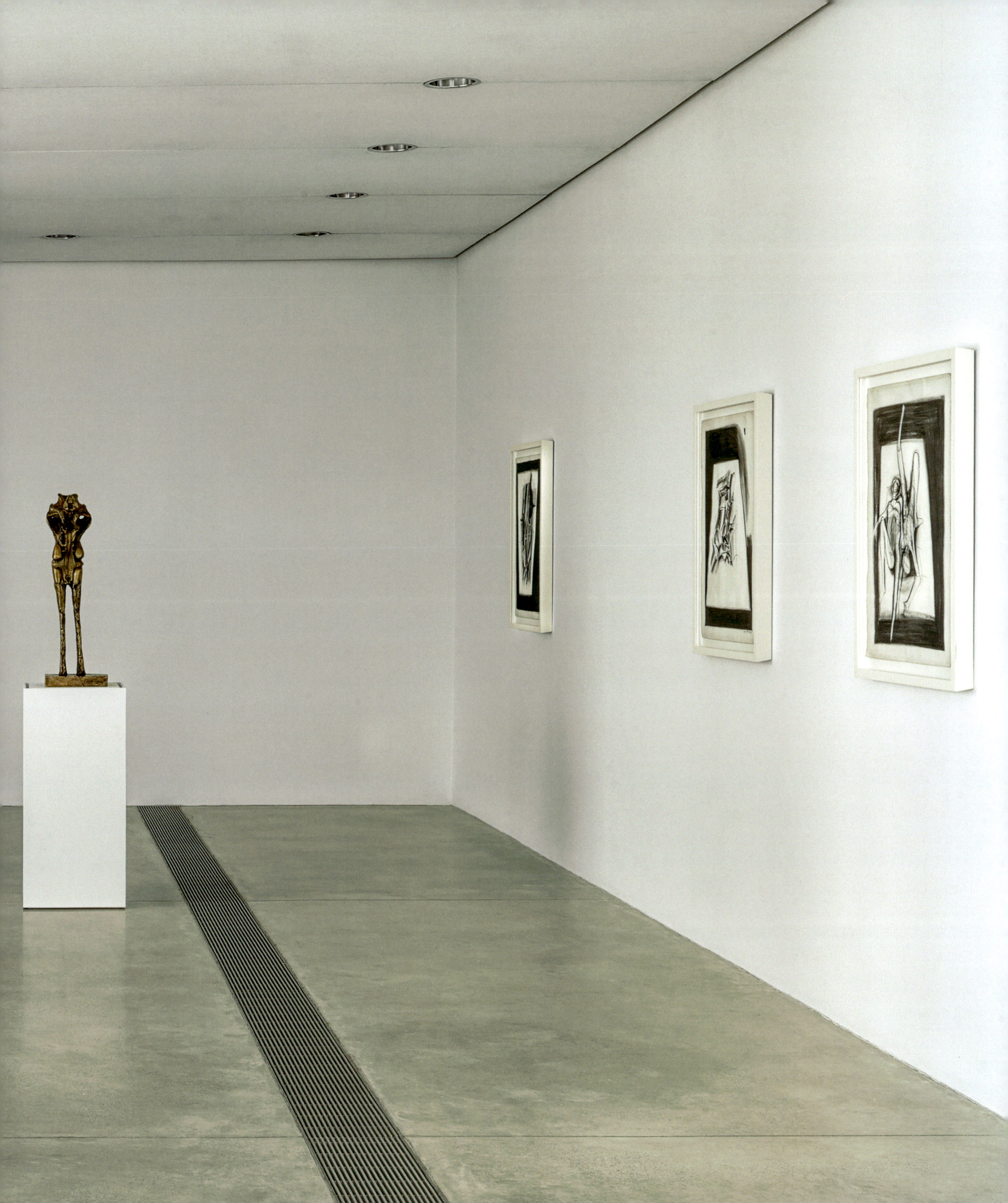

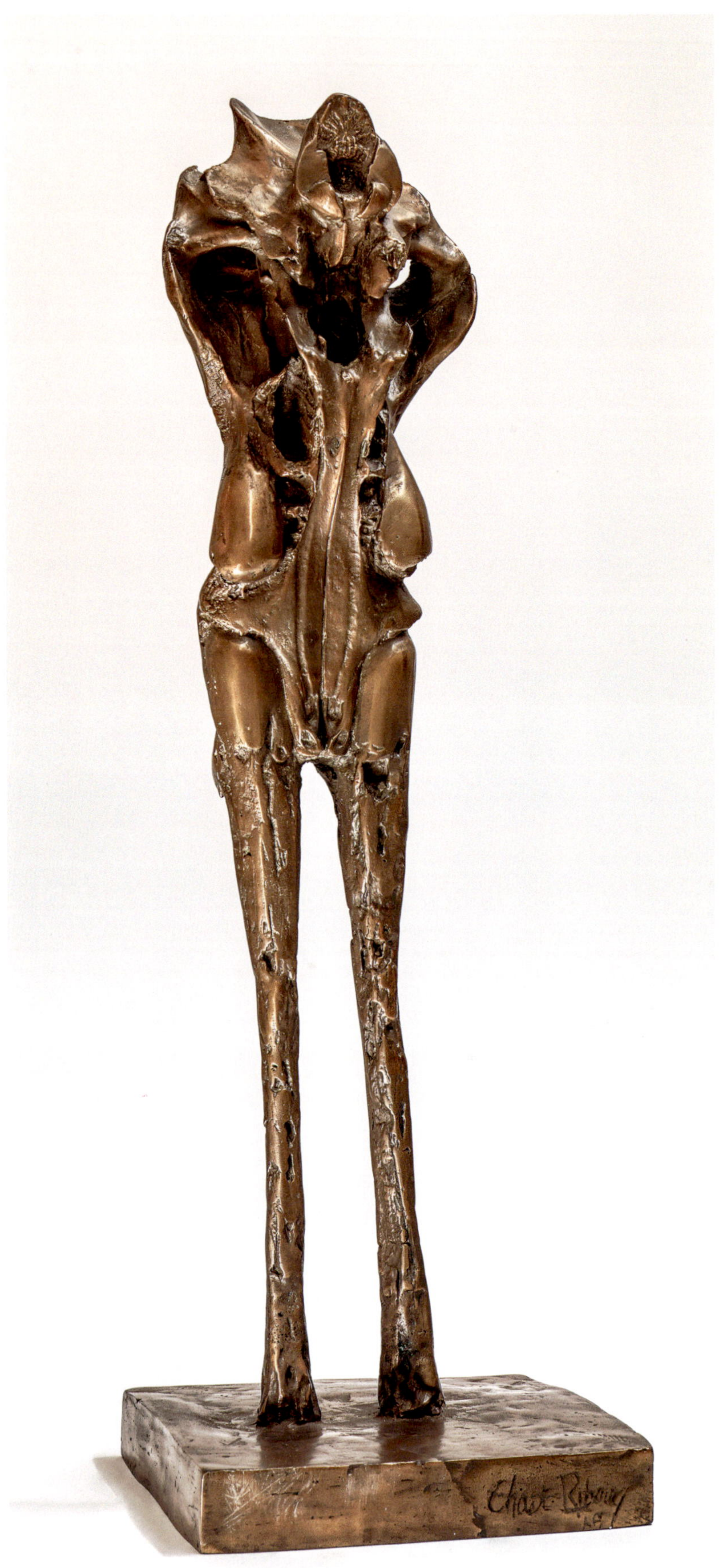

Nostradamus, 1966. Bronze, 30⅝ × 10 × 10 inches (77.8 × 25.4 × 25.4 cm)

Le Lit, 1966. Charcoal, charcoal pencil, and ink with engraving and aquatint on paper, 31½ × 23⅞ inches (80 × 60.6 cm)

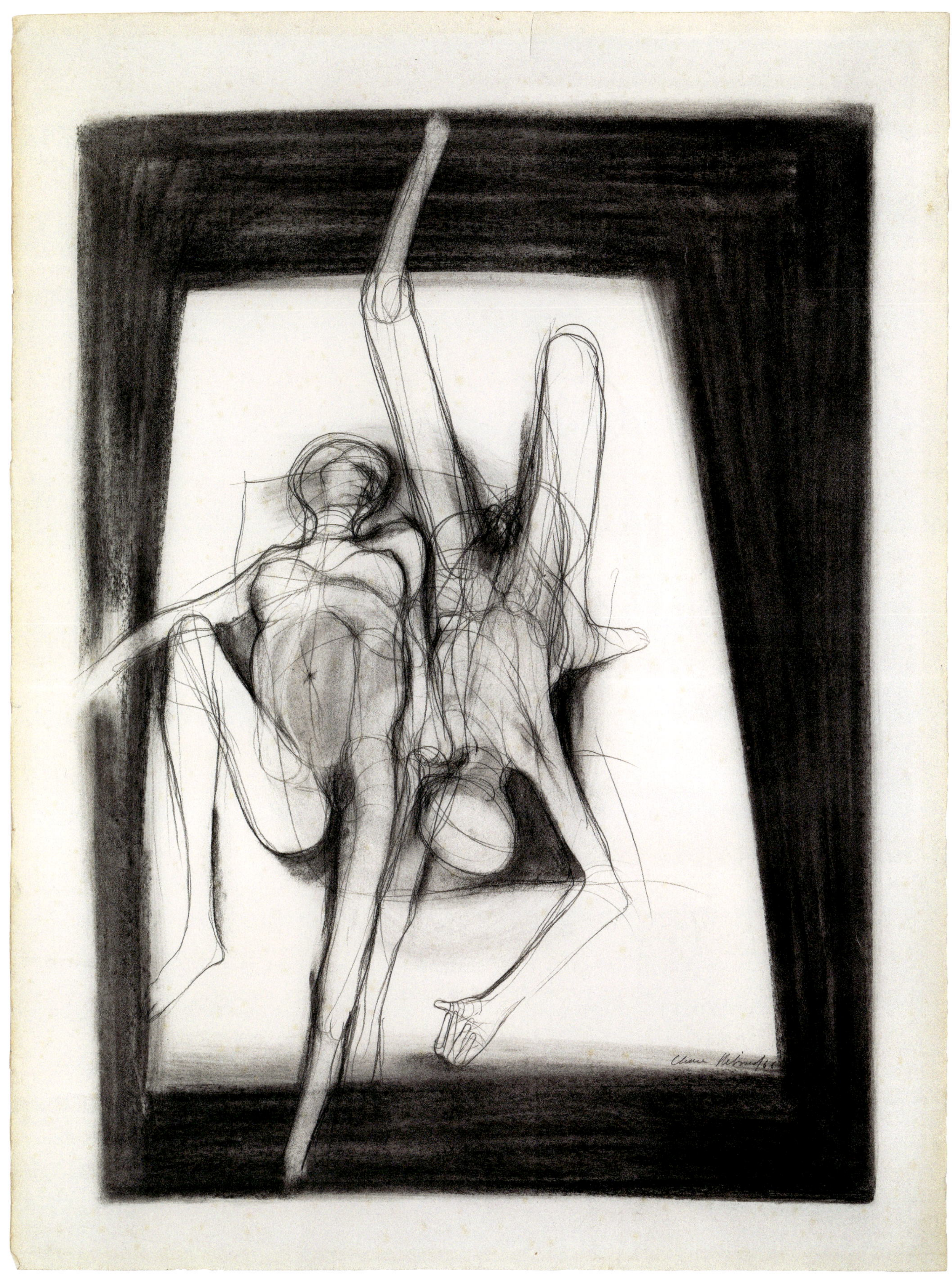

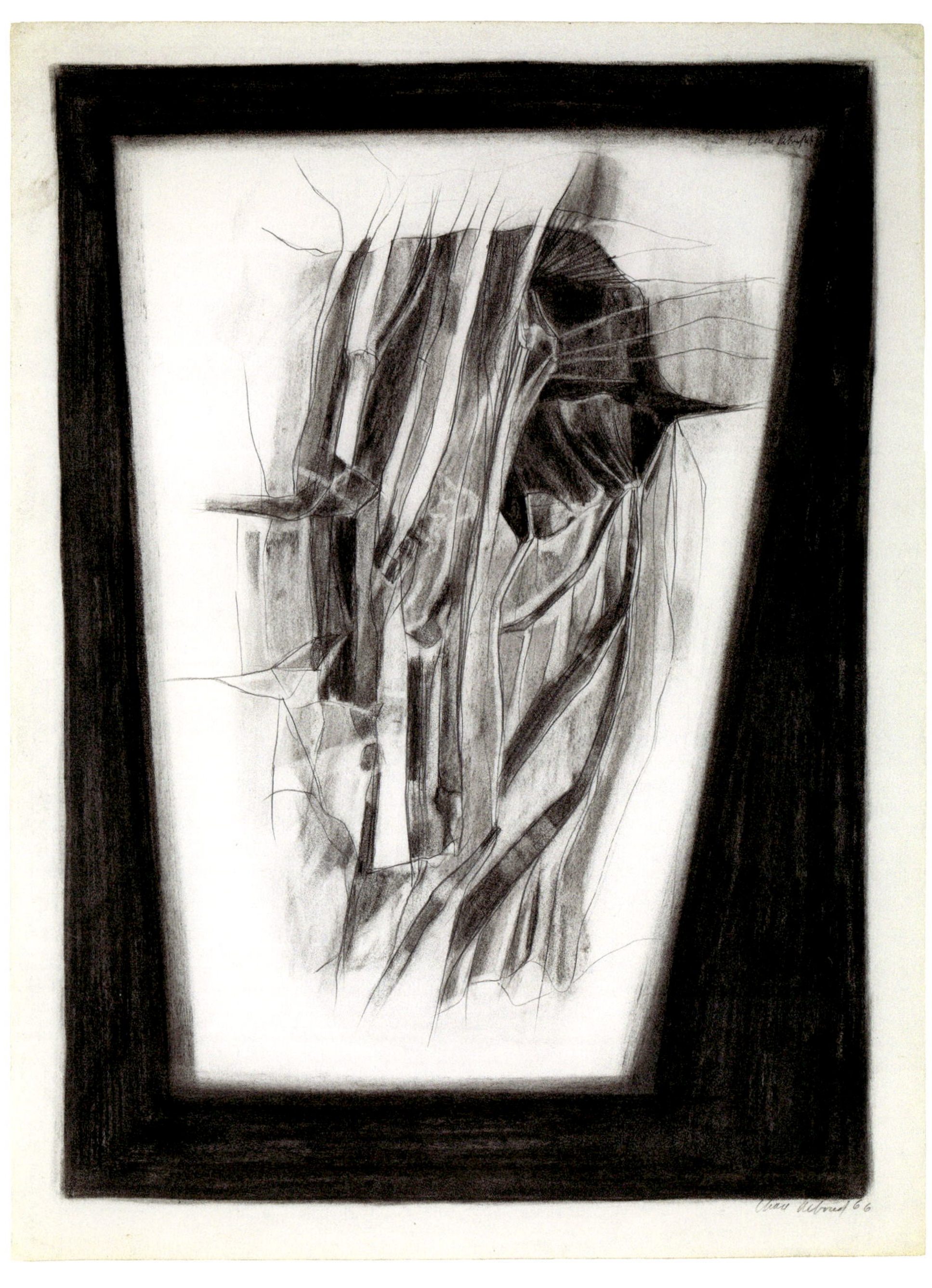

Le Lit, 1966. Charcoal and charcoal pencil
on paper, 30 × 22⅛ inches (76.2 × 56.2 cm)

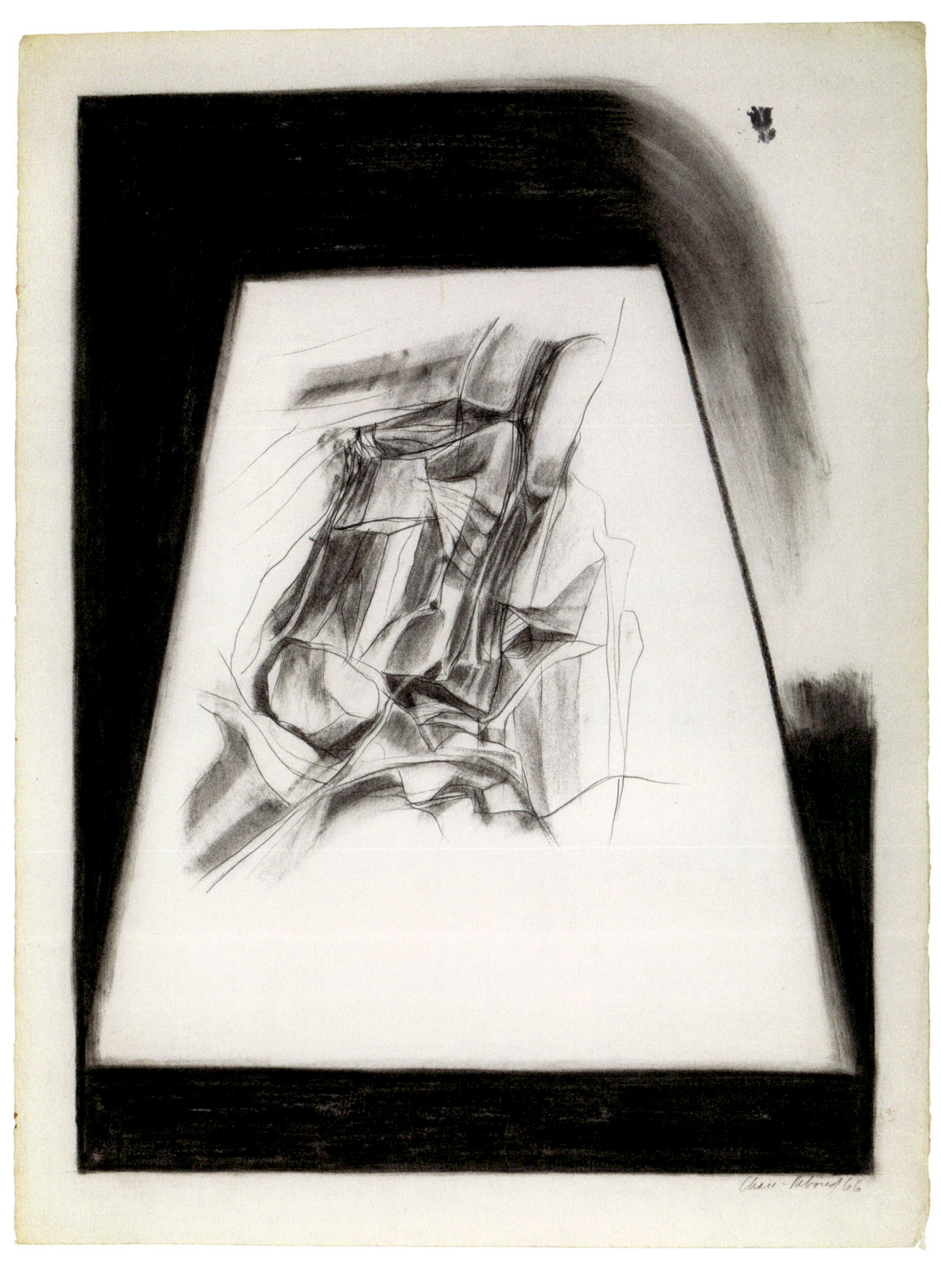

Le Lit, 1966. Charcoal, charcoal pencil, and
ink with engraving and aquatint on paper,
31½ × 23⅞ inches (80 × 60.6 cm)

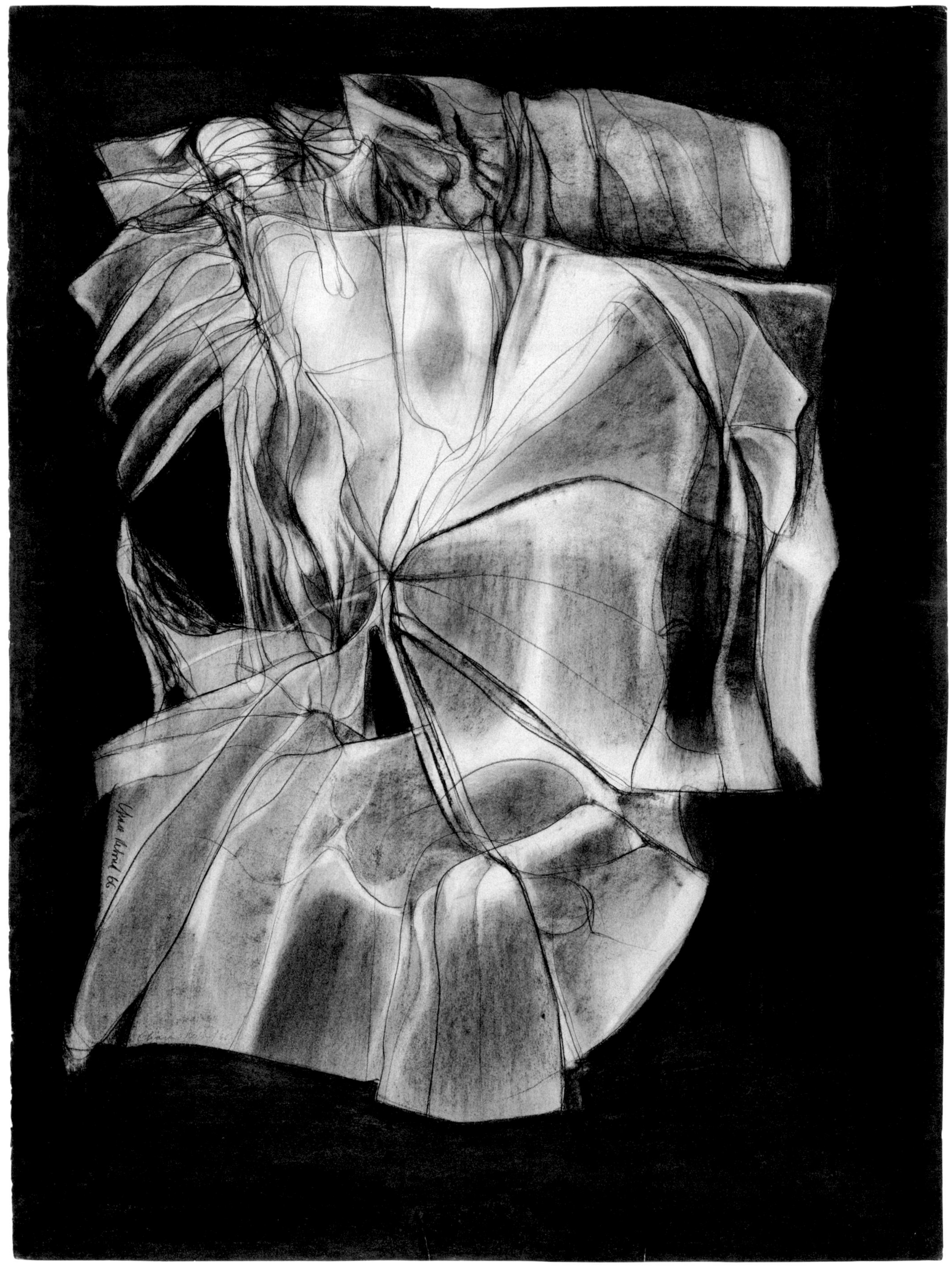

Le Lit

Sullen blizzard of white linen
Lying rumpled
Under the morning sun,
Last night's pressed flesh
Still glowing like the flickering shadows
Of a silent movie,
Contours still raging like burnt-out onion skin
Dry and flaking with
Tiny ridges where a thousand drummed dreams
Swim like microbes.

Pale, rider-less white,
Turning as the sun turns
Into a melancholy monument,
Spent sheets with the pillows on the floor,
Whistling like Memnon at dawn,
Blue-veined as Carrara marble,
Frozen into Alexandrine History,
A tombstone fashioned by some
Second-rate sculptor
To support his family of ten.

Summits like a crumpled Sphinx
Take on a life of their own.
Mesas and mountains rise and fall.
Lake bottoms and craters breathe and sigh
Strangled and tortured in the
Tangled limbs of a forlorn and
More than slightly ridiculous lagoon,
A neglected memorial from the Great War,
Expensively made only to be disfigured by
Disrespectful children.

I ache to soothe those troubled peaks of lust,
To calm the kind contusions of the night,
At least to lay a wreath on you
And sit silently
In my cripple's chair,
Relieved to be alive but not happy,
Straining to read
The half-effaced and fading legend
In Roman letters . . .

    HERE LIED.

Le Lit, 1966–73. Charcoal, charcoal pencil, and ink with engraving and aquatint on paper, 31½ × 23⅞ inches (80 × 60.6 cm)

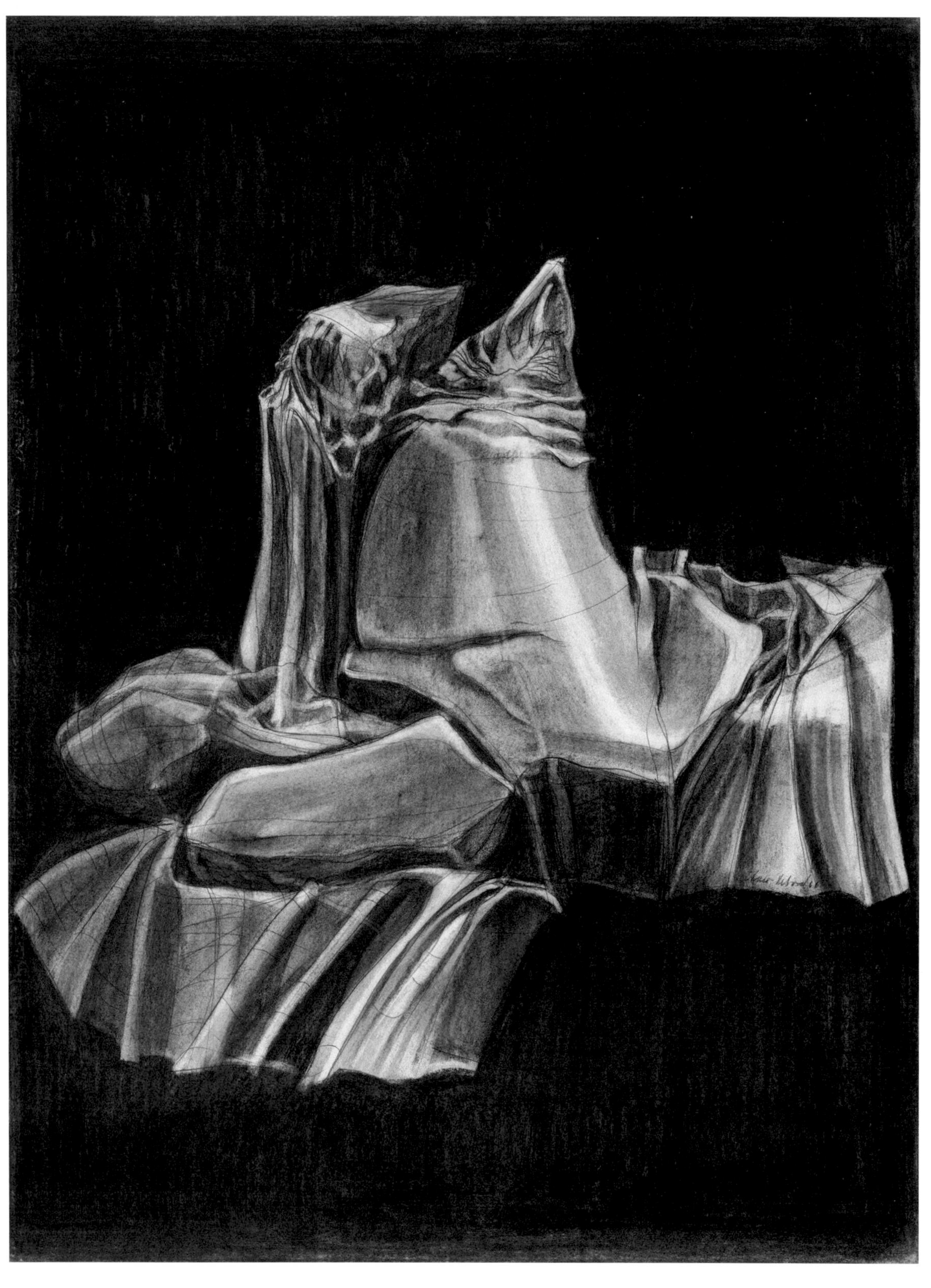

Untitled, 1966. Charcoal on paper, 30 × 21⅞ inches (76.3 × 55.7 cm)

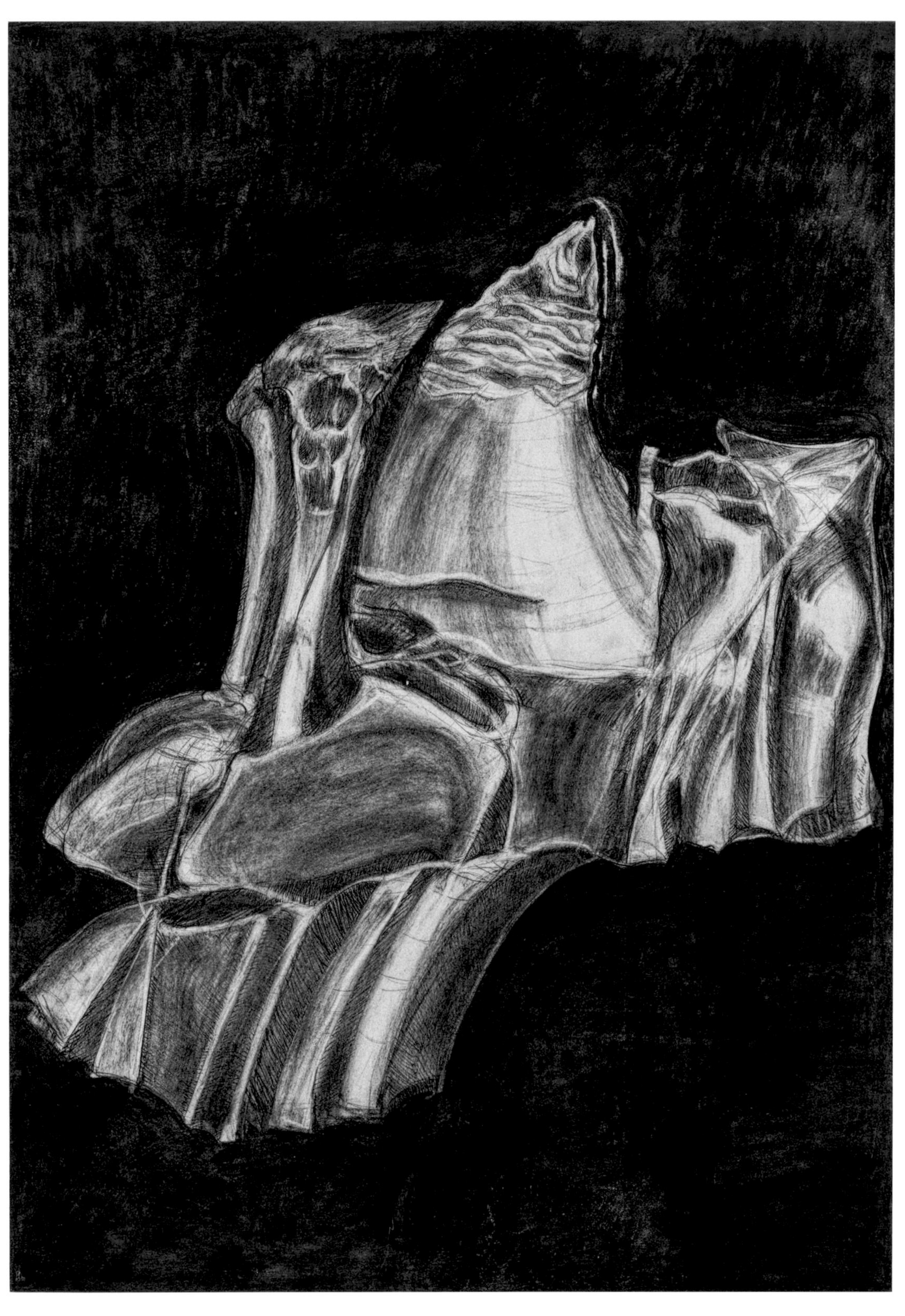

Untitled, 1966. Charcoal, charcoal pencil, and ink with engraving and aquatint on paper, 31½ × 23⅞ inches (80 × 60.6 cm)

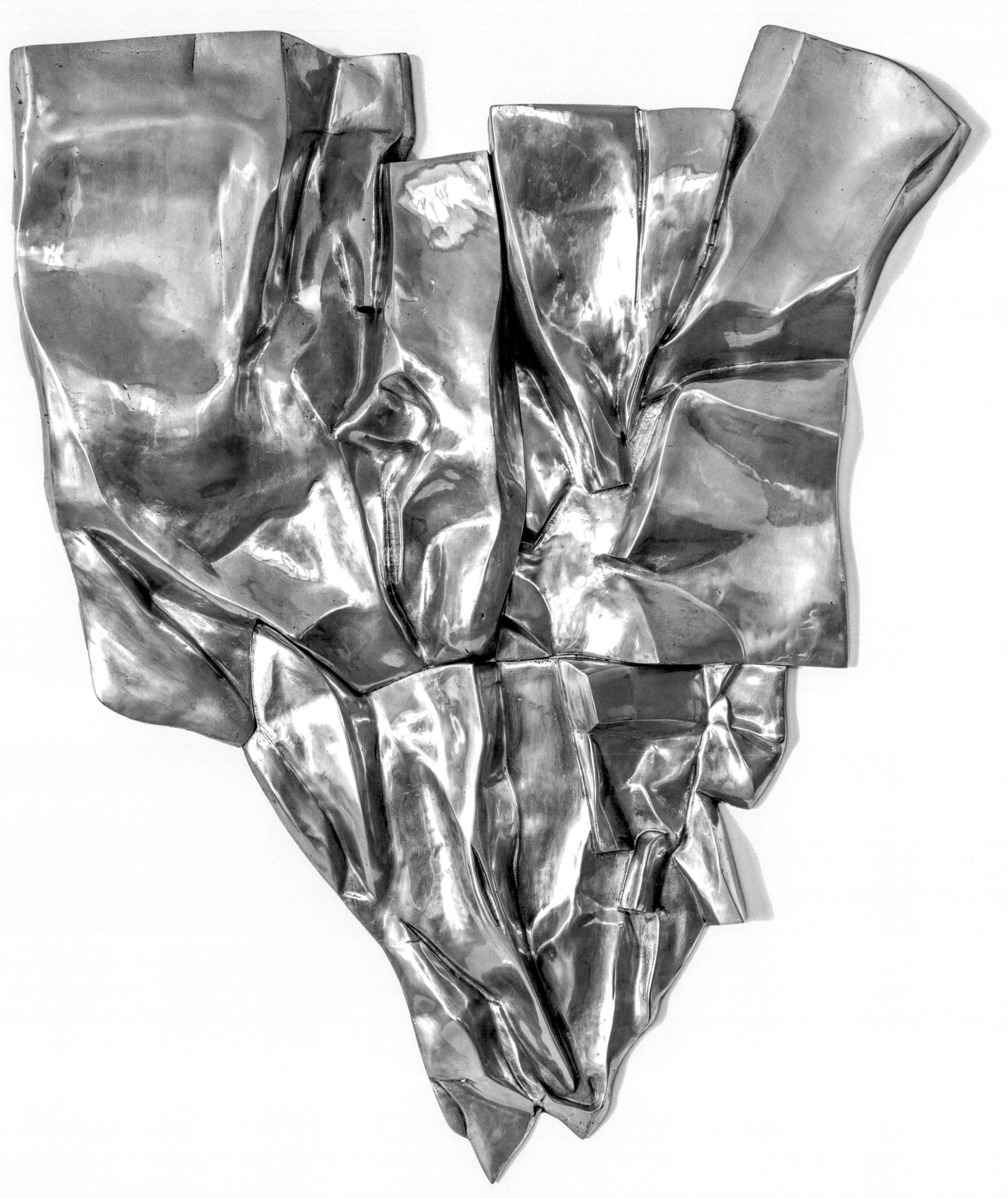

Performance

I

Let's start from the End, not the Beginning,
From the final curtain, not the overture
The Brass and Cymbals reverberate in climax
The roll of drums marks the chorus procession
And flutes and woodwinds accompany us

II

However, the conductor directed, we had a good time,
Our laughter and joie de vivre stole the show
Our performance enchanted the dazzled audience
Which was surprised to learn the concert had to end
Since our duet had always been held up as an example

III

But all music arrives at the last beat one day,
Scores are settled, the orchestra packs up
Its instruments and goes home, the public files out,
The lights dim and then are extinguished for good
Ending the Beginning without so much as an intermission

Time Womb Jacqueline, 1970. Polished aluminum, 61⅛ × 50⅝ × 4⅞ inches (155.3 × 128.6 × 12.4 cm)

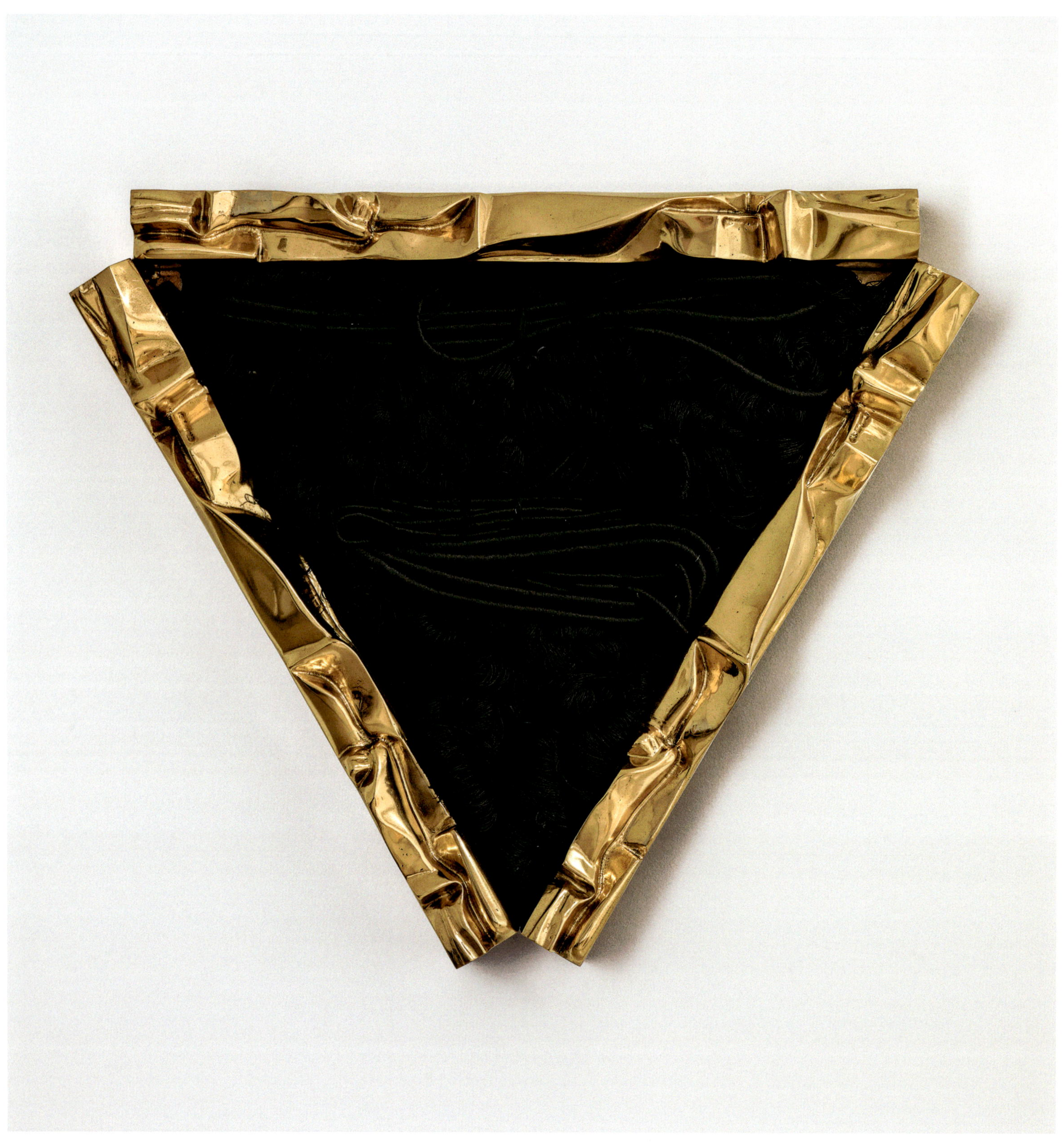

Homage to Gustave Courbet, 1967. Polished
bronze and silk, 29 × 30 × 5½ inches (73.7 ×
76.2 × 14 cm)

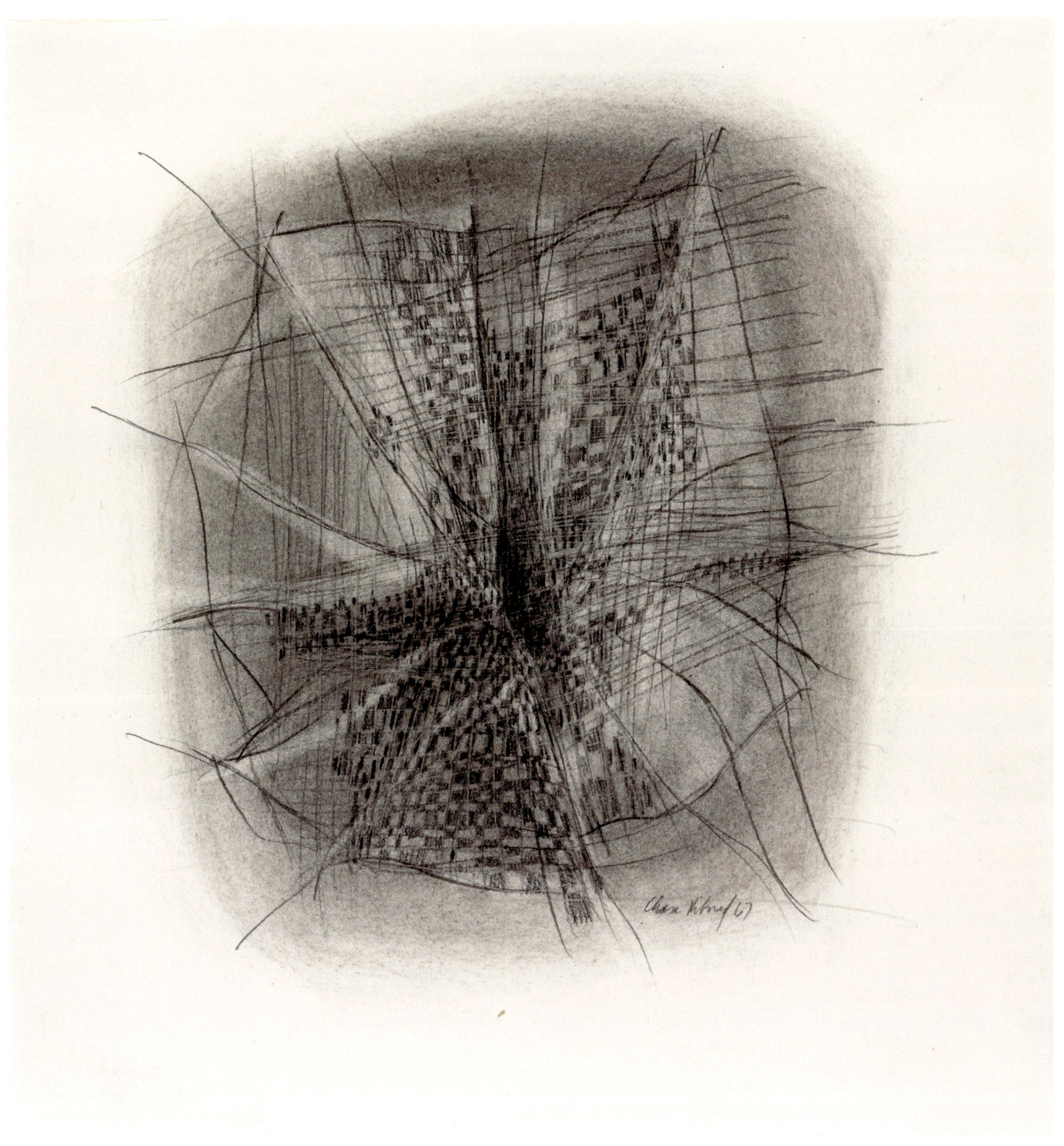

Untitled, 1967. Pencil and charcoal on paper,
11⅛ × 10¼ inches (28 × 26 cm)

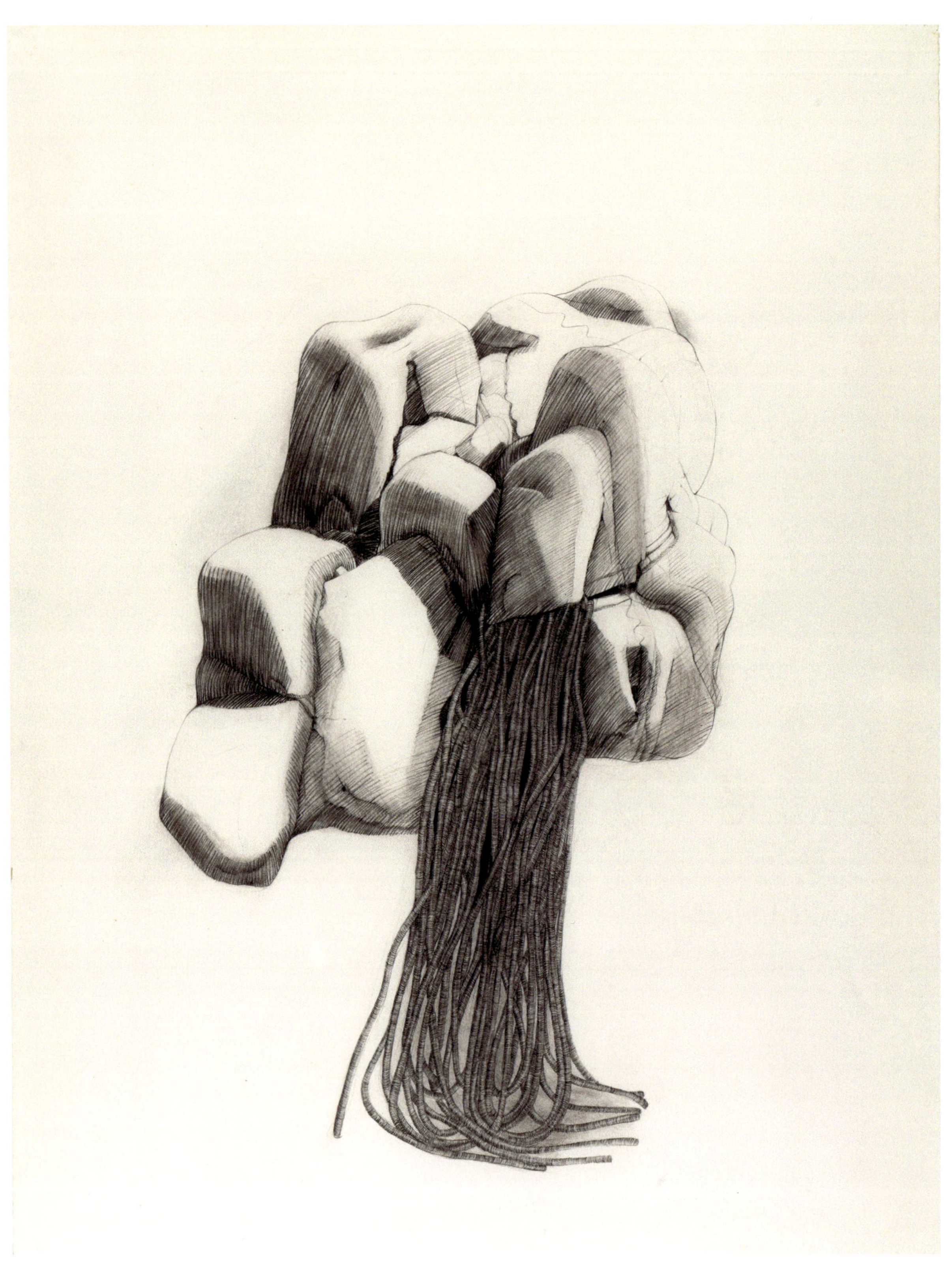

Untitled, 1971. Charcoal and pencil on paper,
29⅞ × 22⅛ inches (76 × 56.4 cm)

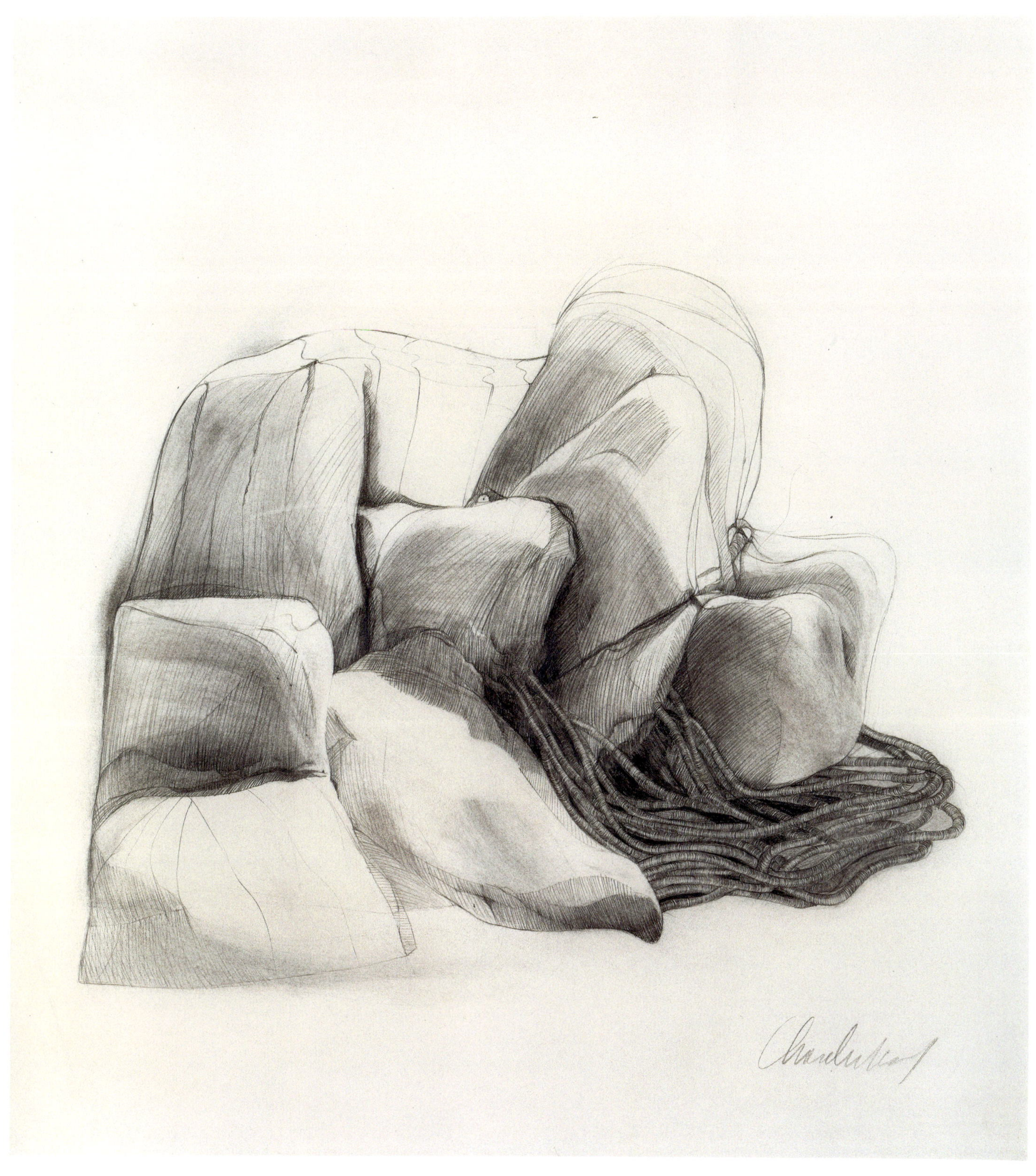

Landscape and Cords, 1973. Charcoal and
charcoal pencil on paper, 22¼ × 19¾ inches
(56.5 × 50.2 cm)

Well of the Concubine Pearl, 1967. Polished
aluminum, silk, wool, linen, synthetic fibers,
and steel chain on painted steel base, 81 ×
30 × 30 inches (205.7 × 76.2 × 76.2 cm)

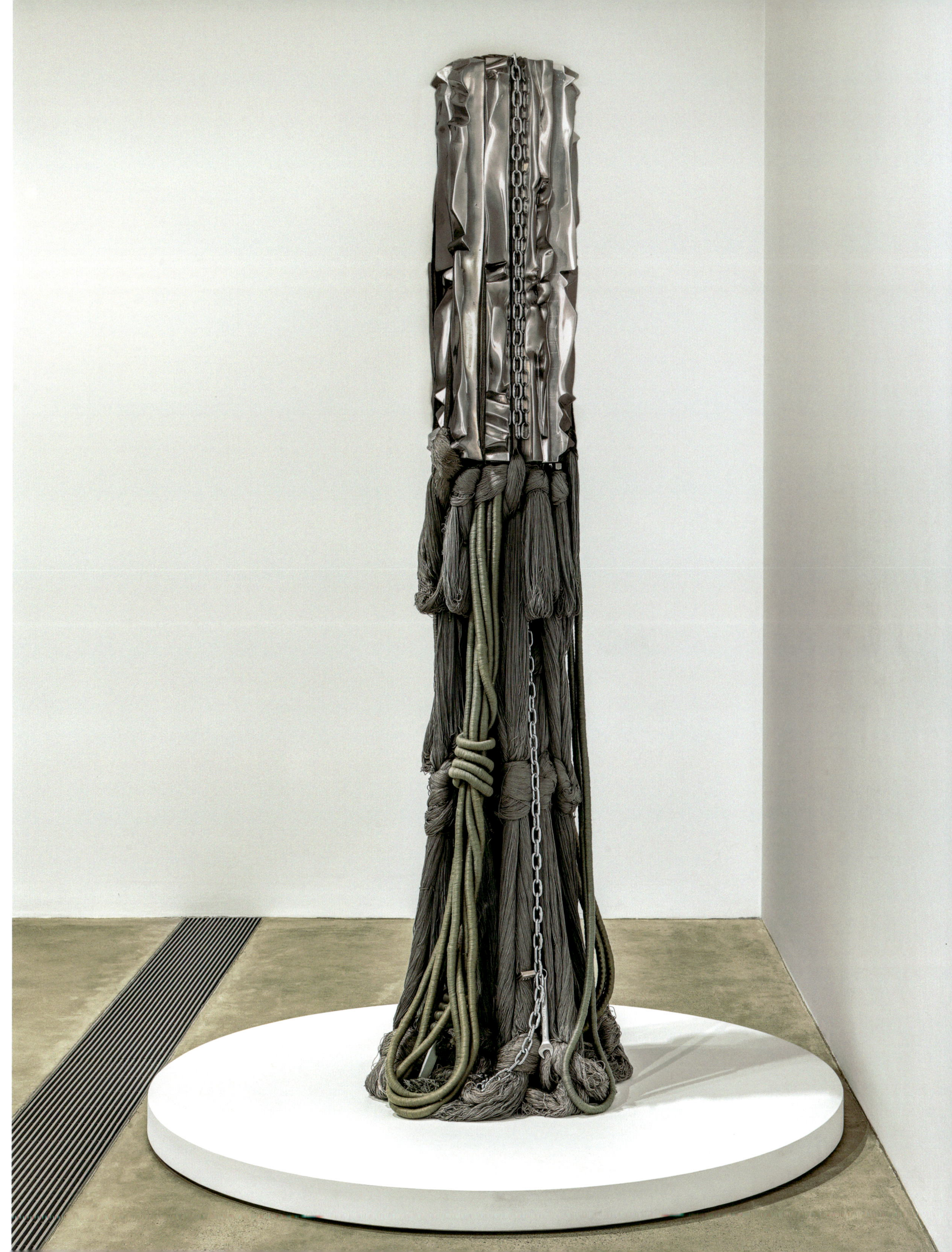

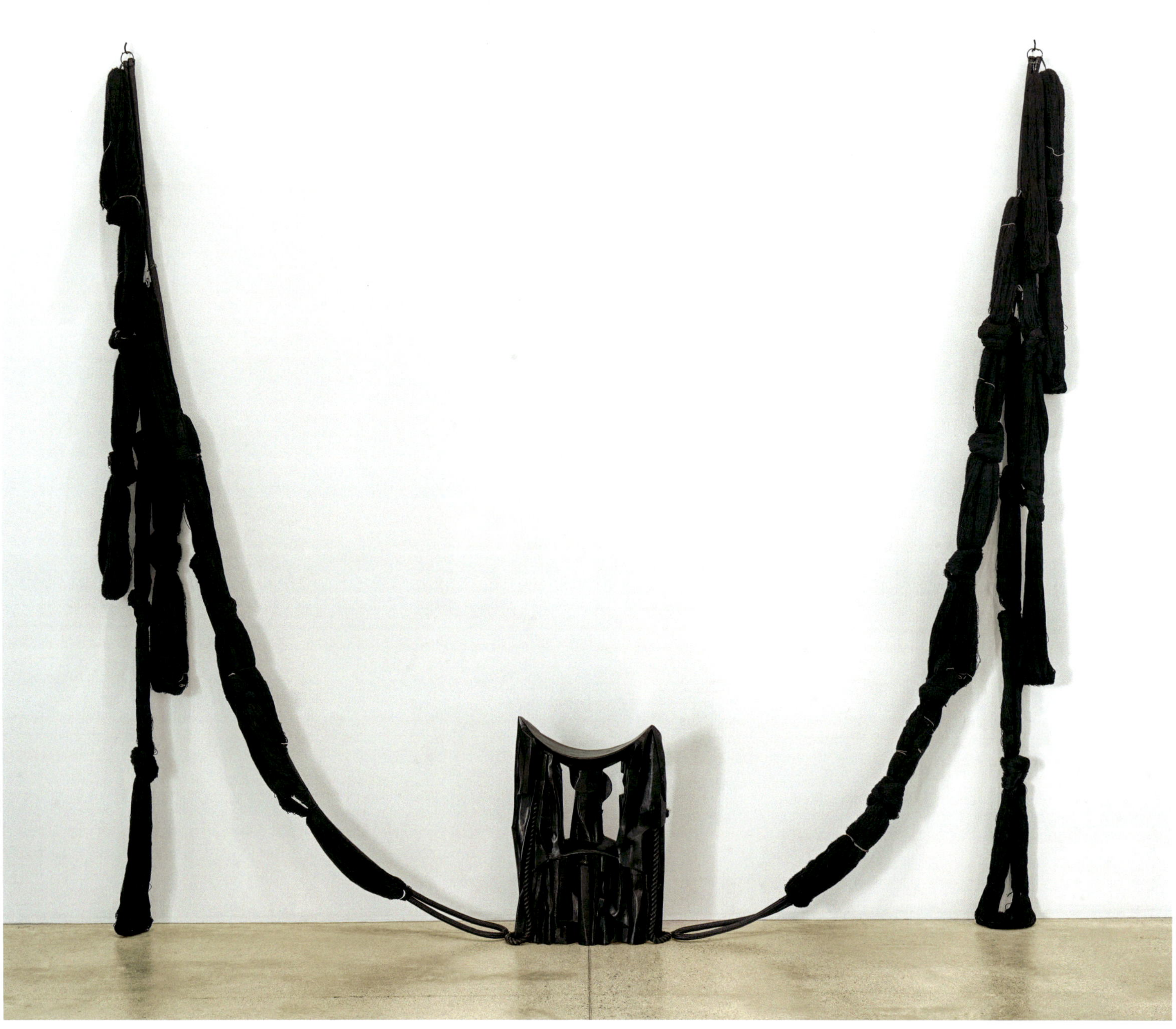

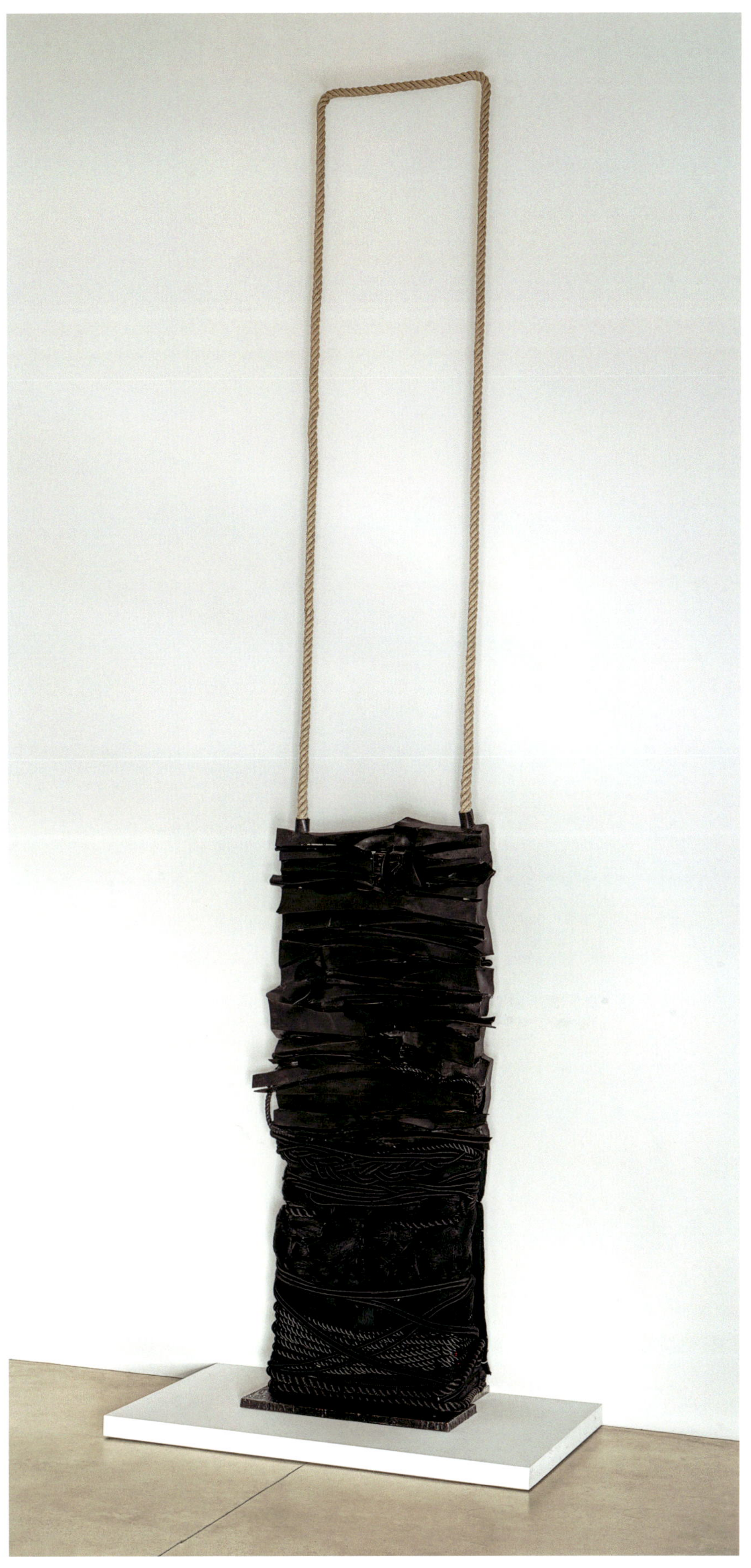

L'Architectura, 1984/2021. Bronze with black patina, wool, and other fibers, 124 × 135½ × 15⅛ inches (315 × 344.2 × 38.4 cm)

Nursery #3, 2007. Black bronze, silk, and rope, 189 × 36⅛ × 24¼ inches (480.1 × 91.8 × 61.6 cm)

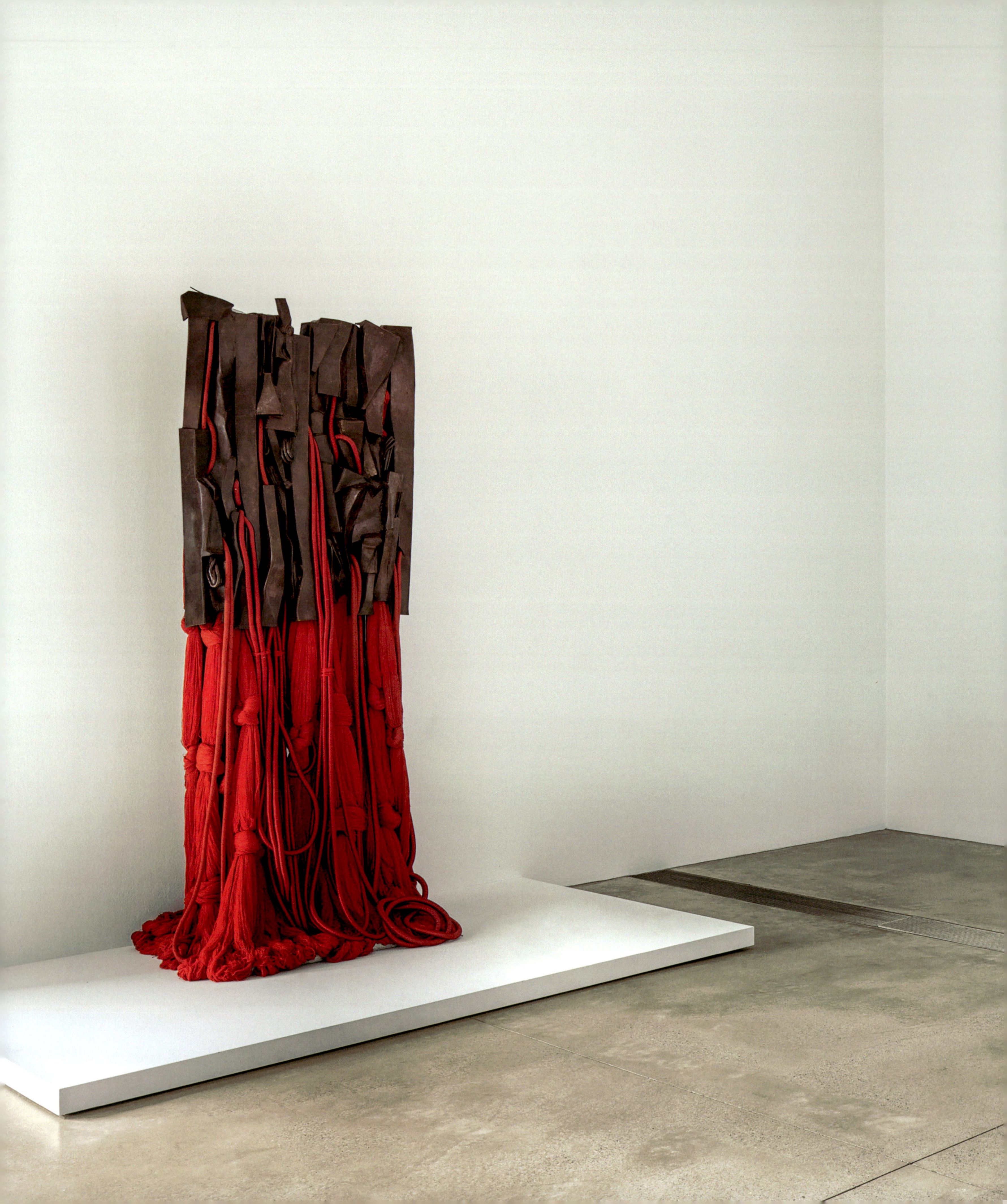

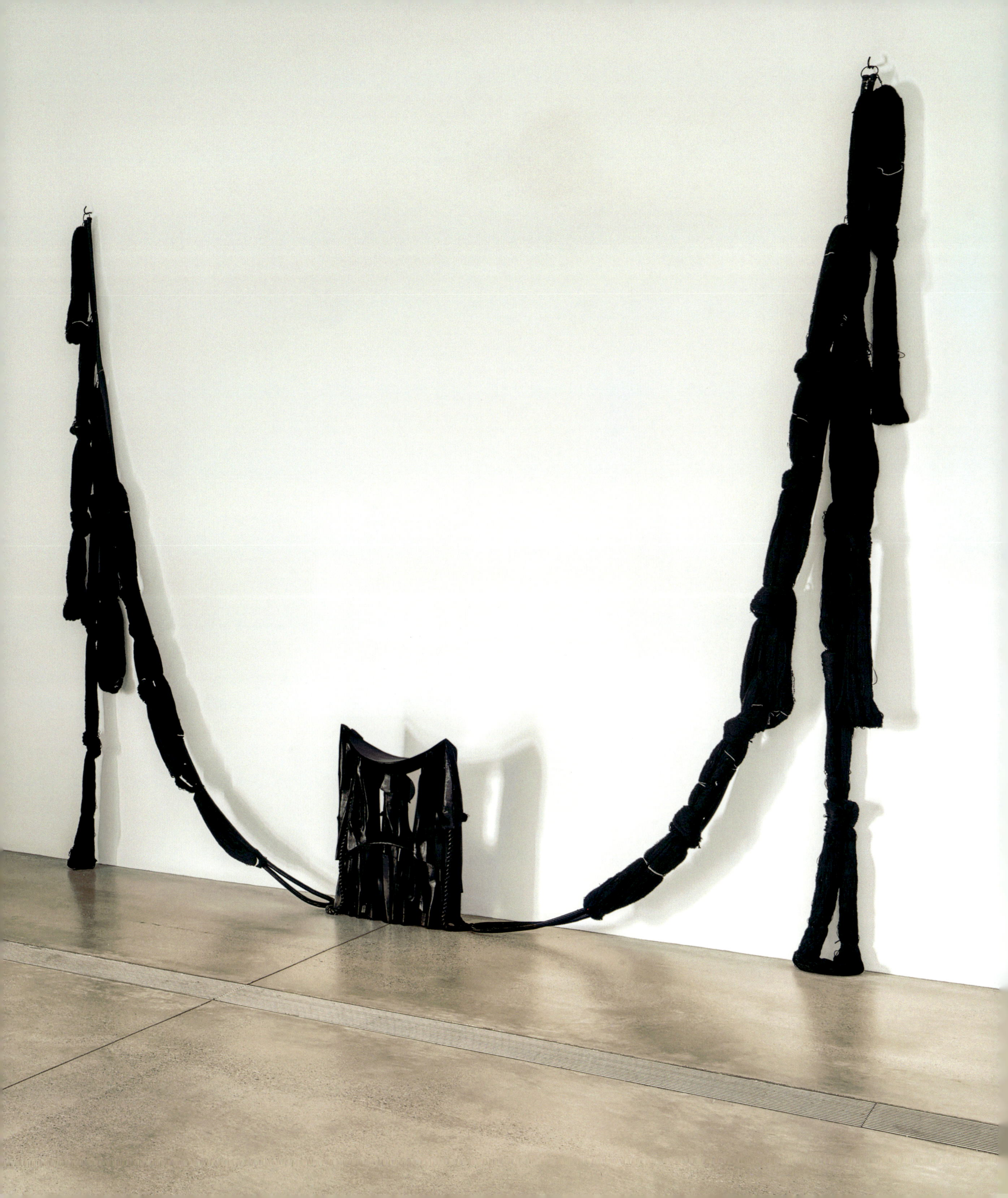

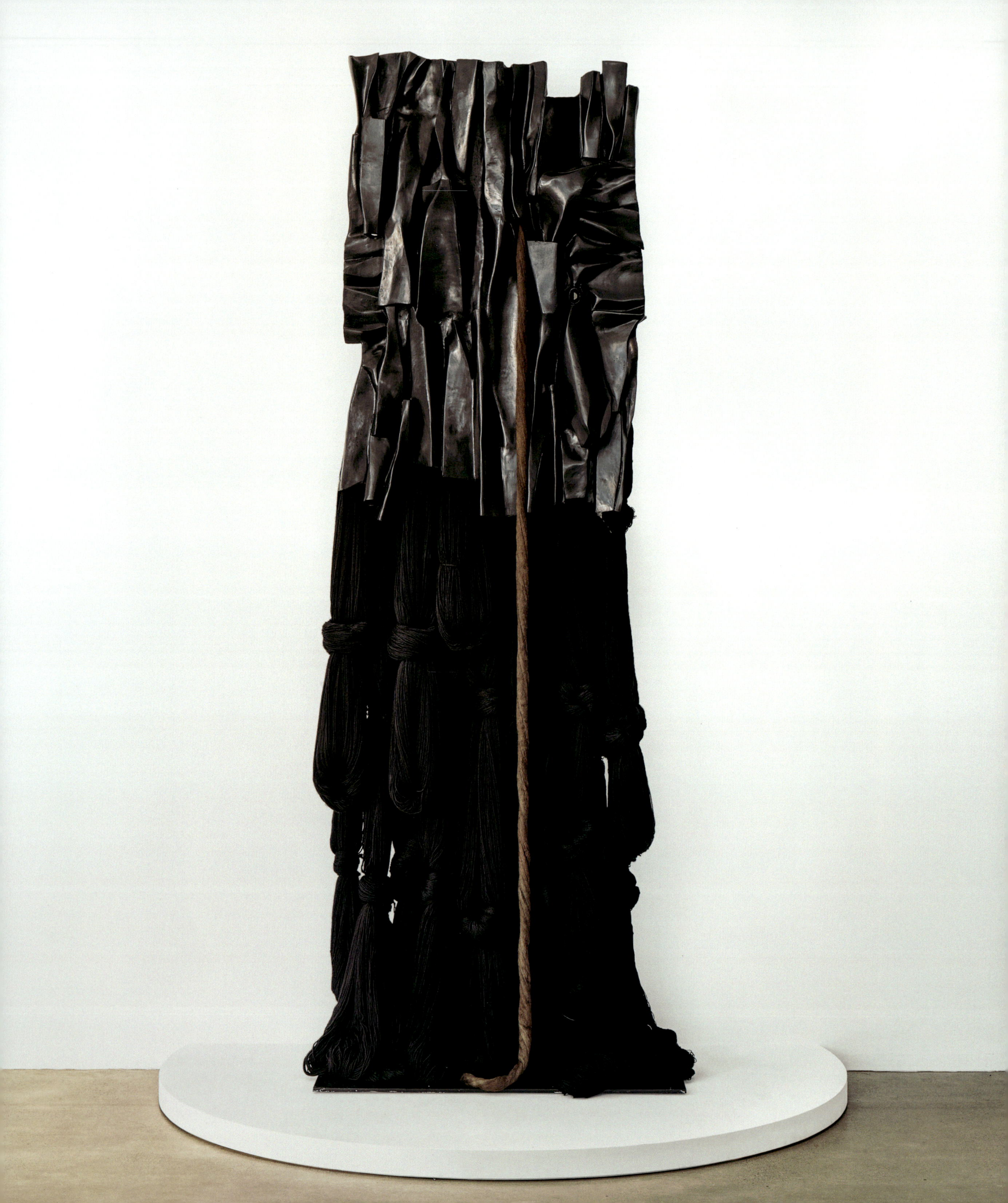

In 1970, Chase-Riboud also began a series of powerful sculptures, which she named *Zanzibar* after the East African island in the Indian Ocean that was an early center of the Muslim slave trade. Discussing the *Zanzibar* group, Chase-Riboud wrote an autobiographical note for the encyclopedia *Contemporary Artists*: "If 'beauty' can be called 'black' in the same way that humor can be called 'black,' then *Zanzibar* can be described as such." The note concludes with, "Sculpture as a created object in space should enrich, not reflect, and it should be beautiful. Beauty is its function." This was not the general attitude taken toward art in the 1970s, when "beauty" was hardly de rigueur. It is all the better, therefore, to read an artist saying so. We might even carry it a step further, to the precept of St. Augustine, who affirmed that beauty is the radiance of truth.

Zanzibar/Black (1974–76 [*sic*]) is endowed with a mysterious beauty, which we also find in some of Chase-Riboud's exquisite charcoal drawings of this period. The same discipline required in making drawings is related to the ordered structure of her poetry. Her incisive poem, "Why Did We Leave Zanzibar?" was actually written in 1969–70, a few years prior to the sculptures of that same [*sic*]. The poem, like the metal and fiber sculptures, fuses sensual celebration with passionate indignation into an epic work. Her deliberations on the history, life, and emotion of the African American—the "dark haloed sister"—does not plead a cause, but transforms this awareness into a delineation of human experience. Her ardent poems and sculptures are, in spite of their rich sensuality, carefully restrained in their basic formal structure. They were, after all, made by the hand of an erstwhile student of architecture.

Excerpt from "Barbara Chase Riboud's Sculpture" by Peter Selz, *Callaloo* 32, no. 3 (Summer 2009): 869.

Zanzibar, 1974. Polished bronze with black patina, silk, wool, and synthetic fibers with steel support, 108¼ × 34⅝ inches (275 × 88 cm)

Why Did We Leave Zanzibar?

Dark haloed sister,
Penumbrae jewel
Burning in dry tobacco leaf beauty,
Brittle and flaking discontent,
Eyes damned with the silt of disappointment,
Lodged and sheltered in Public Housing,
Celled there tapping in Morse Code on the bars of the mind:
The unspeakable that resounds through
The landscape of your nerve ends like orgasm.
Long-fingered, long-necked
Delicate wristed and ankled sister,
Wide-hipped and smelling of honey,
Eyes echoing hollow words and unremembered places,
Fingers stuttering, tearing
And wrapping themselves around
The essential question:

Why did we leave Zanzibar?

Something in the line of the back spells
The irredeemable exhaustion of trying to make ends meet;
Those two butt ends of our amputated history,
Cauterized on the hot iron of self-hate,
Lusting after self-destruction
That we find in split vaginas,
Smeared with the muck of barbarians,
Birthing a race of orphans and madmen
When we could have stayed on the beach,
Heads severed and wombs filled with sand,
Clutching our ancestors,
Rejoicing in sterility,
Reveling in abortion,
Resplendent with infanticide,
Cursing the living with the last breath of strangled children.
You say we had no choice:

There is always one alternative to rape and every woman knows it

Dark-breathed sister,
Sinister survival worshiper,
Ready with the sword to smite the suicides,
Jailer for our prison-makers,
Grinding down our men with religion-pocked
Grins of satisfaction (Jesus Saves),
Crushing our defenseless sons with the jawbone of that Jew's cross,
Dazed and concussed, they stumble into the street to play stickball
Driving their fathers mad with grief and shame
So that their rage is spent in our bodies
(Or better still, the wives and daughters of the enemy);
And how we both glory in it,
Smack our lips in rutting satisfaction,
Tasting curdled blood and milk
Left standing in the sun too long
By absent-minded missionaries:

Benedictus qui venit in
Nomine Domini.

Sassy, sweet-voiced sister,
Moon-browed and night-mouthed
In deepest song,
Lying on your back in cathedrals,
Content that another night has passed
Without murder,
Lying on your back in cathedrals,
Masturbating with the true cross (Sweet Jesus)
While black men thrash around with white flesh,
Listening for your hysterical screams resounding in the tabernacle,
Staining stained glass: those Technicolor prisms of Middle-Eastern legend.
And over all, Cleopatra's asp hovers:
Sliding between legs,
That perpetually open route to power,
Posing the essential question on split tongue:

Why did we leave Zanzibar?
Sweet fragrant mango-stenched beach,
Breasts pressed flat against steamed sand,
Seeping through sieve-like flesh,
Carrying carats of ancestor dust,
Rattling like pearls in oyster shells.

Sleek, earth-dyed sister,
Madness glistening at your throat,
We could have stayed on the beach,
Clinging to the rocks like bats,

REFUSING TO MOVE OUR WOMBS,

Scraping them with flint,
Soaking the continent with the holy blood of martyrs.
Plum-lipped sister,
Sad and wild-eyed with my reflection,
I touch one apricot breast
As you touch one brassy one,
And we gaze into each other's eyes
Like the criminals that we are,
Dark brown gall rising to the surface like oil on water,
Casting up that bottle-wrapped question
Flung into the sea by some desperate hand so many murders ago:

Why did we leave Zanzibar?

73

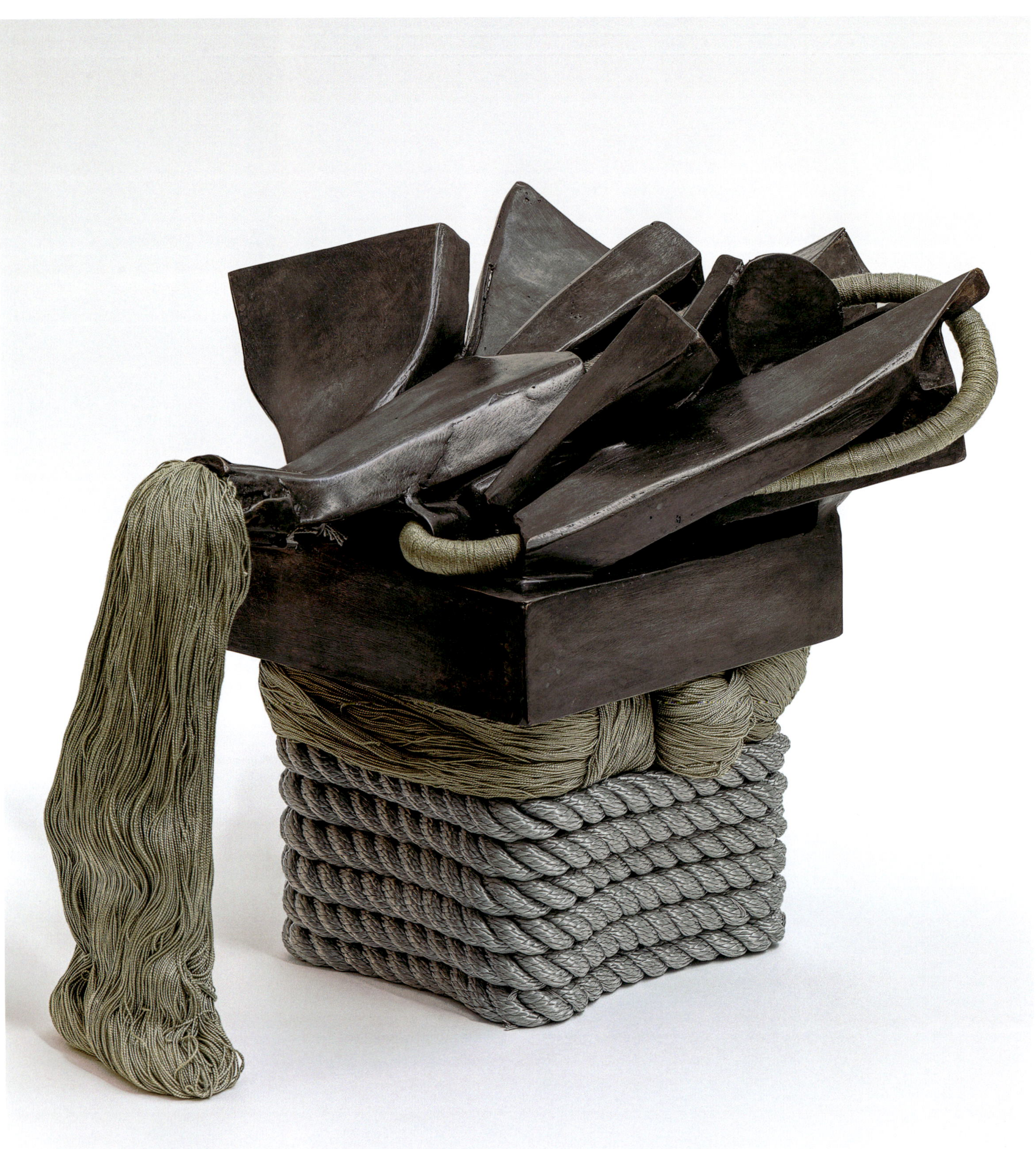

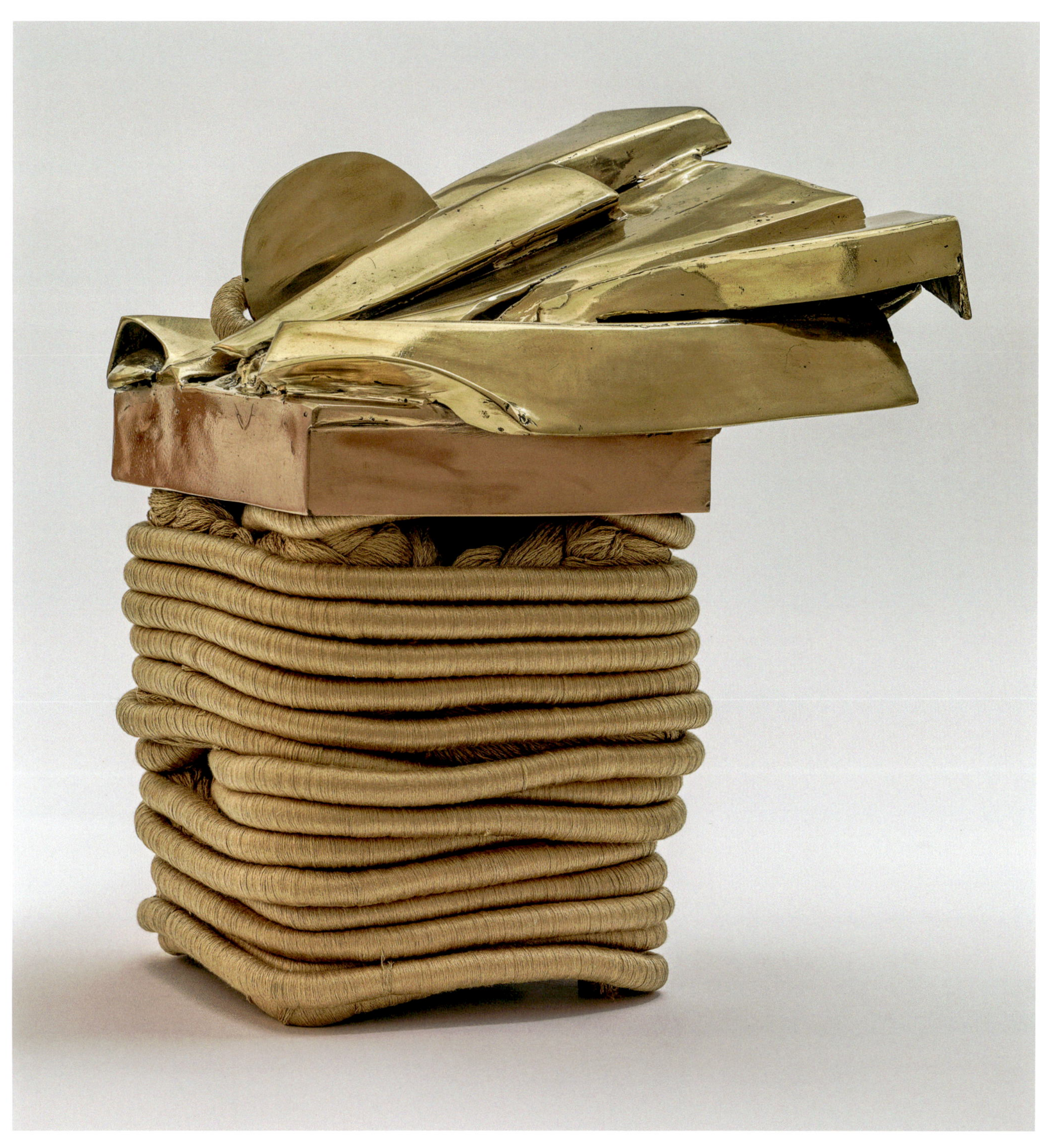

Zanzibar Table Black #2, 1972. Bronze with
black patina, silk, linen, and synthetic fibers,
13½ × 12½ × 17 inches (34.3 × 31.8 ×
43.2 cm)

Zanzibar Table Gold, 1972. Polished bronze
and silk, 15¼ × 13 × 12¾ inches (38.7 × 33 ×
32.4 cm)

Rue des Plantes
2001

Rue des Plantes (White Drawing), 2021.
Synthetic white silk on Arches paper,
25½ × 19⅝ inches (64.8 × 49.8 cm)

Following pages

Jeanne Amoor (White Drawing), 2021.
Silk on Arches paper, 29½ × 21⅝ inches
(75 × 55 cm)

His Phallus in Hand (White Drawing), 2020.
Silk on Arches paper. 29½ × 21⅝ inches
(75 × 55 cm)

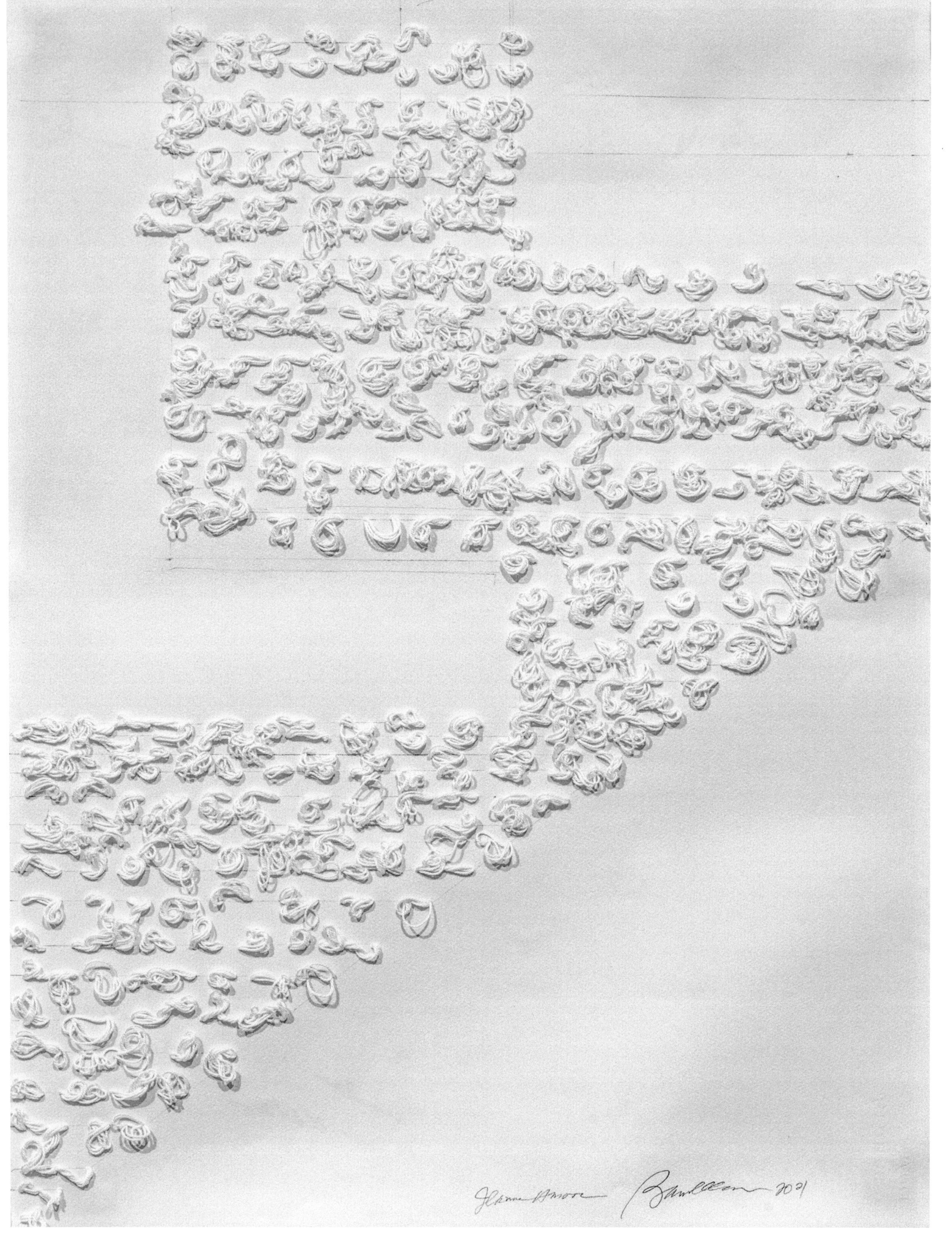

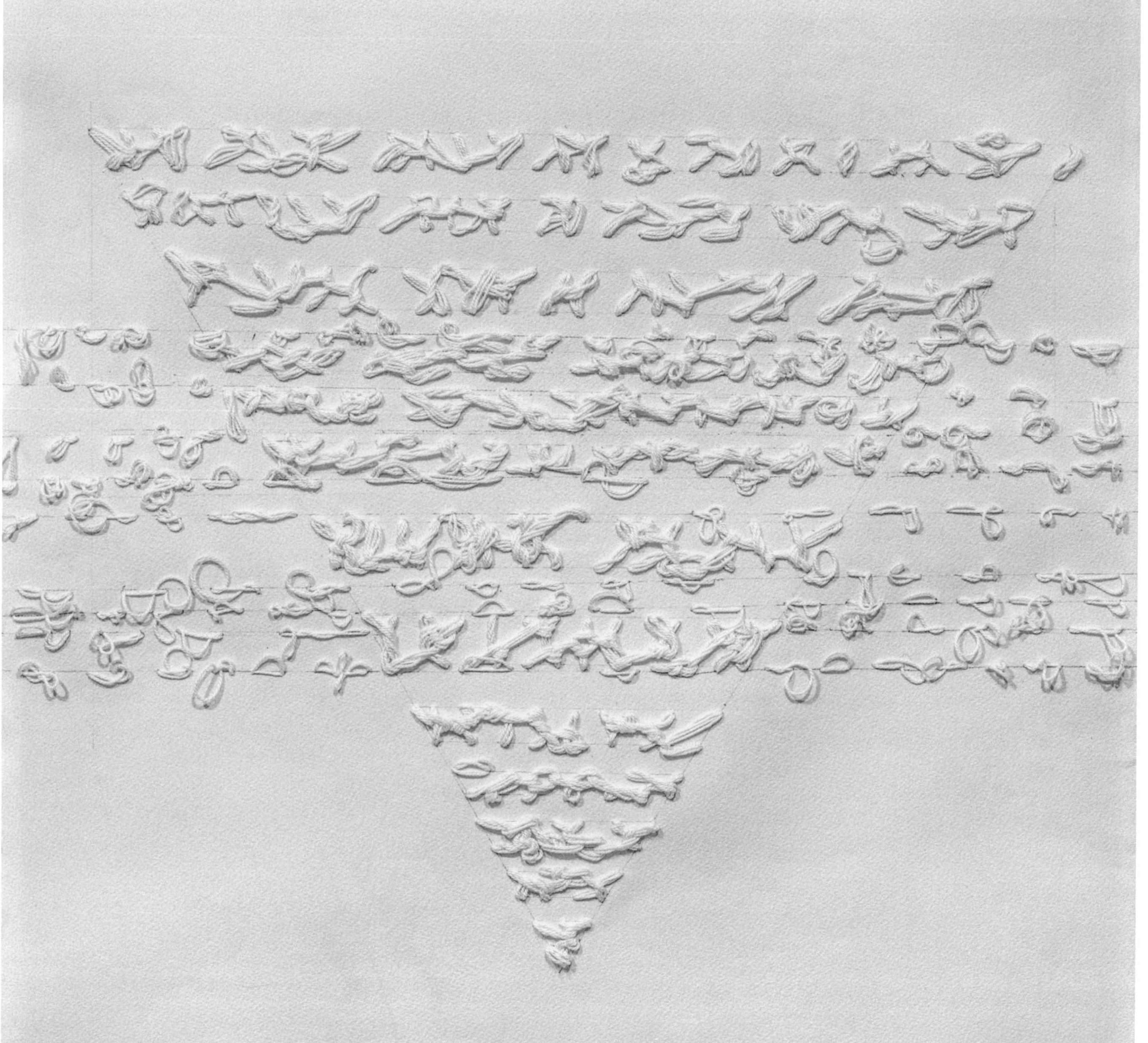
His Phallas in Hand...   Chase Riboud 2020

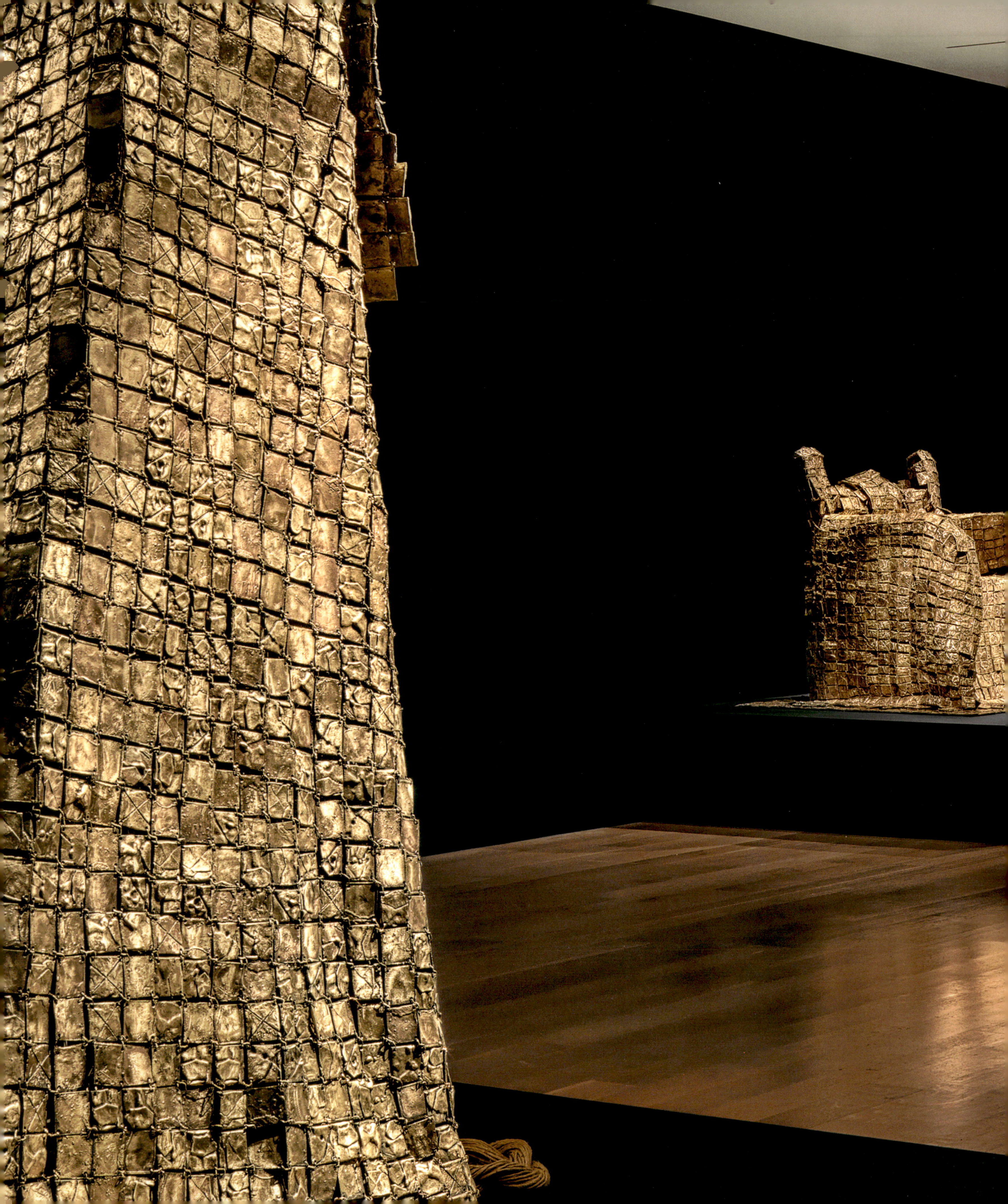

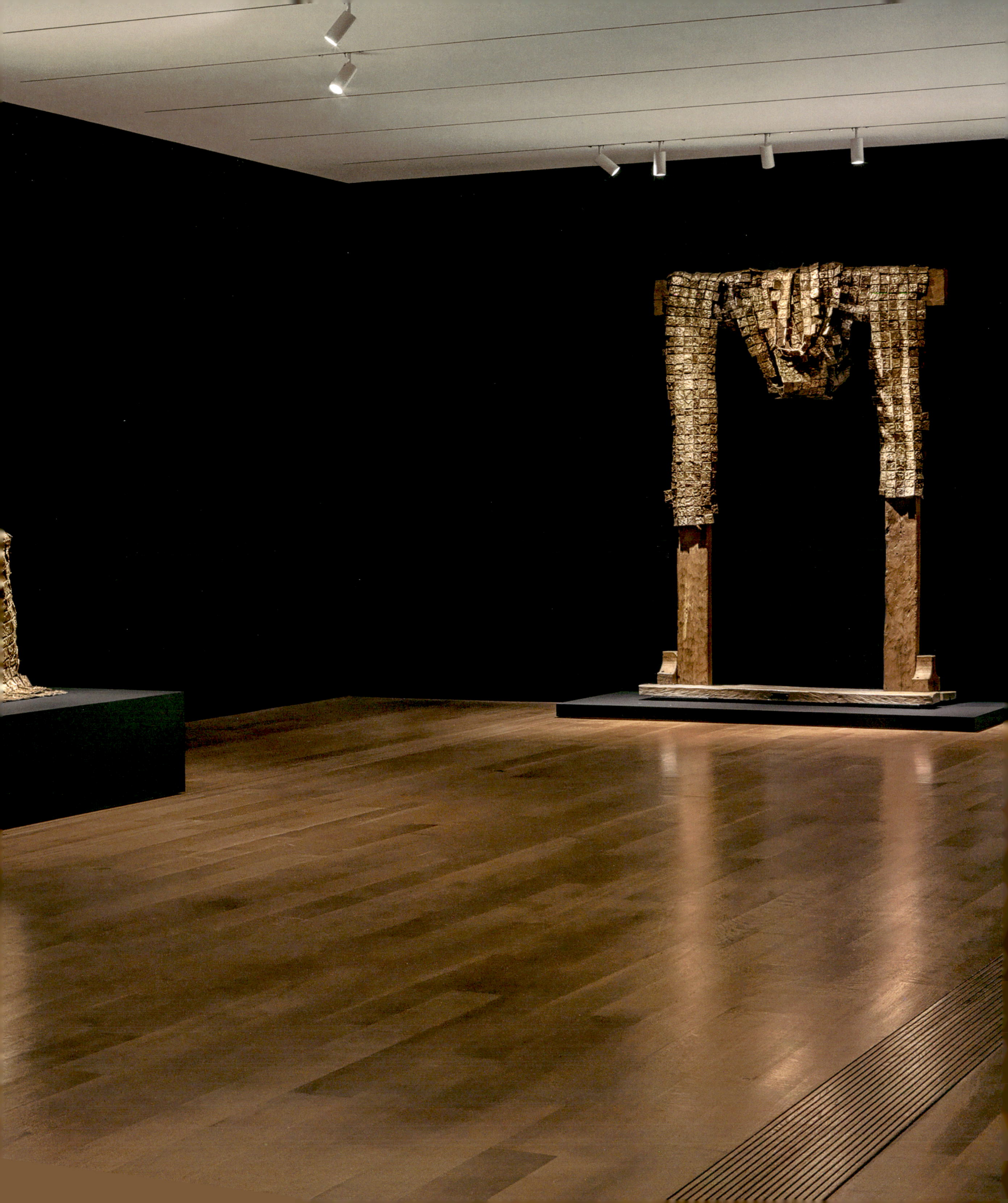

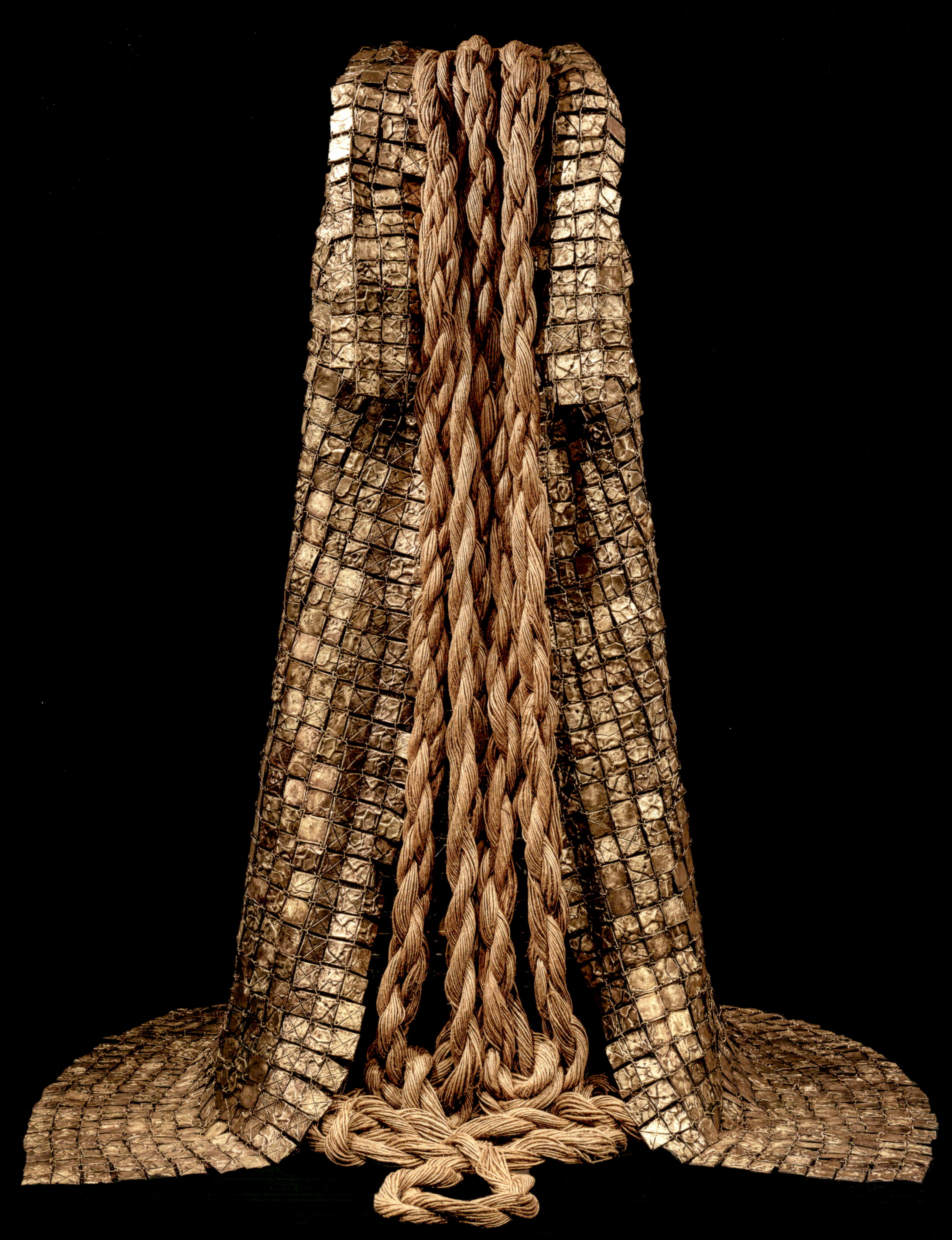

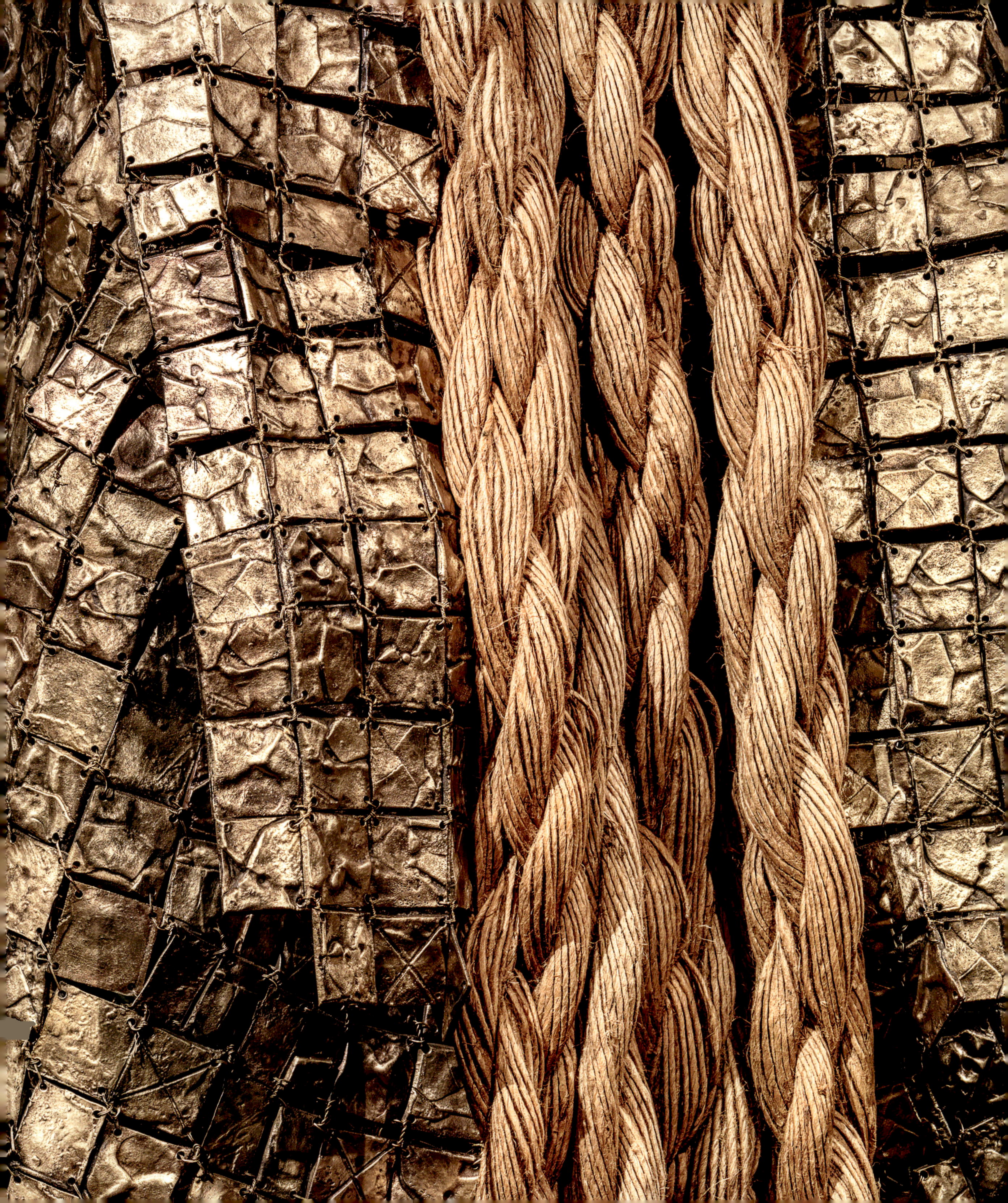

Suzettte Spencer Your meditations on Cleopatra are quite extensive and, more importantly, they also offer us an important place to think about the intersection of literature and sculpture. In what ways, if any, do you imagine the relationship between the poetics of the Cleopatra poems [*Portrait of a Nude Woman as Cleopatra*] and the Cleopatra sculptures? There seems to be an insistence on intimacy, concealment, and disclosure that cuts across genres?

Barbara Chase-Riboud Cleopatra was a literary theme I was determined to keep separate from my sculpture but in the end spilled over into visual expression, because in 1974, my first husband wrote me a letter from China (I had not accompanied him on this trip) describing a new archeological discovery he had photographed: the famous eighth century Han Shrouds made of tiny pieces of square cut jade woven together with gold wire—a phenomenal, world class discovery of which he had the first photographs. Before I actually saw the shrouds, I dreamed up the *Cleopatra* series, the first of which was the *Cape* made up of small squares of multicolored cast bronze held together with cooper wire and draped with a hemp braid. Then I saw photos of the shrouds which were published on the cover of *Art News*. I have since produced, over twenty years, five sculptures in the series when the spirit hits me. *Cleopatra's Staircase* is the last of the series: *Cleopatra's Cape*, *Cleopatra's Door*, *Cleopatra's Bed*, and *Cleopatra's Wedding Dress*. The *Wedding Dress* was completed in 2003. At what point did the sculpture and poetry merge into *Portrait of a Nude Woman as Cleopatra*? I'm not sure.

Excerpt from "On Her Own Terms: An Interview with Barbara Chase-Riboud" by Suzette A. Spencer, *Callaloo* 32, no. 3 (Summer 2009): 752.

Le Manteau (The Cape), or *Cleopatra's Cape*, 1973 (detail)

Cleopatra's Door, 1984. Multicolored
cast-bronze plaques over oak, 98½ × 59 ×
19¾ inches (250 × 150 × 50 cm)

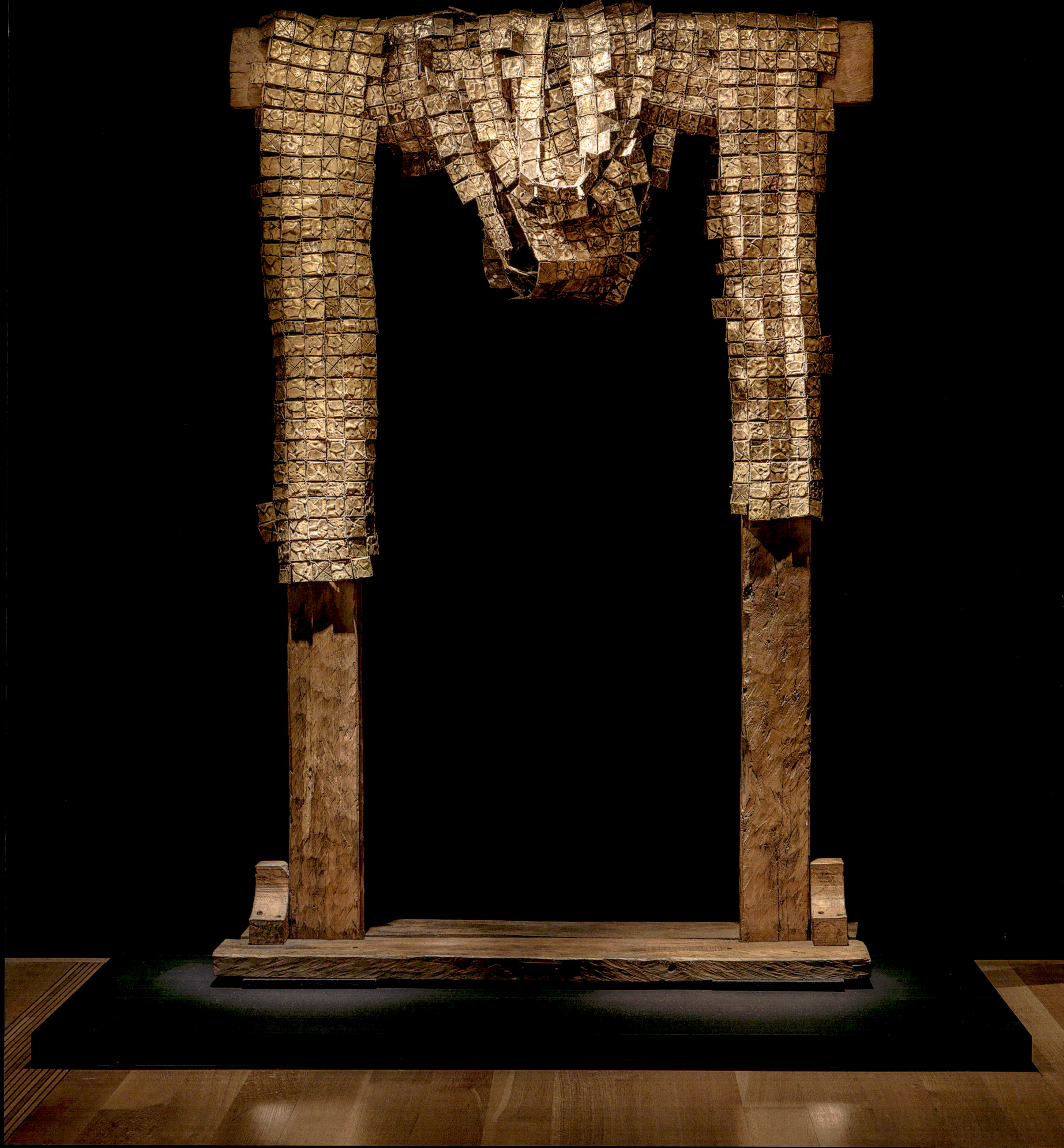

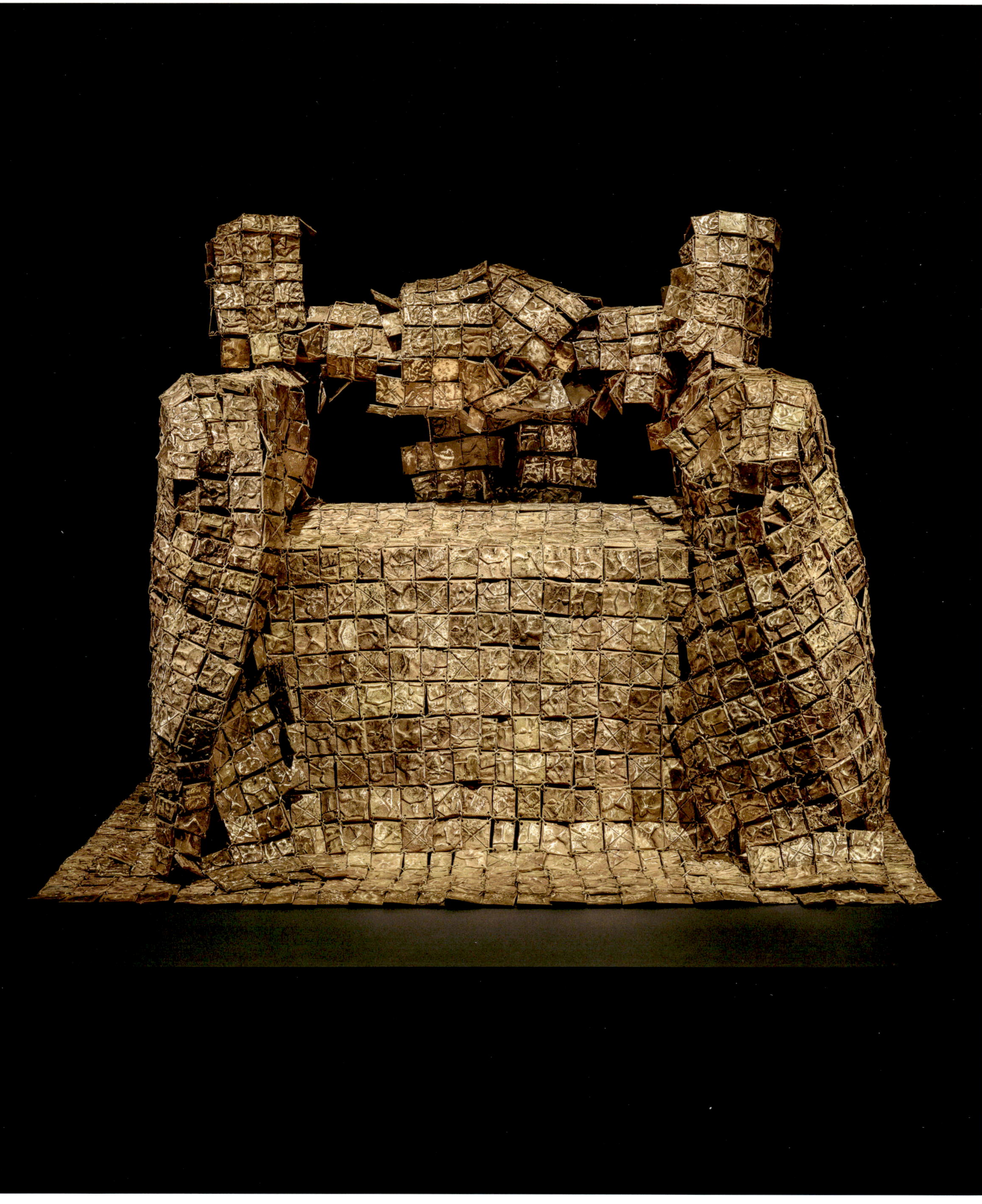

Cleopatra LIV

I'm leaving this place, cheeks swollen with
Puffed breaths of desperate Life, swaddled in
Silk sails embroidered delicately by infant hands
I have glided from mistake to mistake,

Striking my colors for all to see,
For I am the Signifier, the Way is in me.
I've unsealed it in one blinding Wound.
Drumrolls of sound break the pain spiralling towards

The high-arched vaults of Delphi, rancid as the
Oracle's breath and smooth as a divine phallus—
A Hallelujah of crescending spasms, tiny splinters

Of agony pressing bone like the Moon of your thumb,
And serpents lick the convulsions of new chromosomes
That transforms the woman.

Cleopatra's Chair, 1994. Multicolored
cast-bronze plaques over oak, 39⅜ × 49⅝ ×
43¼ inches (100 × 126 × 110 cm)

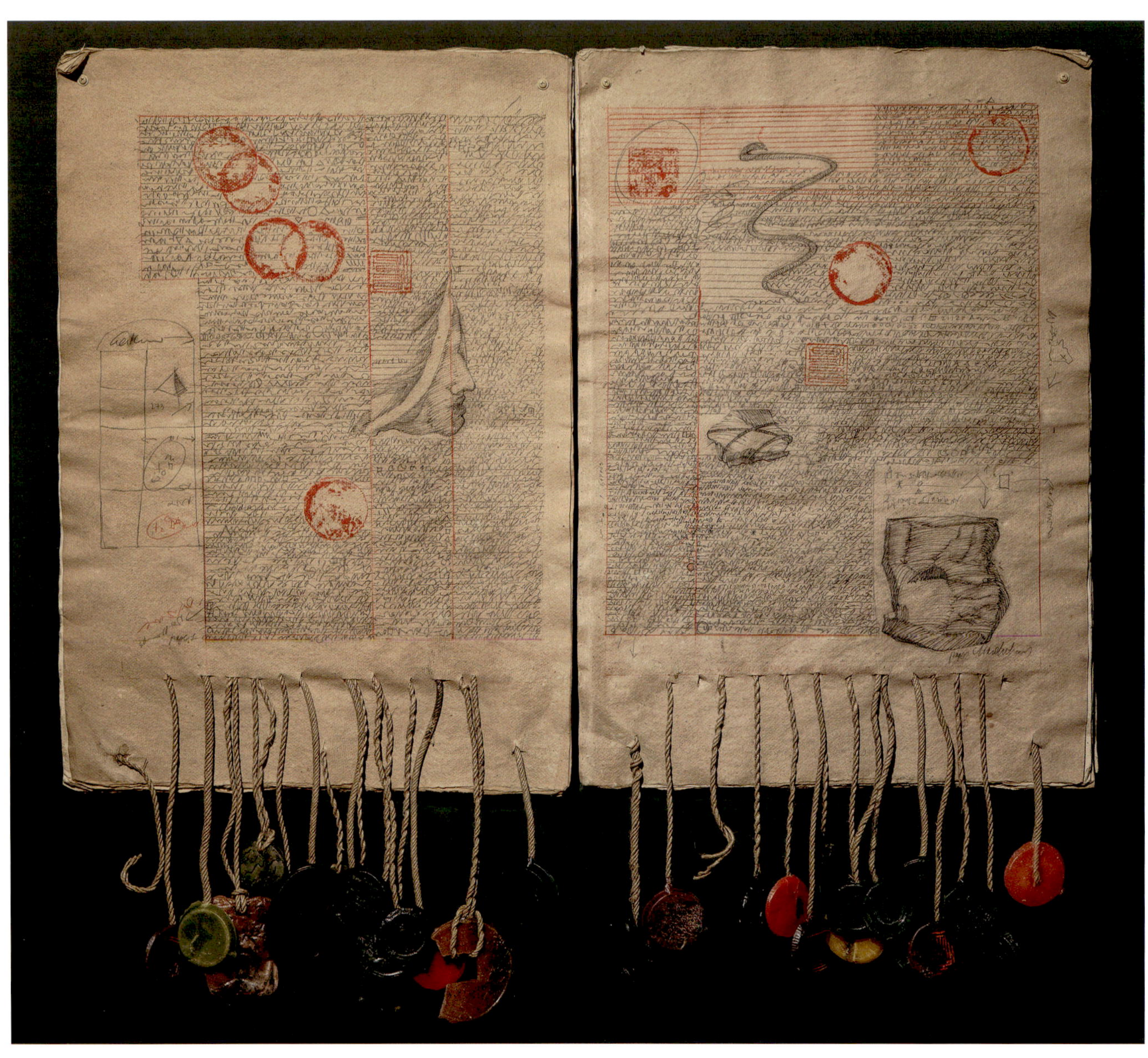

Cleopatra's Marriage Contract, 2000.
Handmade paper, graphite, ink, wax,
and cord, 39 × 42 × 1 inches (99.1 ×
106.7 × 2.5 cm)

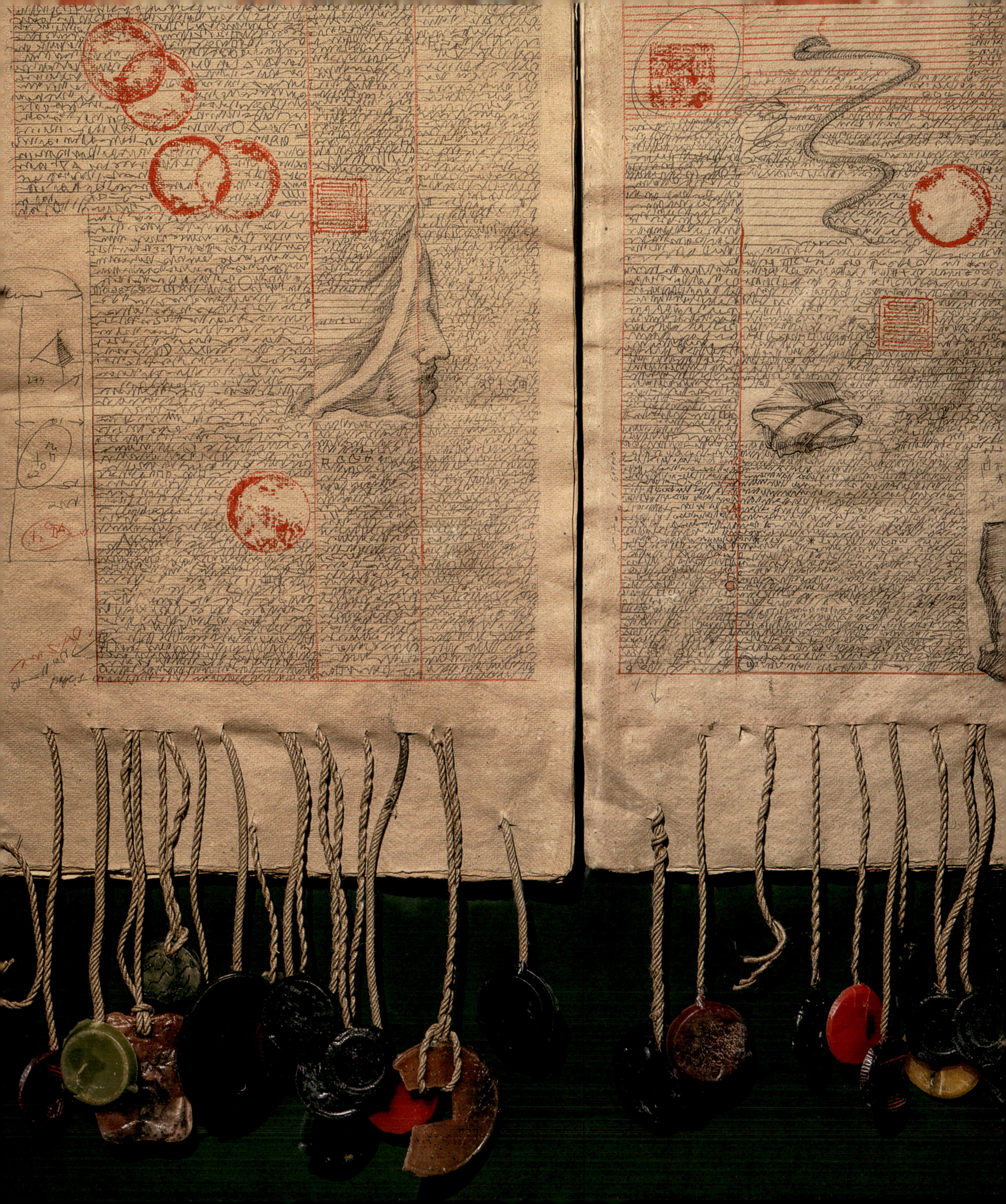

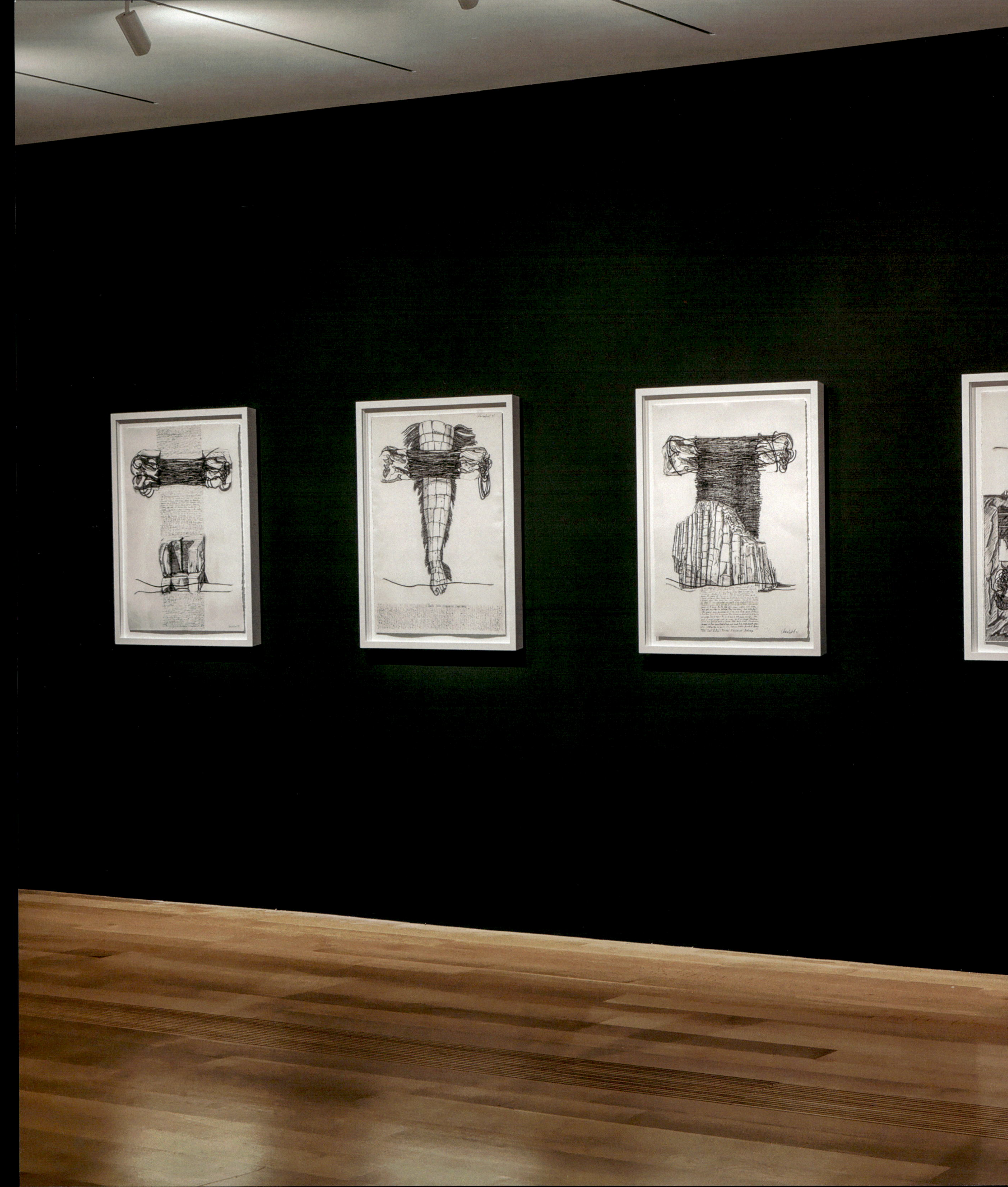

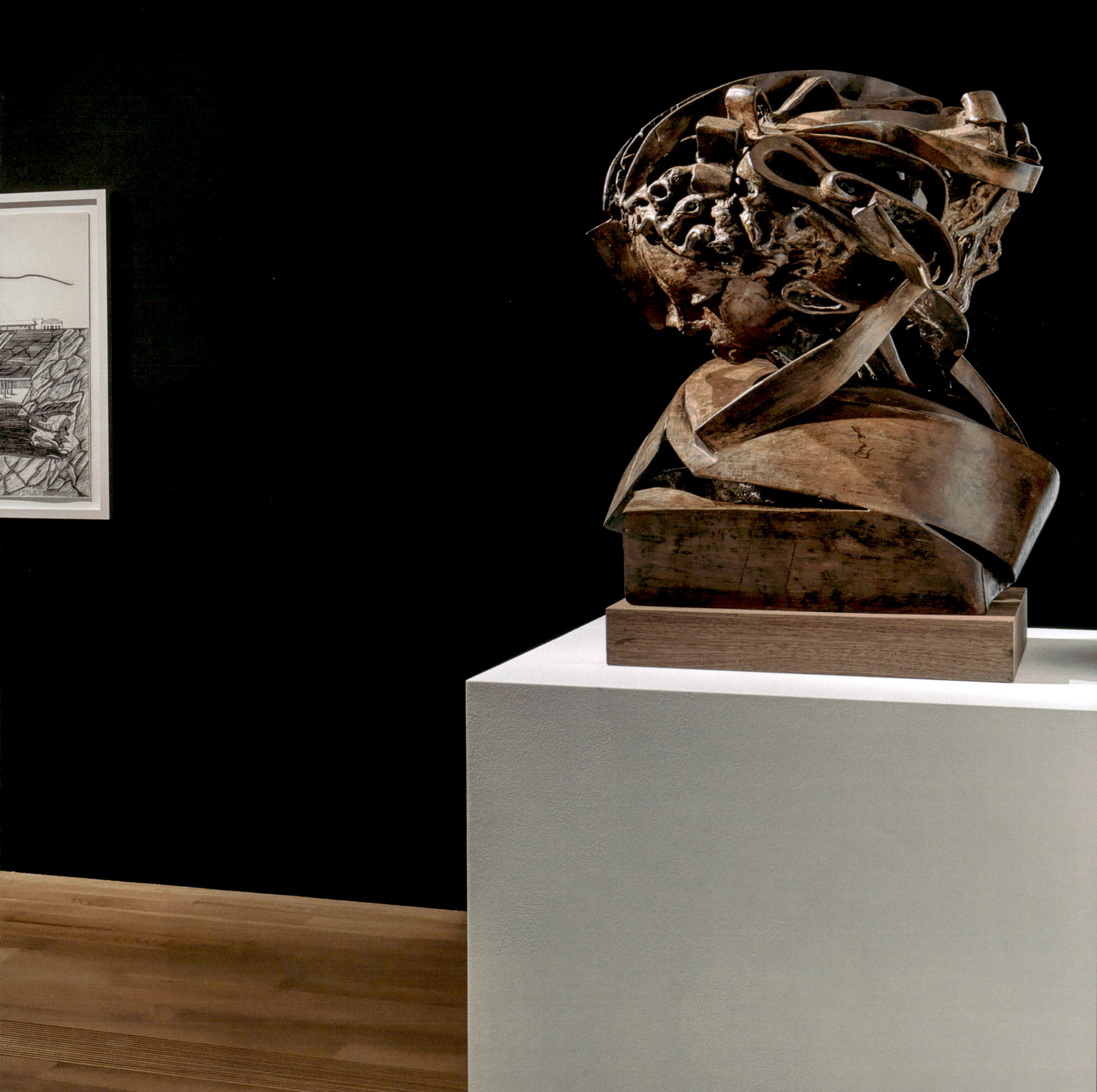

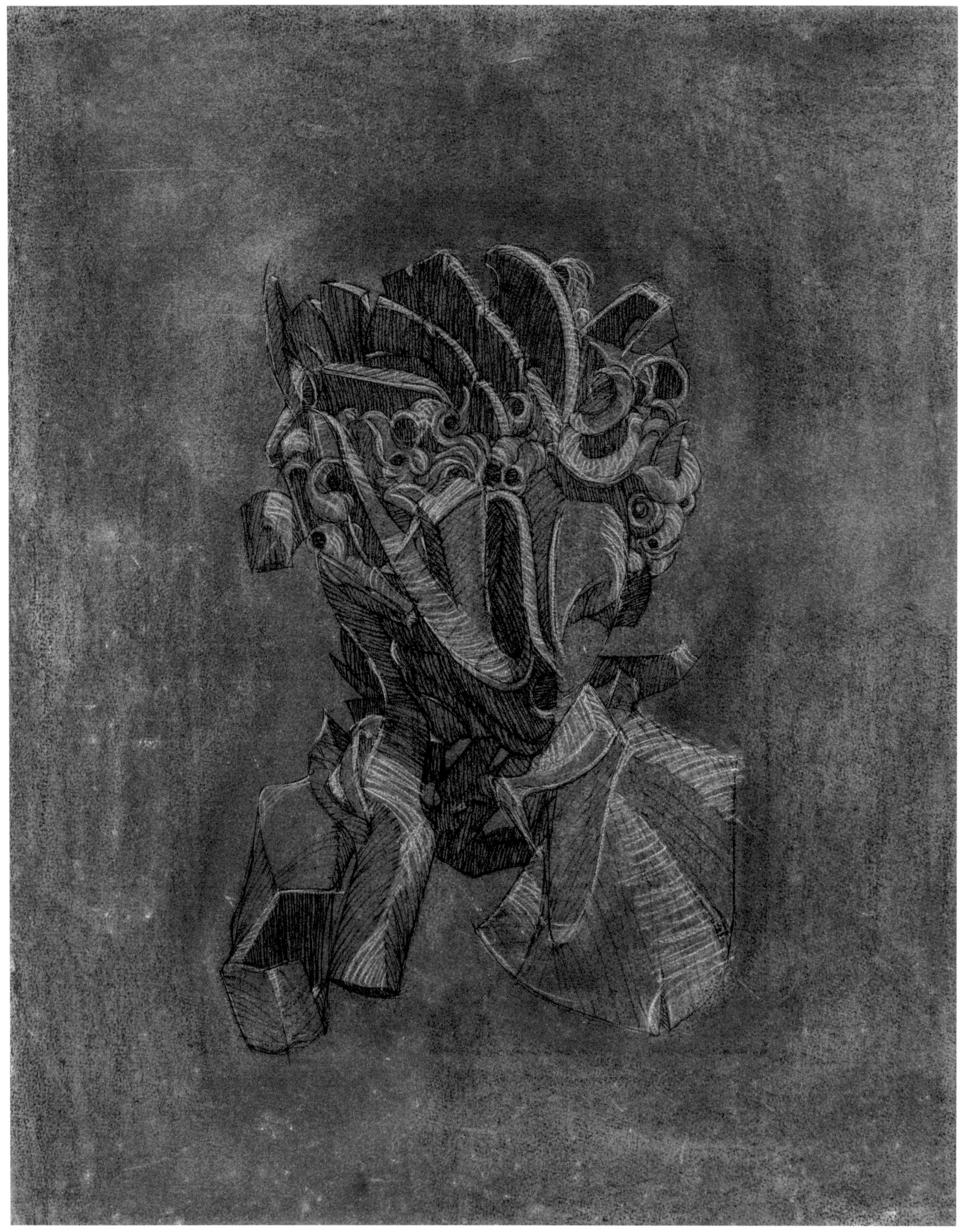

Sarah Baartman Red Drawing #4, 1997.
Pastel and graphite on paper, 28 × 20 inches
(71.1 × 50.8 cm)

Suzette Spencer Certainly, writing is a different art form than sculpture, but while they are different I see meeting points, especially in the relation between your sculpture *Africa Rising* and your novel *Hottentot Venus*.

Barbara Chase-Riboud The African Burial Ground [*Africa Rising*] is where sculpture met literature in my career. It is where they crossed for the first time and where I strove for a sculptural language which could confront the challenge of history in terms of a sublime aesthetic that could merge the demands of a public sculpture with the objectives of a postmodernist monument of beauty. For once the message was the subject matter, and the sculpture not only preceded the novel, it was intimately intertwined with the novel in that it was only upon completing the sculpture (1998) that I decided to write the novel as my last word on Sarah Baartman (2003).

Would I have written the book if I hadn't done the sculpture? I don't know really. All I know is that I had had the research on Baartman for a decade and had never gotten around to using it until I had to confront the necessity of an icon for one of the most charged historical sites in America: the place where mainstream history meets and merges with subterranean history. For a long time, however, I insisted that there was a big separation between literature and sculpture, because I did not want to be perceived as a dilettante. I did not want to be perceived as a sculptor who writes books or as a writer who makes sculpture. It's my biggest problem because there is this kind of condemnation of people who do two things.

Excerpt from "On Her Own Terms: An Interview with Barbara Chase-Riboud" by Suzette A. Spencer, *Callaloo* 32, no. 3 (Summer 2009): 750–51.

Africa Rising Bust Overcast #1, 1998. Bronze with silver patina, 25⅜ × 17 × 18½ inches (64.5 × 43.2 × 47 cm)

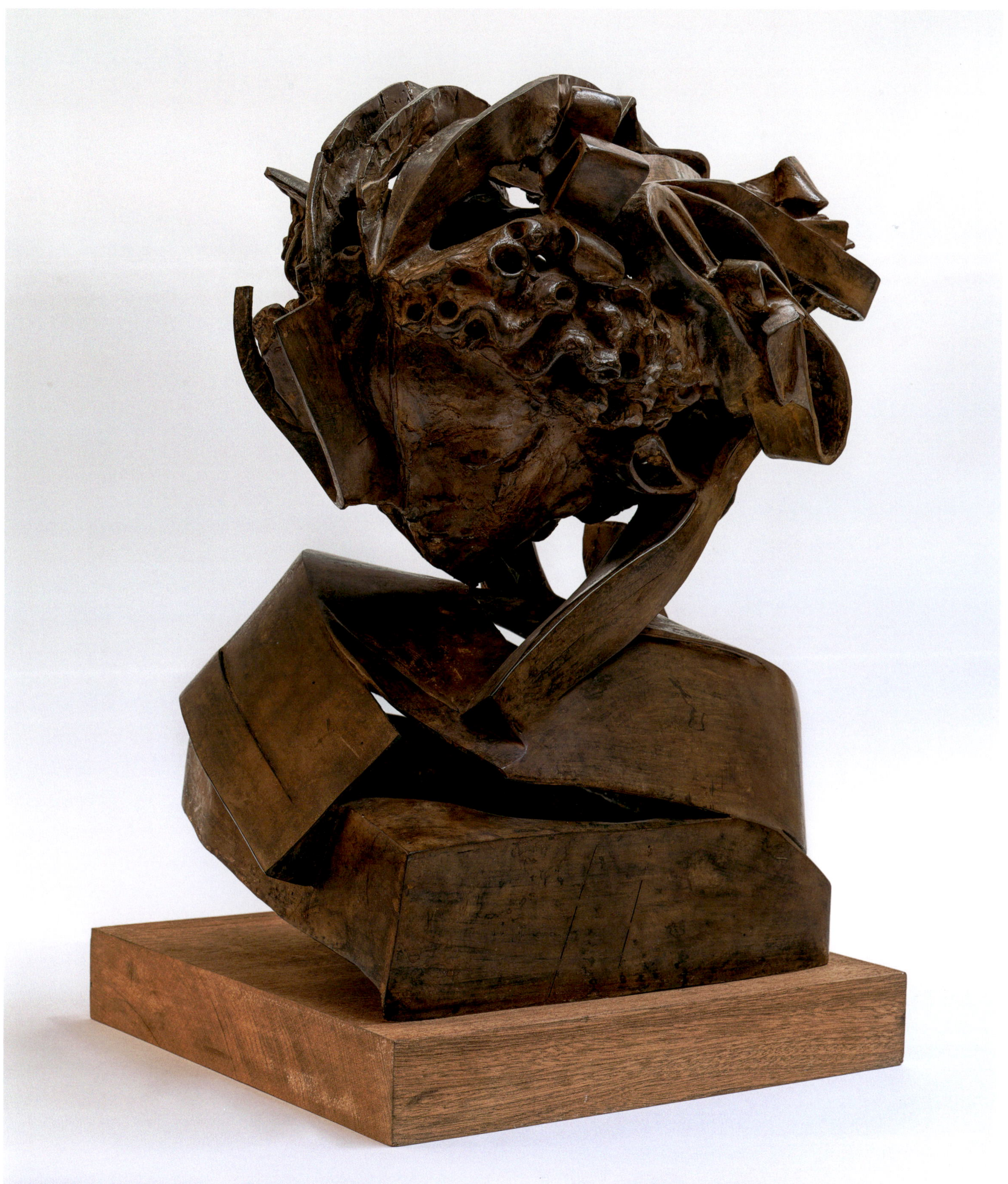

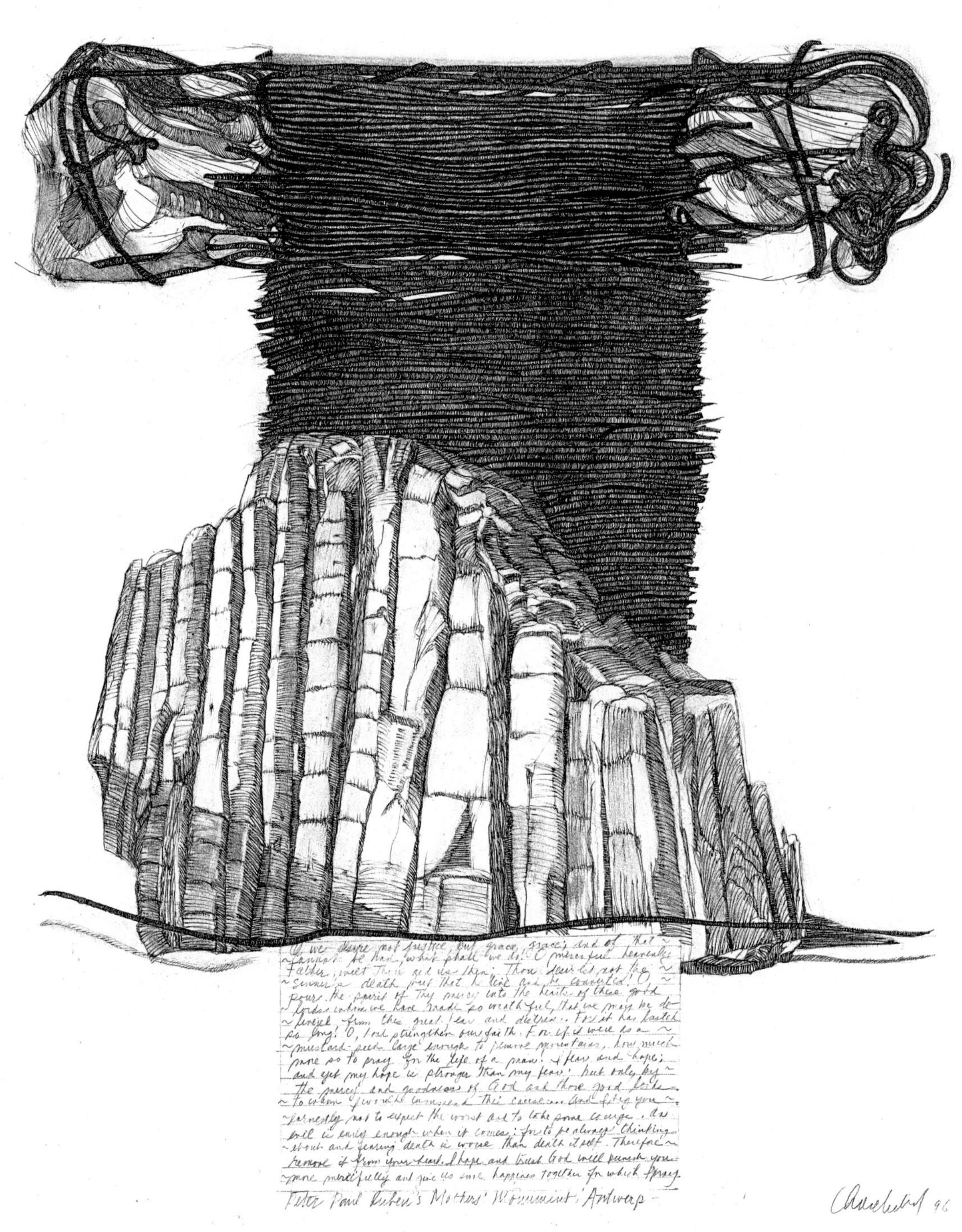

*Peter Paul Rubens' Mother's Monument,
Antwerp*, 1996. Charcoal, charcoal pencil,
and ink with engraving and aquatint on
paper, 31½ × 23⅞ inches (80 × 60.6 cm)

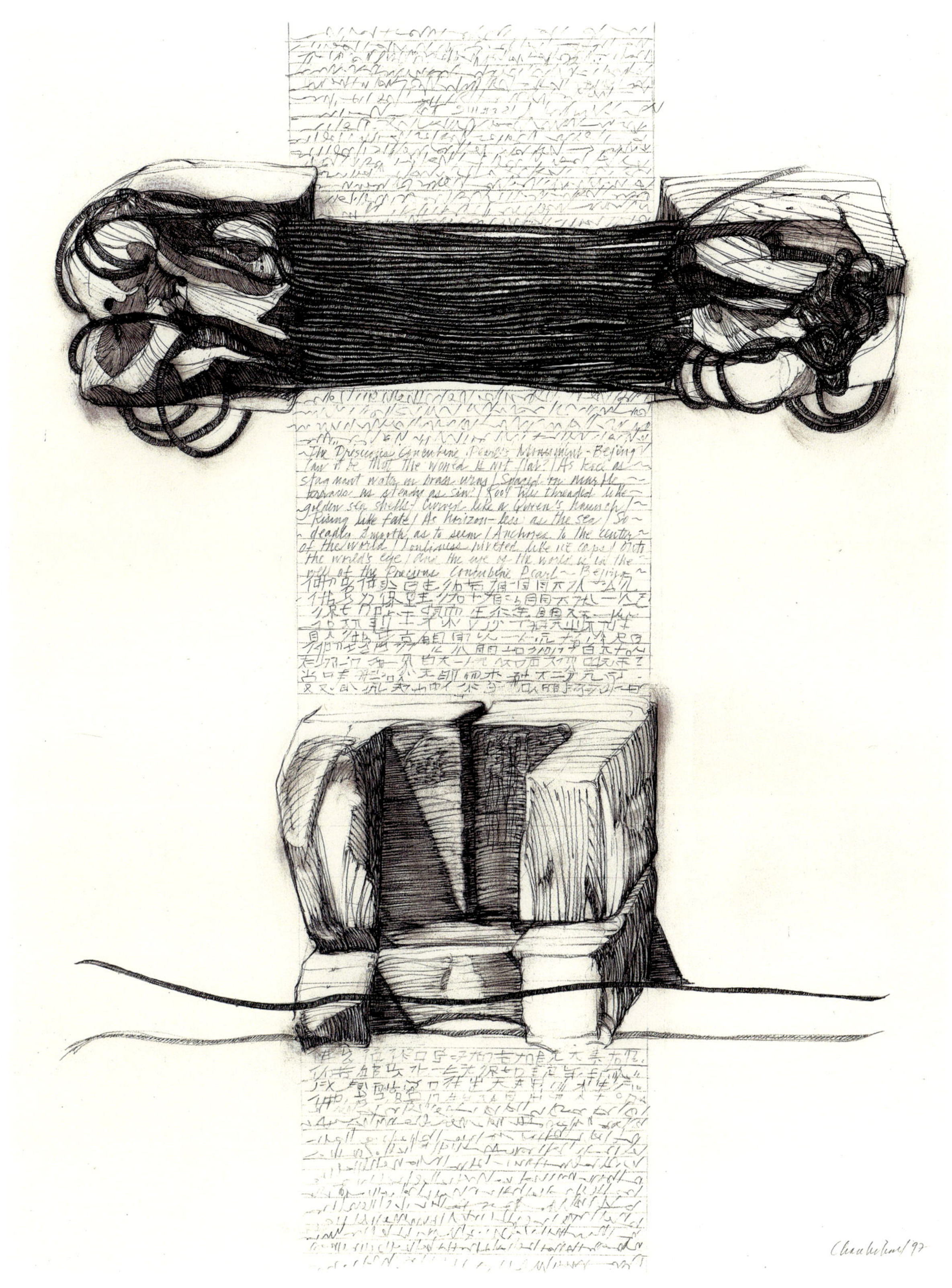

*The Precious Concubine Pearl's Monument,
Beijing*, 1997. Charcoal, charcoal pencil, and
ink with engraving and aquatint on paper,
31½ × 23⅞ inches (80 × 60.6 cm)

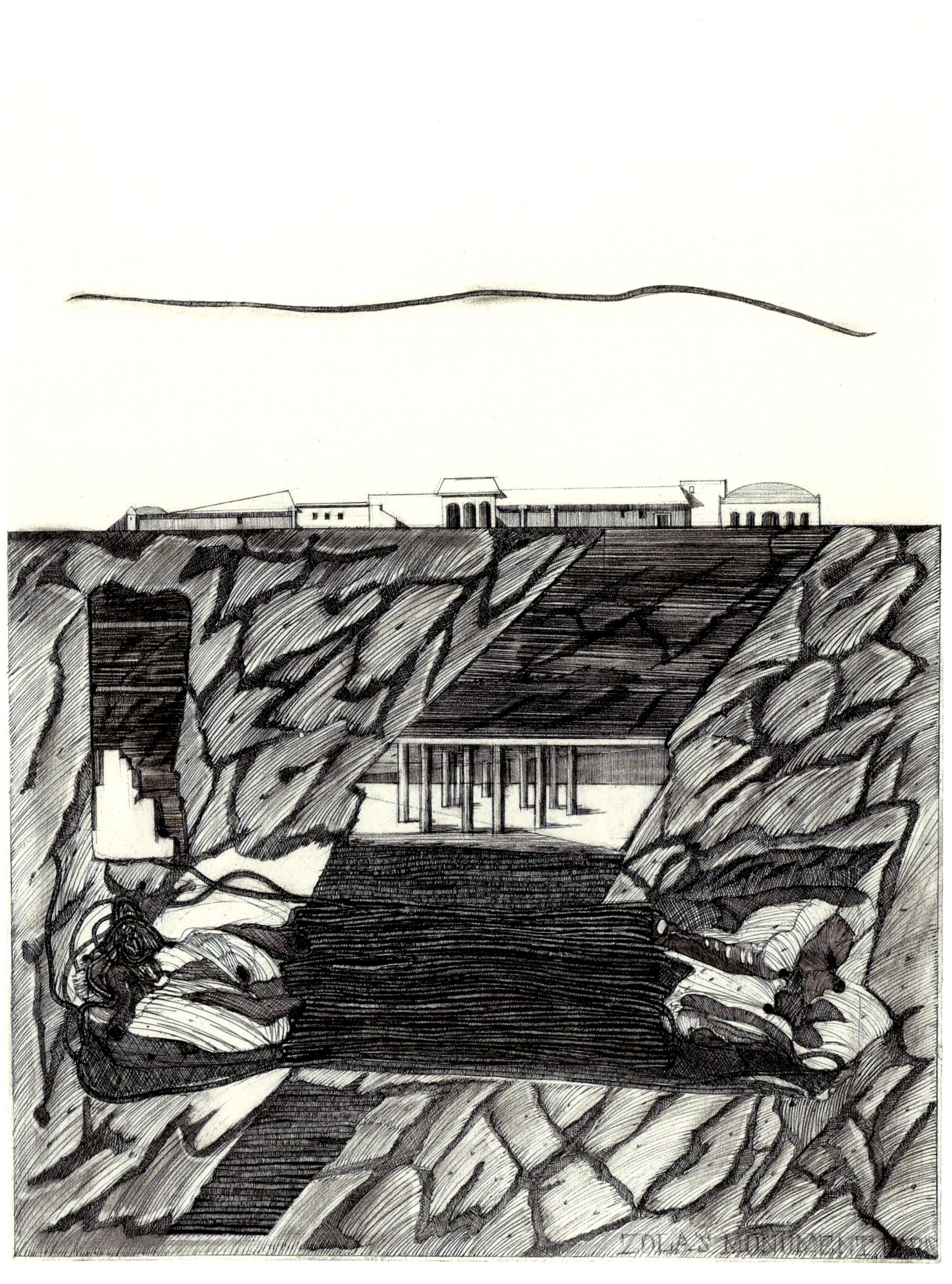

Zola's Monument, Paris, 1996. Charcoal, charcoal pencil, and ink with engraving and aquatint on paper, 31½ × 23⅞ inches (80 × 60.6 cm)

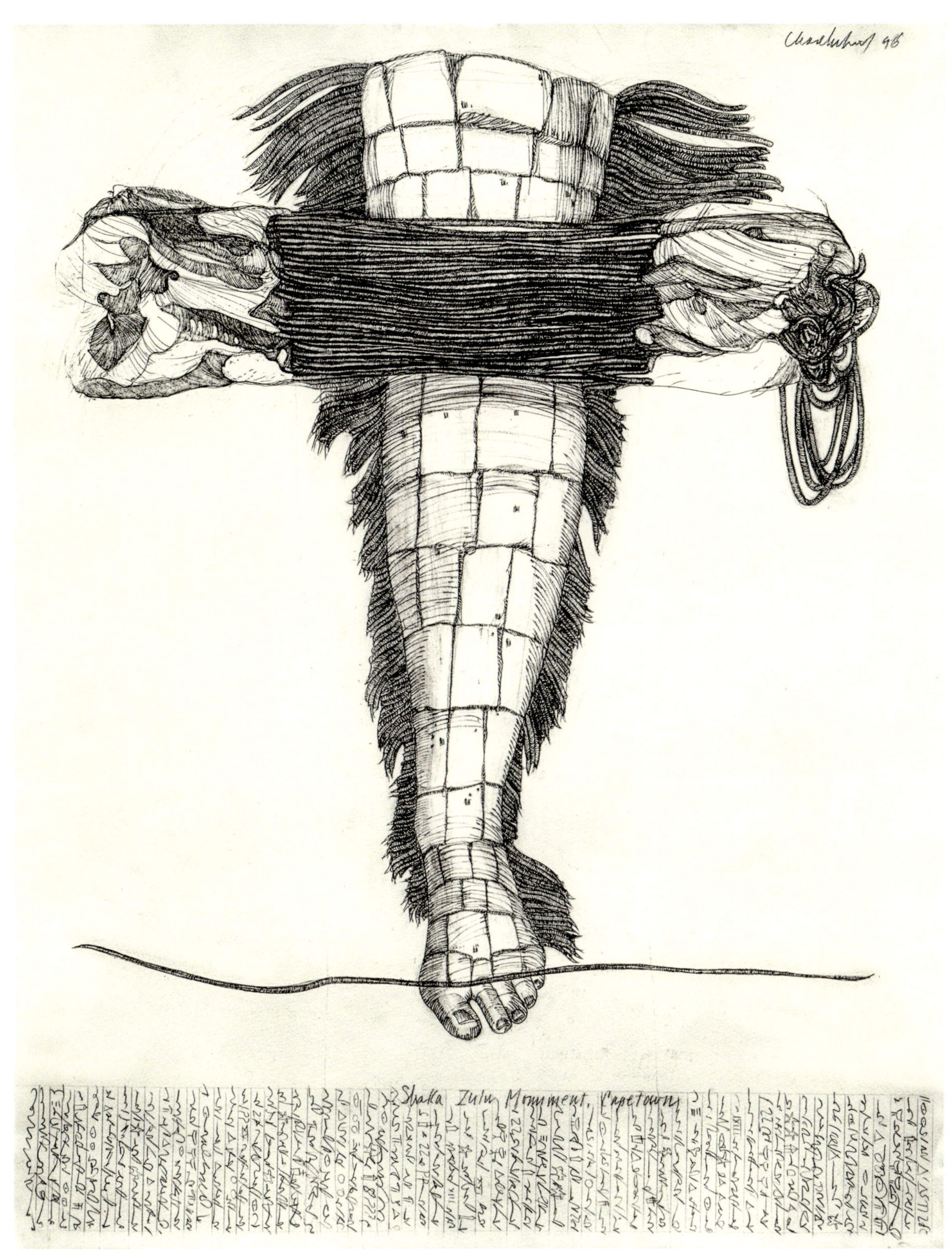

Shaka Zulu Monument, Capetown, 2007.
Charcoal, charcoal pencil, and ink with
engraving and aquatint on paper, 31½ ×
23⅞ inches (80 × 60.6 cm)

Woman's Monument, 1998. Bronze, 31 ×
30¼ × 18½ inches (78.7 × 76.8 × 47 cm)

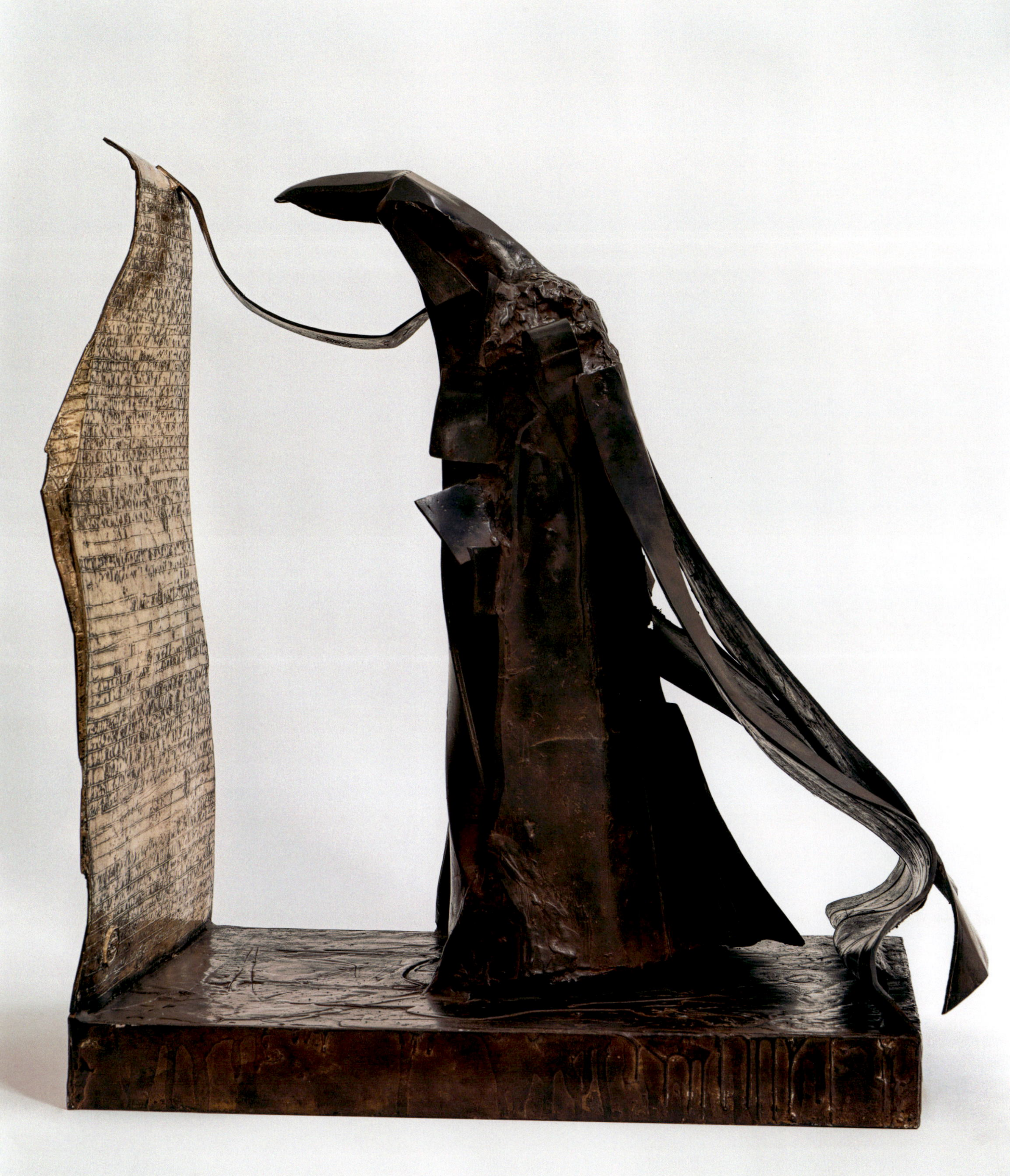

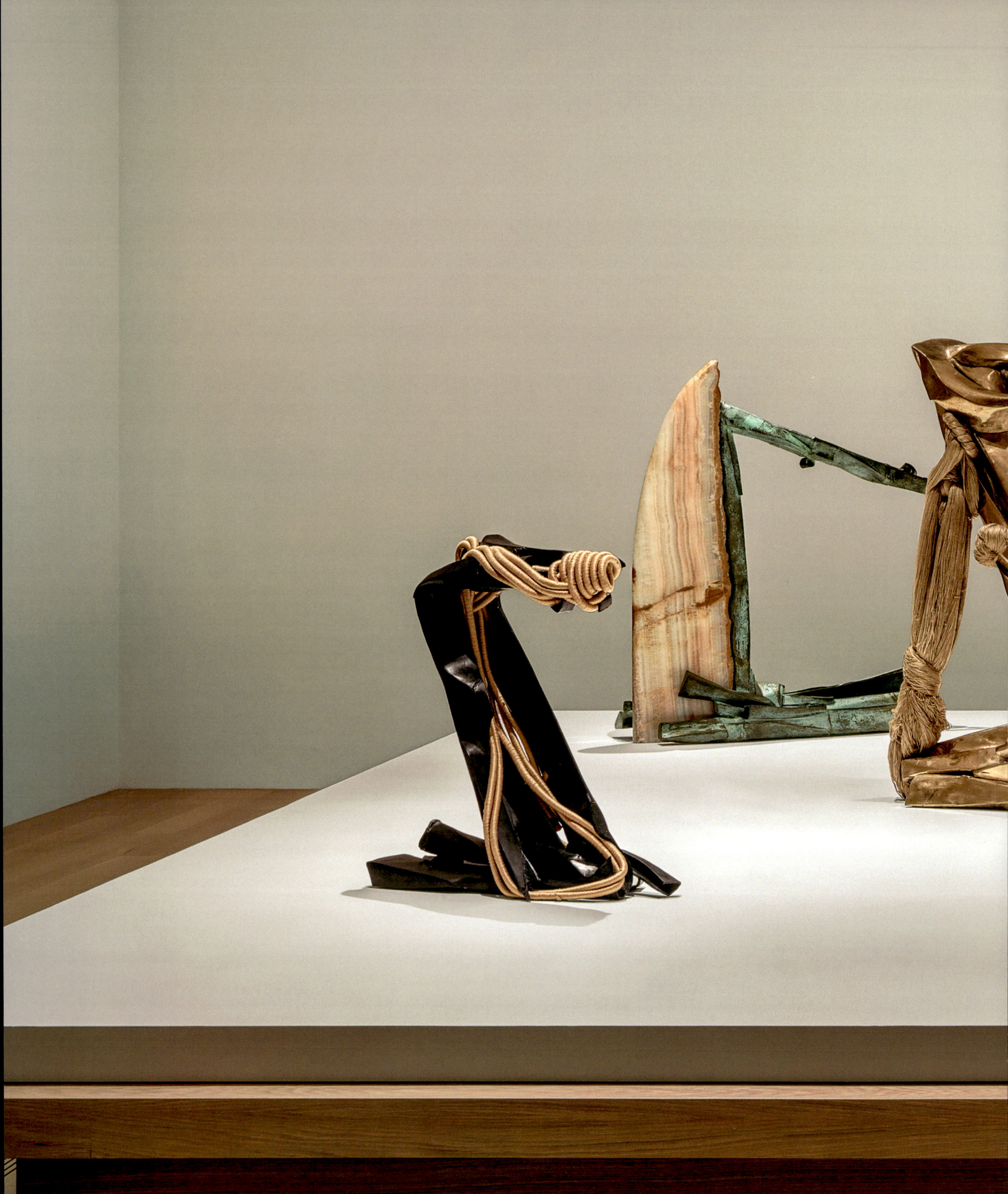

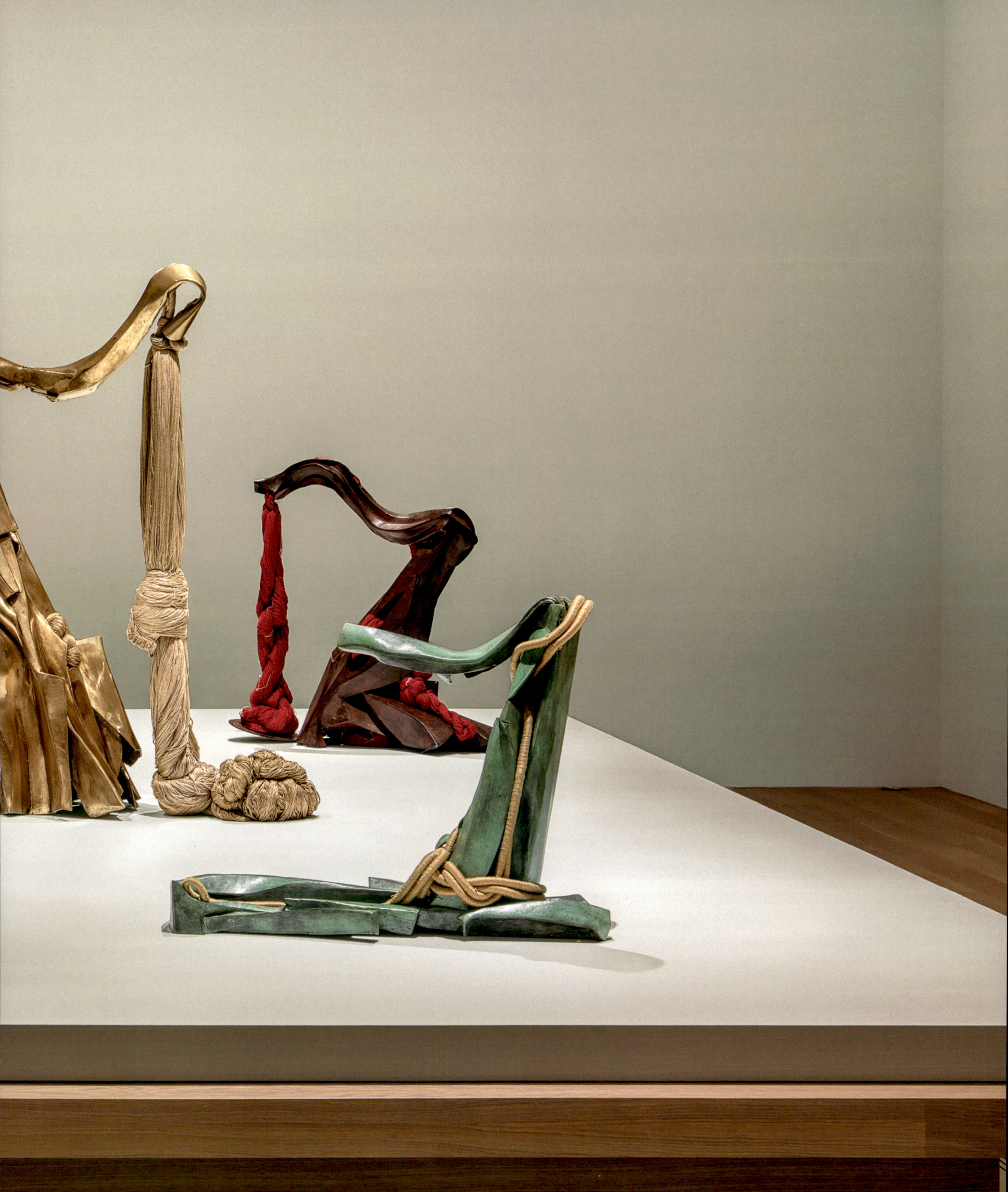

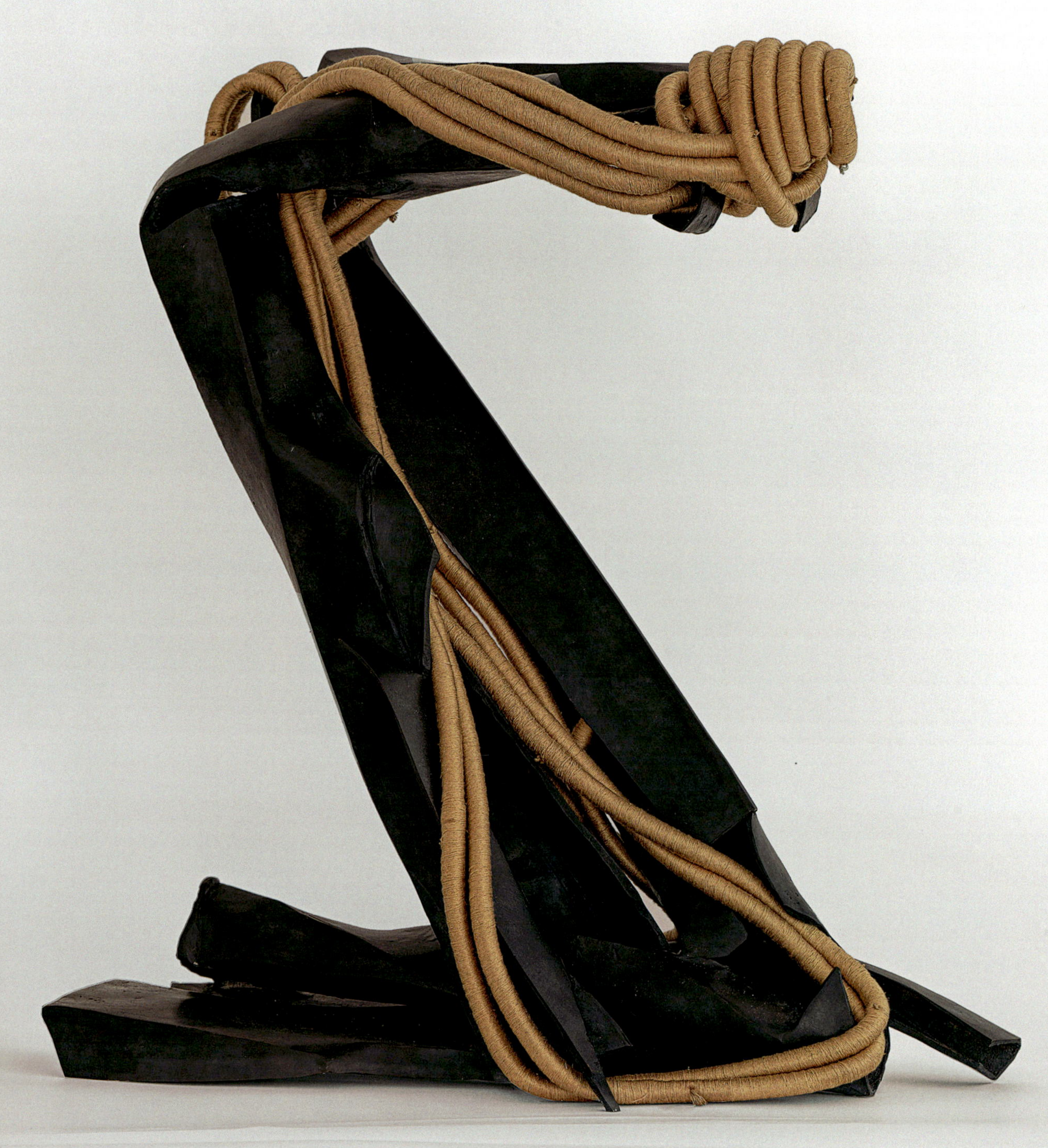

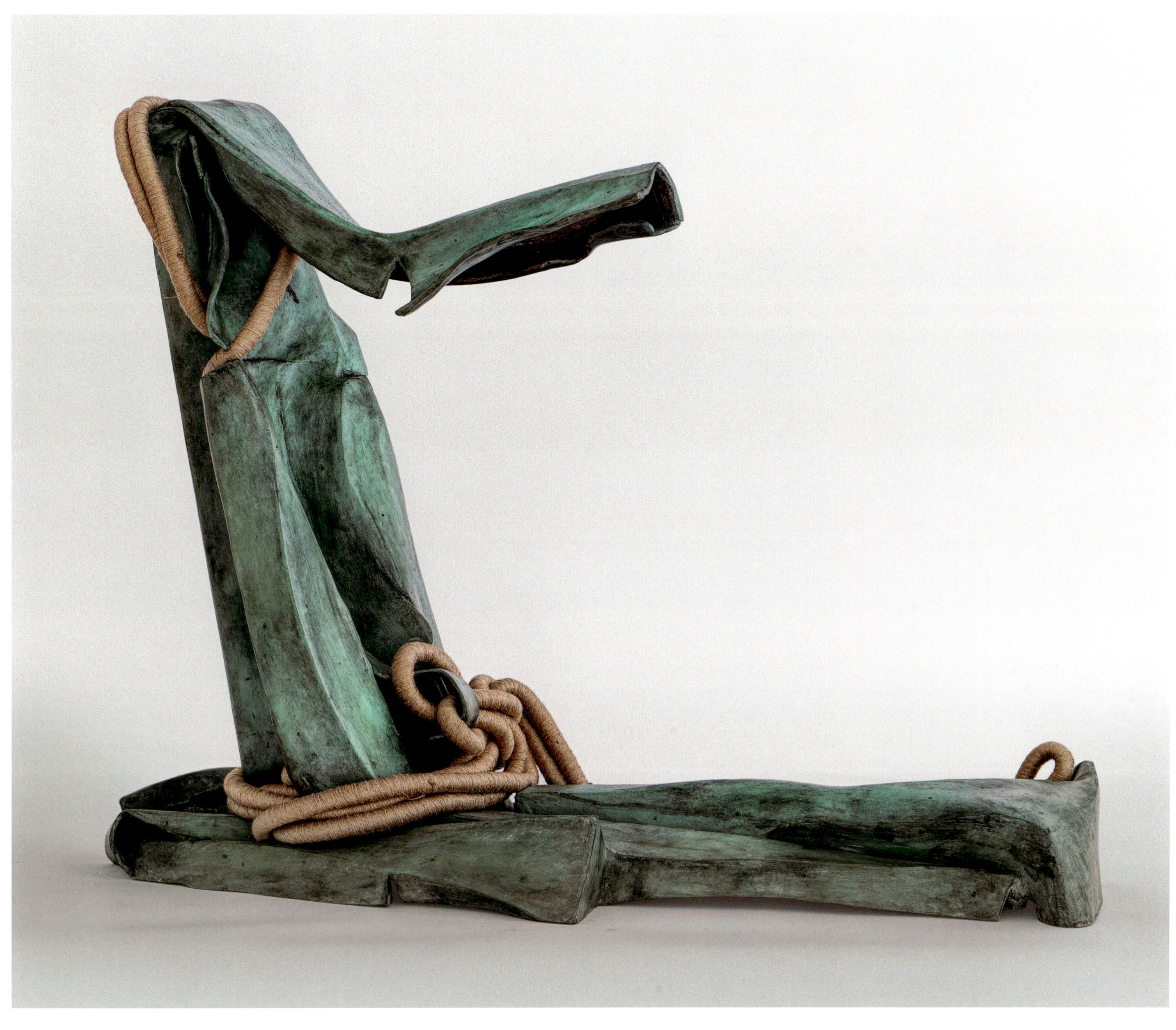

La Musica Black #1, 1998. Bronze with black patina and silk, 23⅞ × 21¼ × 9⅝ inches (60.6 × 54 × 24.4 cm)

La Musica Archaeological, 2003. Bronze and silk cord, 21 × 26¾ × 11 inches (53.3 × 67.9 × 27.9 cm)

La Musica Alabaster, 1998. Bronze and alabaster, 40½ × 35 × 12 inches (102.9 × 88.9 × 30.5 cm)

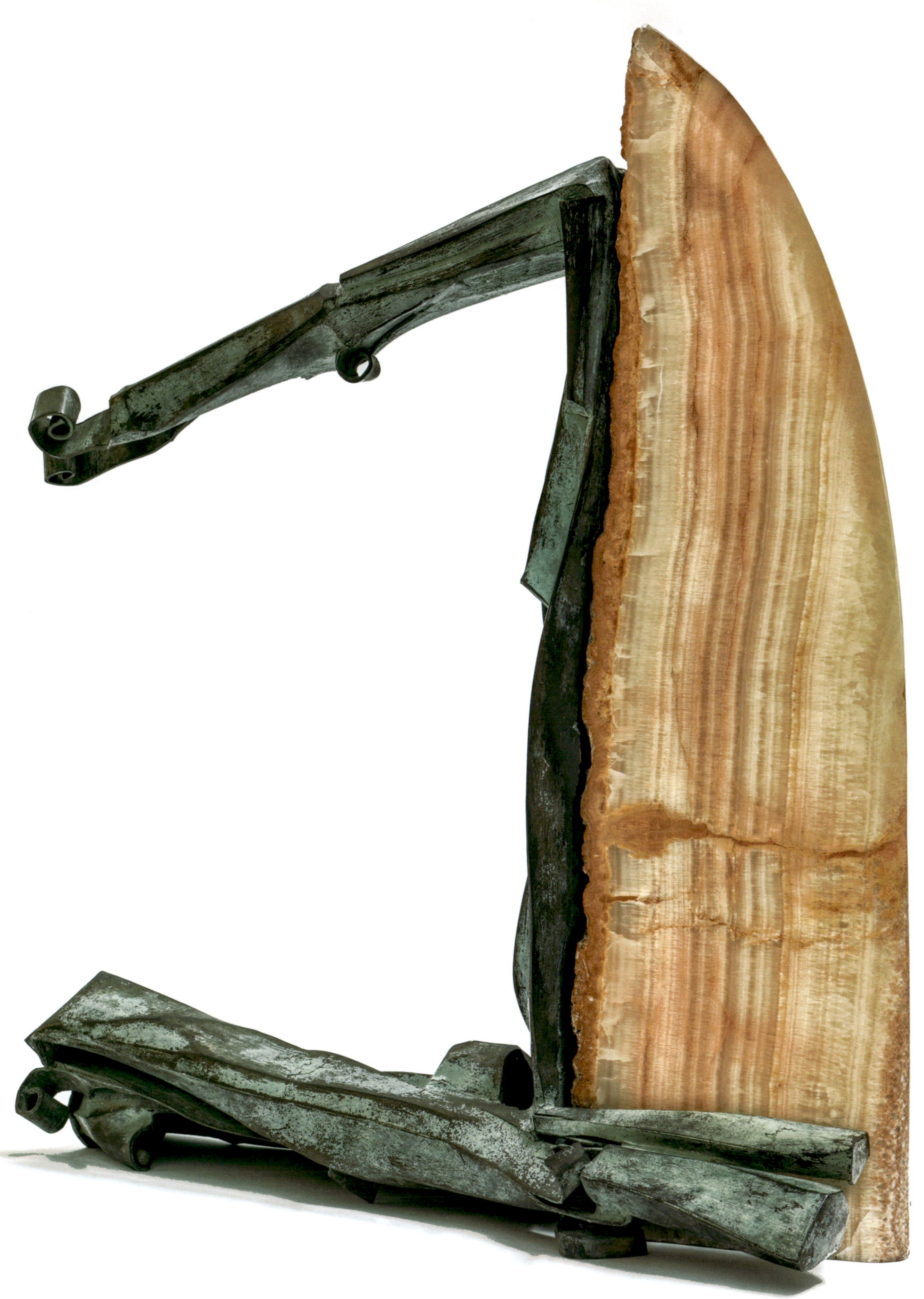

On Hearing Marian Anderson

A woman's voice is rushing like the wind,
Black it seems and damp of the night…
Rich velvet rising from the scent of
Ferns and glossy moss touched by moonlight,
The low breath of resurrection.

Her voice compels the hundred thousand
Assembled on the Mall to hear her bewitch
The Washington Monument defiantly
Lifting the spirits of the dispossessed
As if there was no grave,

Something in it of silver and fabulous
Silken scarves flung out throughout Bach's equations
Caught in the draft of genius
Low and grave and sonorous as steel
Slowing the heartbeat to Bach's own rhythm

A woman's voice is rushing like the wind,
Hard, simple and pure as diamonds,
Making her music impossible to ignore
The beat of its wings
As mysterious as a flight of stairs.

La Musica Marian Anderson, 2003. Bronze,
silk, and synthetic fibers, 45¼ × 25⁹⁄₁₆ ×
10⅝ inches (115 × 65 × 27 cm)

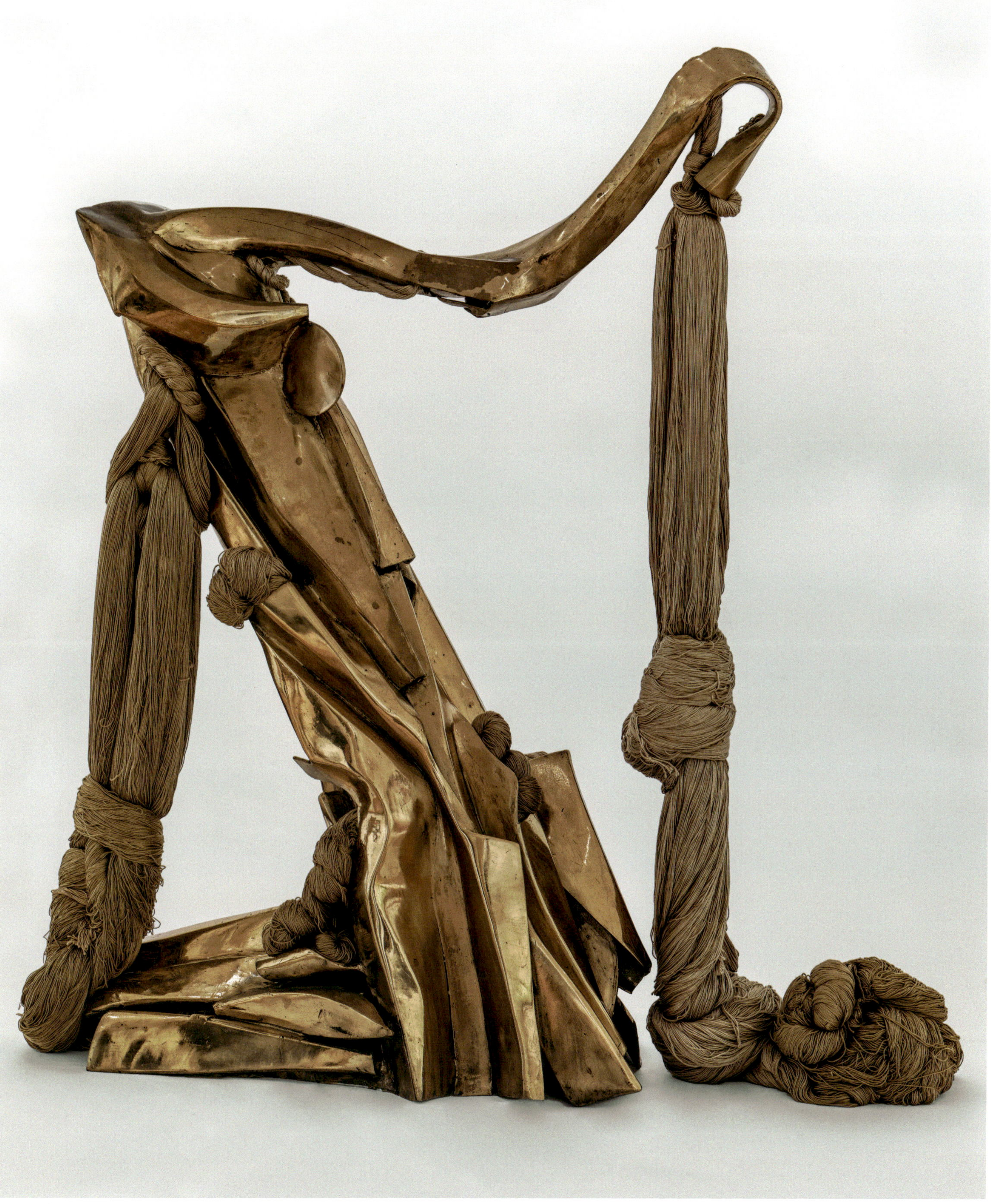

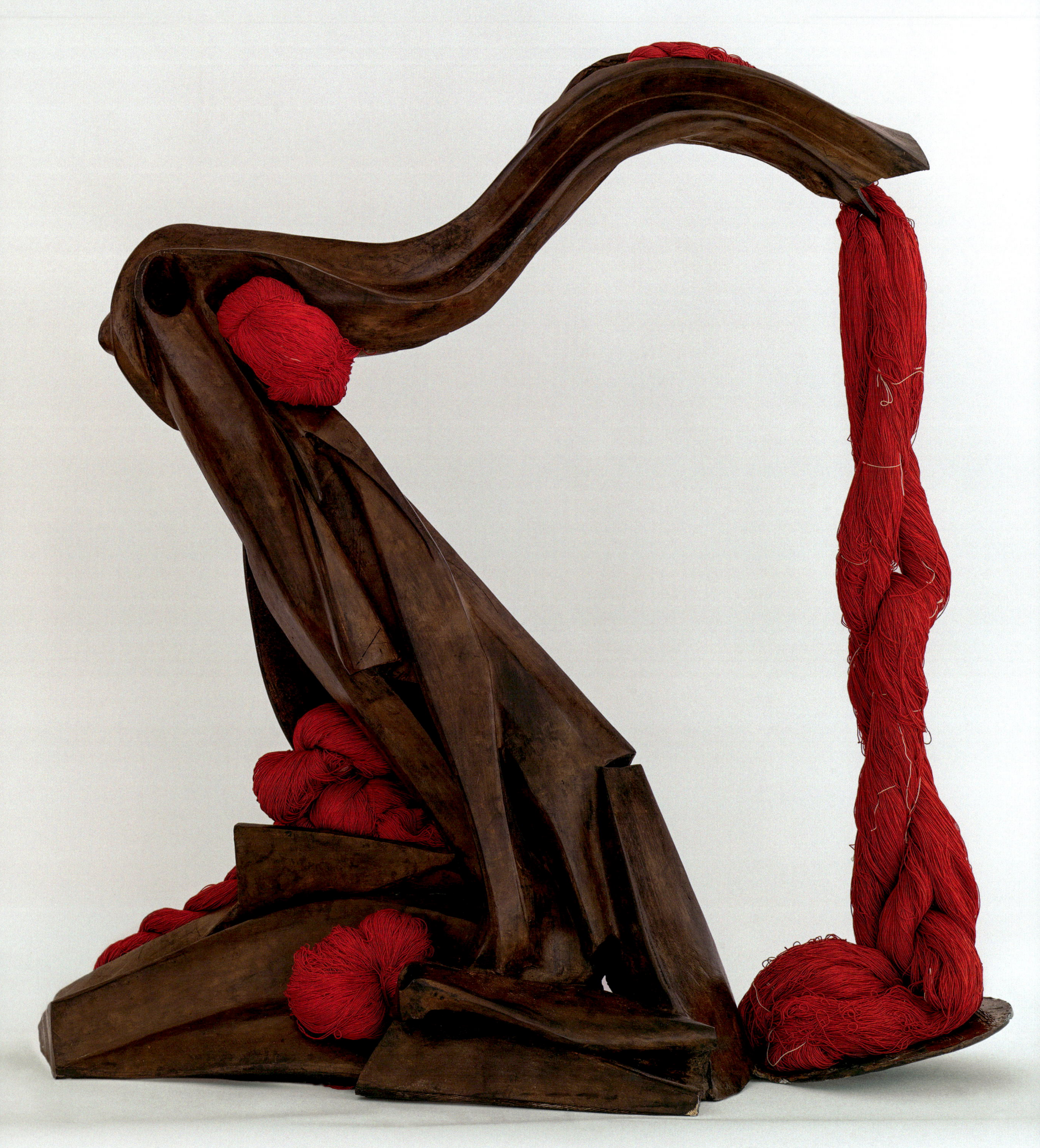

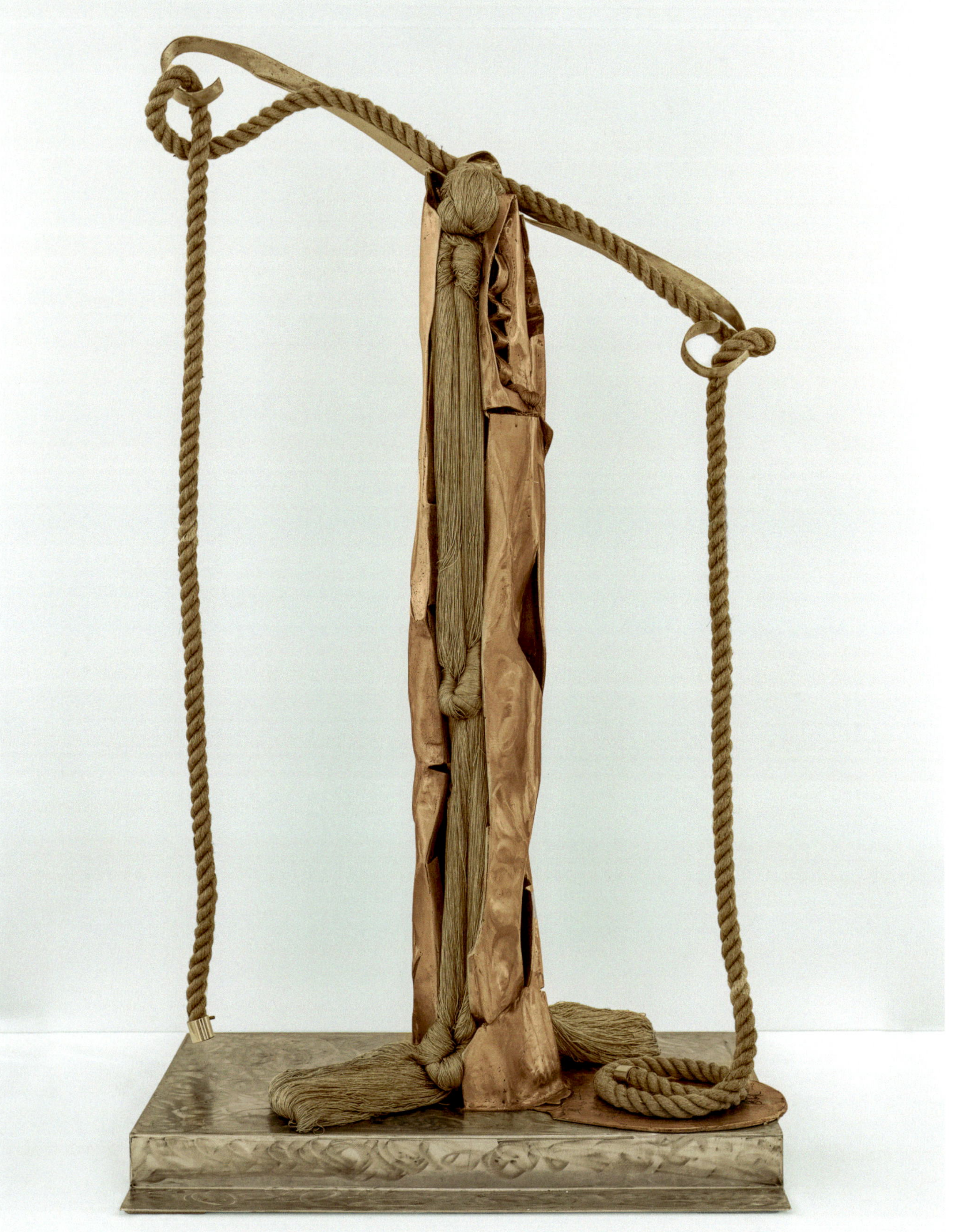

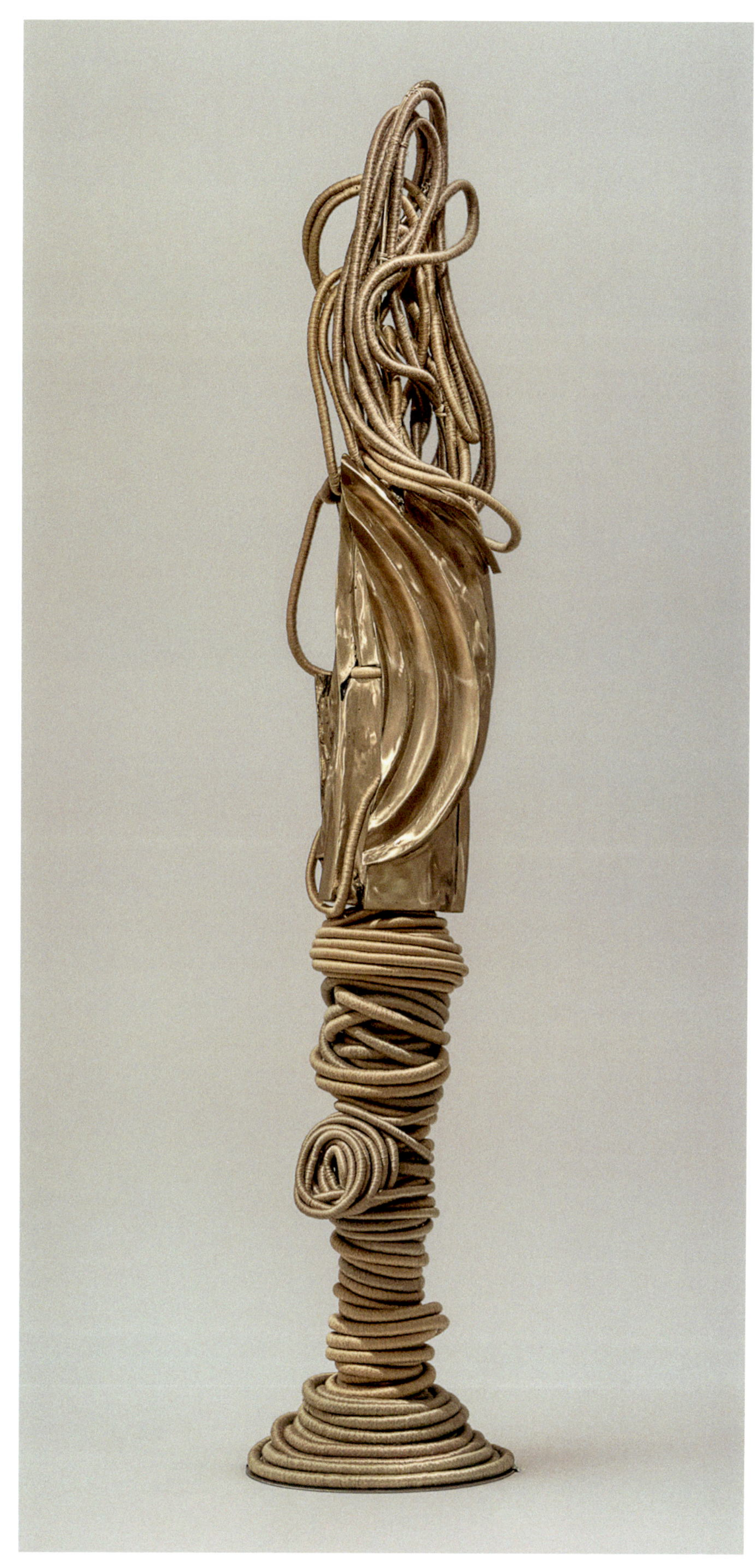

Twin Towers, 2007. Polished bronze and silk with steel base, 65¾ × 36⅜ × 25¾ inches (167 × 92.4 × 65.4 cm)

Anne d'H, 2008. Bronze and silk, 73 × 13½ inches (185.4 × 34.3 cm)

Anne d'Harnoncourt—1943–2008

I lit a candle beneath Bernini's canopy
In Saint Peter's Basilica,
Laid a wreath of red roses on Raphael's tomb
In the Pantheon,
Scraping tidbits of our last conversation
From the stones of the Venice Biennale.
I have knelt before Caravaggio's saints
Like a Pilgrim and
Like a Pilgrim, wondered through the Roman Forum
On the point of tears.

Pausing in the Palatino to ponder all that was
Excellent in you, burdened by Life's fragility,
And what is real and what is un-real, reconciling
The possible and the impossible while you sleep,
Anne, the Validé, Philadelphia's Athena,
With your lynx eyes and Etruscan smile, your Herculesian
Voice & aristocratic lisp that turned p's into th's,
The scepter your father bequeathed you held
Draped in Tanagrino scarves, shading that
Brilliance that glows like Leonardo's moon.

Like a sister I revolt at this un-timeliness & waste,
Of a free and generous spirit, seeped
In choice and dedicated to that empire of color,
The red Degas, rest, rest, rest, removed,
Not so much because Life is untimely & wasteful,
But because the house you lived in was the essence
Of timeliness and the enemy of waste,
It was the opposite of emptiness—a rose figured
Lekythos Vase overflowing with the eternal
Fascination of Perfection.

At Petra, I stand on the rock of Isis,
In Cairo, I weep on the granite of Sphinx
Barefoot, I walk the labyrinth of Chartres' Cathedral,
At Aya Sophia, I kneel on a silk prayer rug,
And cover my face and hair in grief, gazing,
Neither to the right nor the left,
But somewhere in that Netherland where Art dwells,
Immobile & irreducible & still living . . .
The only proof that anything
Has ever happened in the past.

Anne d'H, 2008 (detail)

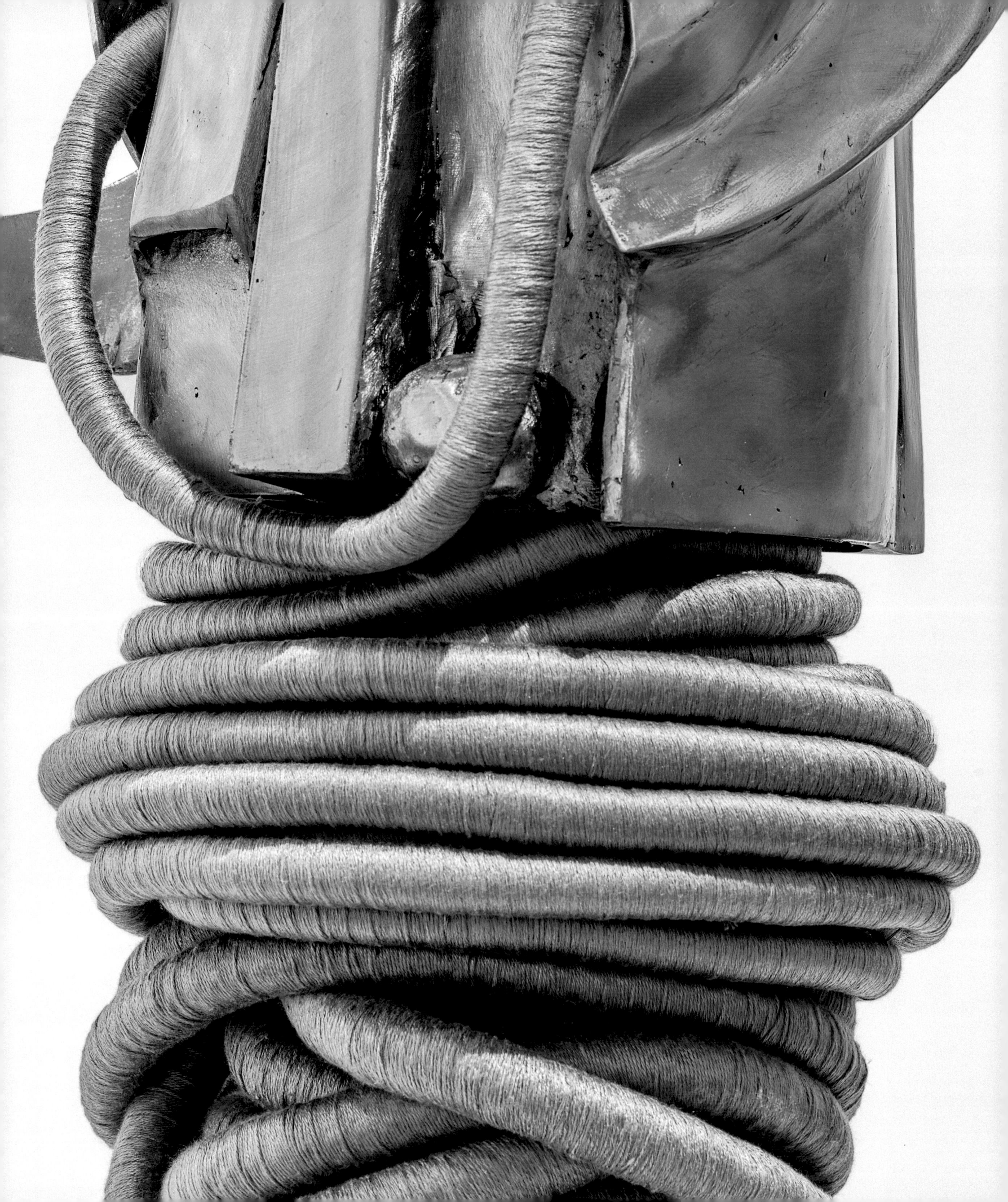

La Musica Red Parkway, Josephine, 2007.
Bronze with red patina and silk, 72⅞ × 49 ×
19 inches (185.1 × 124.5 × 48.3 cm)

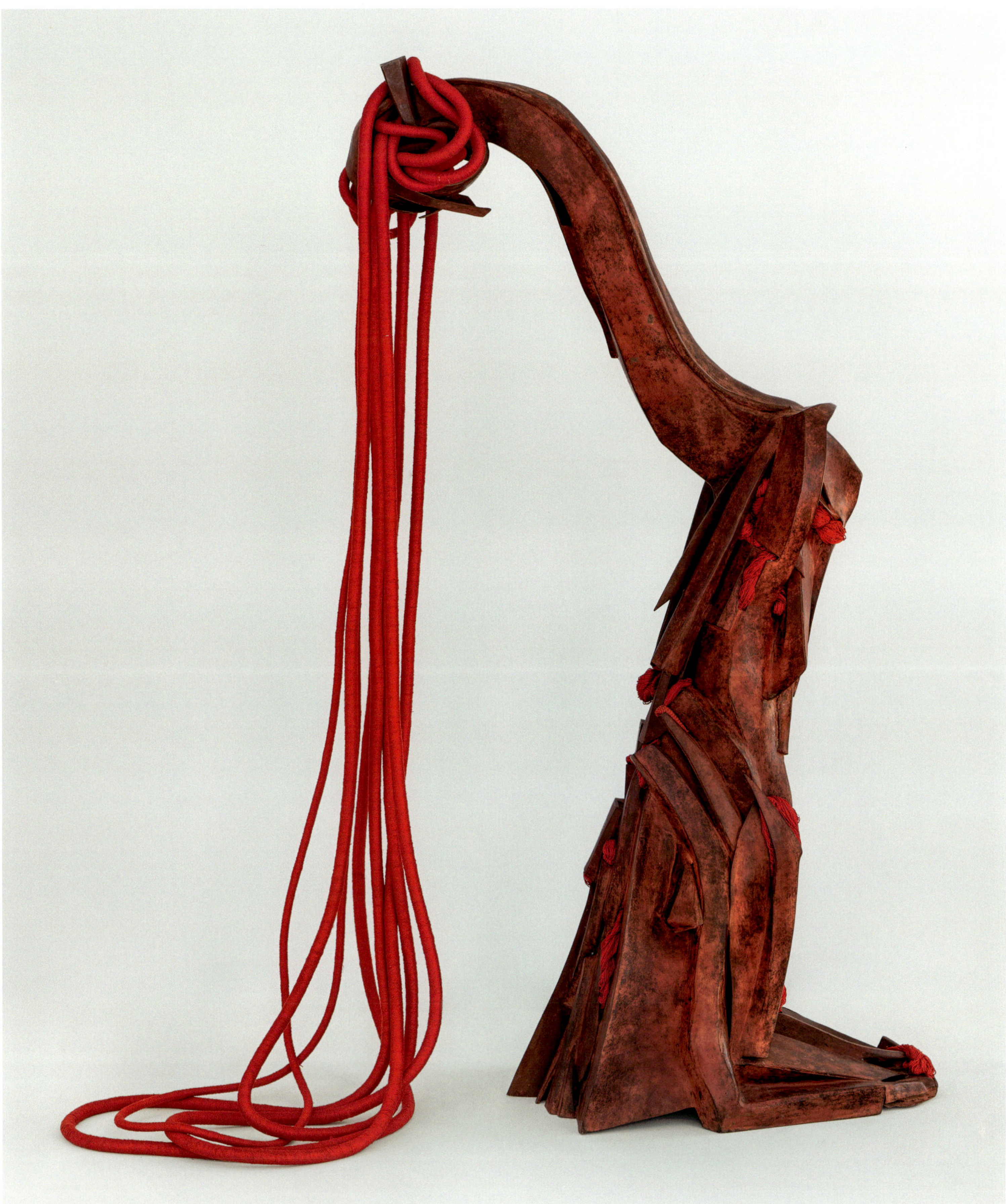

FROM MALCOLM TO JOSEPHINE

A Manifesto for Sculpture in Pursuit of Futurism

Barbara Chase-Riboud and Reginald Jackson

Too long has our art been freighted with demands for strict resemblance, to reflect the rectitude of portraiture. Sculpture wanes, beset by faultless ratios that decant its noblest aspiration. Survey these funerary slabs, emplaced like pompous sentries, all too often lustrous, laden, and bereft. Who shackled them to reverence? What bled them of all ardor? Such awful pains to snuff out any motion liable to inhabit sculpted forms!

The blues remind us that requiems only resonate so far. So today we scrap dirges for buoying refrains: Come, quit the cemeteries littered with decorum. Come, crawl past crumbling plinths to cull momentum from debris. Come, smelt our ore for something more than busts, and chains.

Left: Marcel Duchamp (1887–1968), *Nude Descending a Staircase (No. 2)*, 1912. Oil on canvas, 57⅞ × 35⅛ inches (147 × 89.2 cm). The Philadelphia Museum of Art, The Louise and Walther Arensberg Collection, 1950

Right: Pablo Picasso (1881–1973), *Head of a Woman (Fernande)*, 1926–27. Bronze, 16¼ × 9¾ × 10½ inches (41.3 × 24.8 × 26.7 cm). The Metropolitan Museum of Art, Leonard A. Lauder Cubist Collection, Gift of Leonard A. Lauder, 2021 (2021.33)

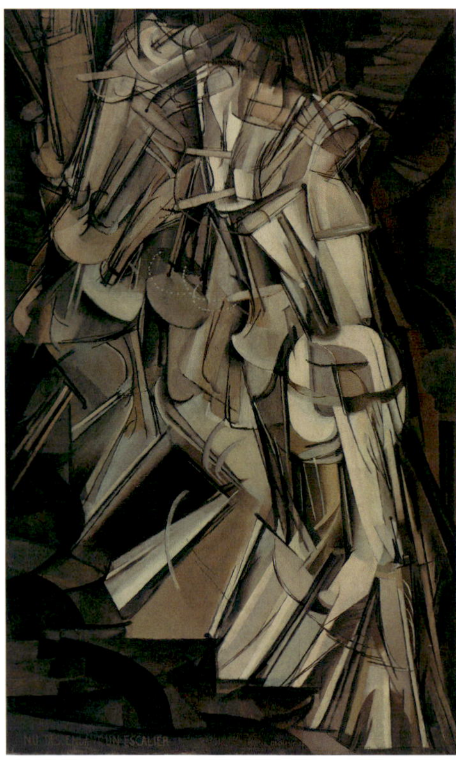

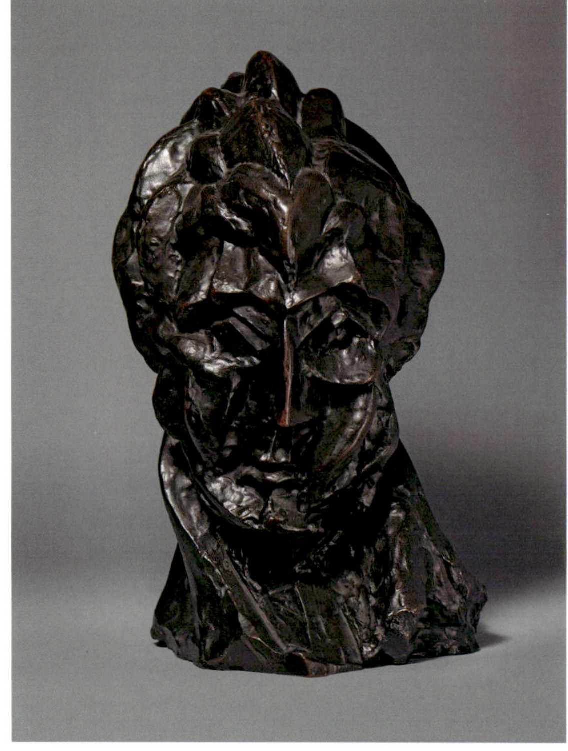

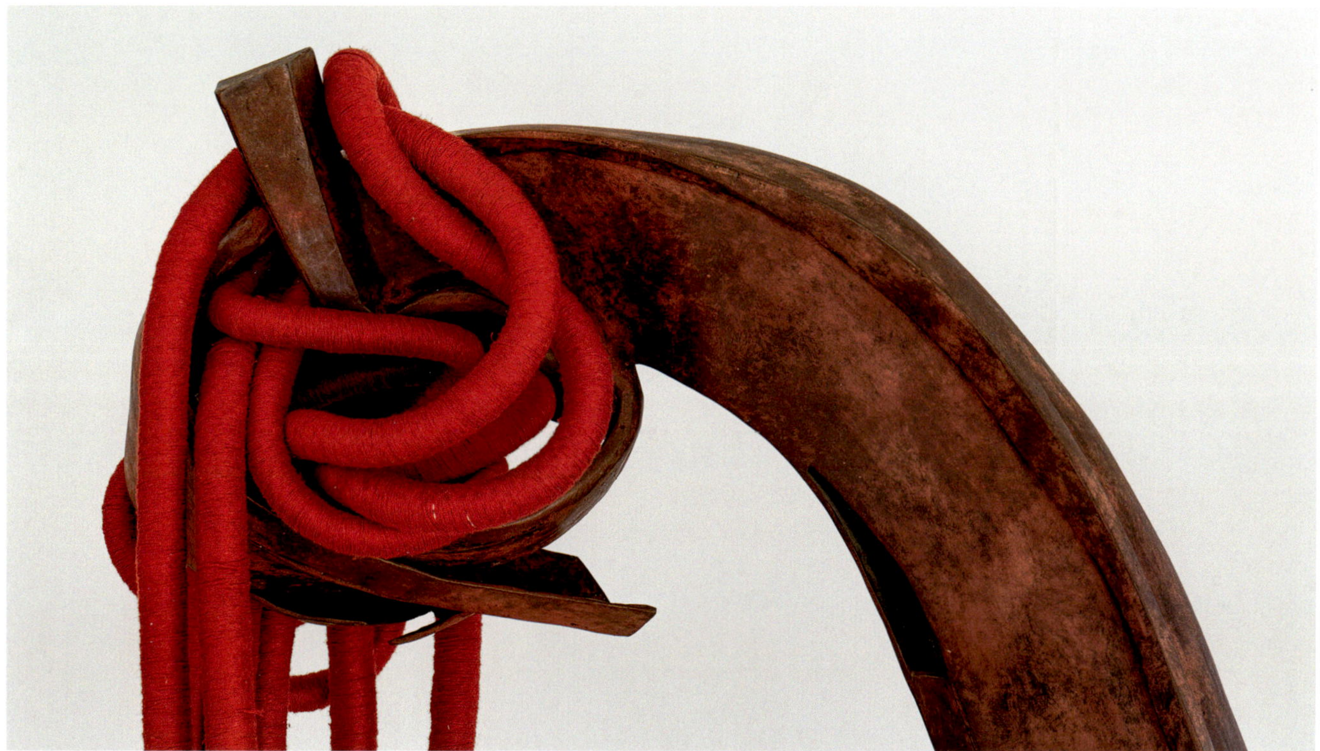

Let us jettison the stale geometry of these remnants and clear terrain to host a raucous, swinging romp. Sculpture must not sit still.

Pillars fail to capture all the zeal *Josephine*'s Muse emits. Note the rift between sculpture wrought to anchor sites, and sculpture spurred to refract snatches of an essence. *Josephine* flouts likeness, revels in abstraction.

Josephine strides forth in the wake of the serial permutations *Malcolm X* and *Zanzibar*. *Josephine* becomes possible once pleas for utter gravitas subside. Instead, like the Futurists, "enriched by a new beauty: the beauty of speed," *Josephine* seduces with its raw yet harnessed surge. No time to loiter with monoliths! Dispense with preening monuments! Let us abandon them like sullen husks, hurl ourselves ahead and forego that which is not fervent, raw, and swift.

With brash radiance *Josephine* dares us to peel off any crippling patina. It strikes one's eyes like obsidian and fresh blood. We pledge to splinter templates lest they ration lust to cinders. Hence, no more:

- poignance
- pastel postures
- mausoleums
- jagged edges gnawed by etiquette
- rage or passion

Our craft must prove kinetic! Watch the bearing of its base shift: ricochet from floor, to wall, to a spiral sweep in a quest to mine and convey energy and attitude through evolving armature. We resolve to make sculpture *dance*.

We've come to suspect frigid planes and axes. Let throbbing rhythm thaw Giacometti's brittle toothpick limbs. Skeletons can't withstand the

La Musica Red Parkway, Josephine,
2007 (detail)

Barbara Chase-Riboud, *Pushkin's Horse*, 1994. Bronze, approx. diam.: 23½ inches (60 cm). Mott-Warsh Collection, Flint, MI

rhythm's course. Volcanic in its thrust, *Josephine* explodes then saunters routes right past their bones.

La Musica's ebb and flow arranges stalks of creased metal as they branch and lean against draped or knotted fabric in their midst. But *Josephine* boosts the shades of red to different heights and bolder ends. It sheds the heft of boulder-swollen silk, pares massive densities down to ligatures prone to spring to life. Demure knotting is no more: *Josephine*'s svelte loops cascade willowlike and sultry, its crimson cords flirting with the ground like it were lava.

Watch the molten blood-red bough scythe skyward while the scarlet reins sway loose. Marrow garlands appear to drape a bonsai limb. Silk vines caress charred steel to trigger alchemy. We glean verve from this conjuncture. So, let red and red entwine, make red and red combust! Behold a wayward spirit steeped in rouge and rouge. Discern the scent, the stance, the tone, the flaming vault and whirl of *Josephine*.

Jazz prompts us to carve melodic riffs through space. No more columns tethered to a stoic grid. We must evade the architectural to extrude the gestural. Puncture planar elevations! Make standard axes swerve toward something restive. Syncopate! *Josephine* introduces an extra beat—or more—to basic vectors, distending uniform segments into fuller lines of action. Wary of enclosure, sculpture that nears dance detaches from these framing habits, molting out of scaffolds to sketch calligraphic routes and lay the gesture's vibrancy bare.

Josephine's staccato thrust takes us further than Boccioni's *Unique Forms* and the robotic slice of Duchamp's *Nude Descending* into the arms of Picasso's Fernande—all of which inspire still. Only *Pushkin's Horse* suggests the vibrancy of static but moving forms changing shapes, as Peter Selz remarked in his 1972 essay: "Before our very eyes as Chase-Riboud's silken cords summon contours no less potent once channeled and woven like cursive ligatures that fashion shadows with motions."

La Musica Red Parkway, Josephine, 2007 (detail)

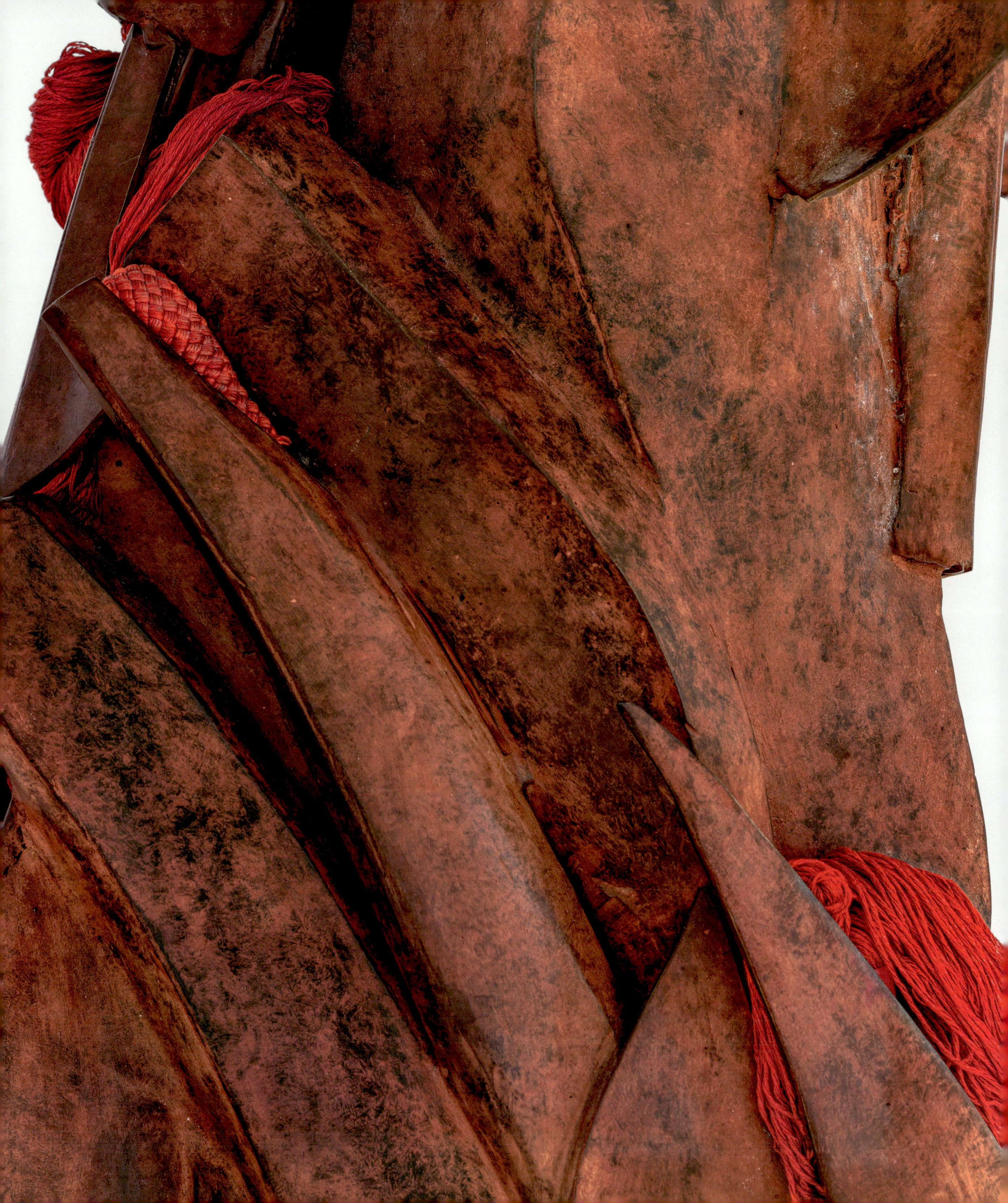

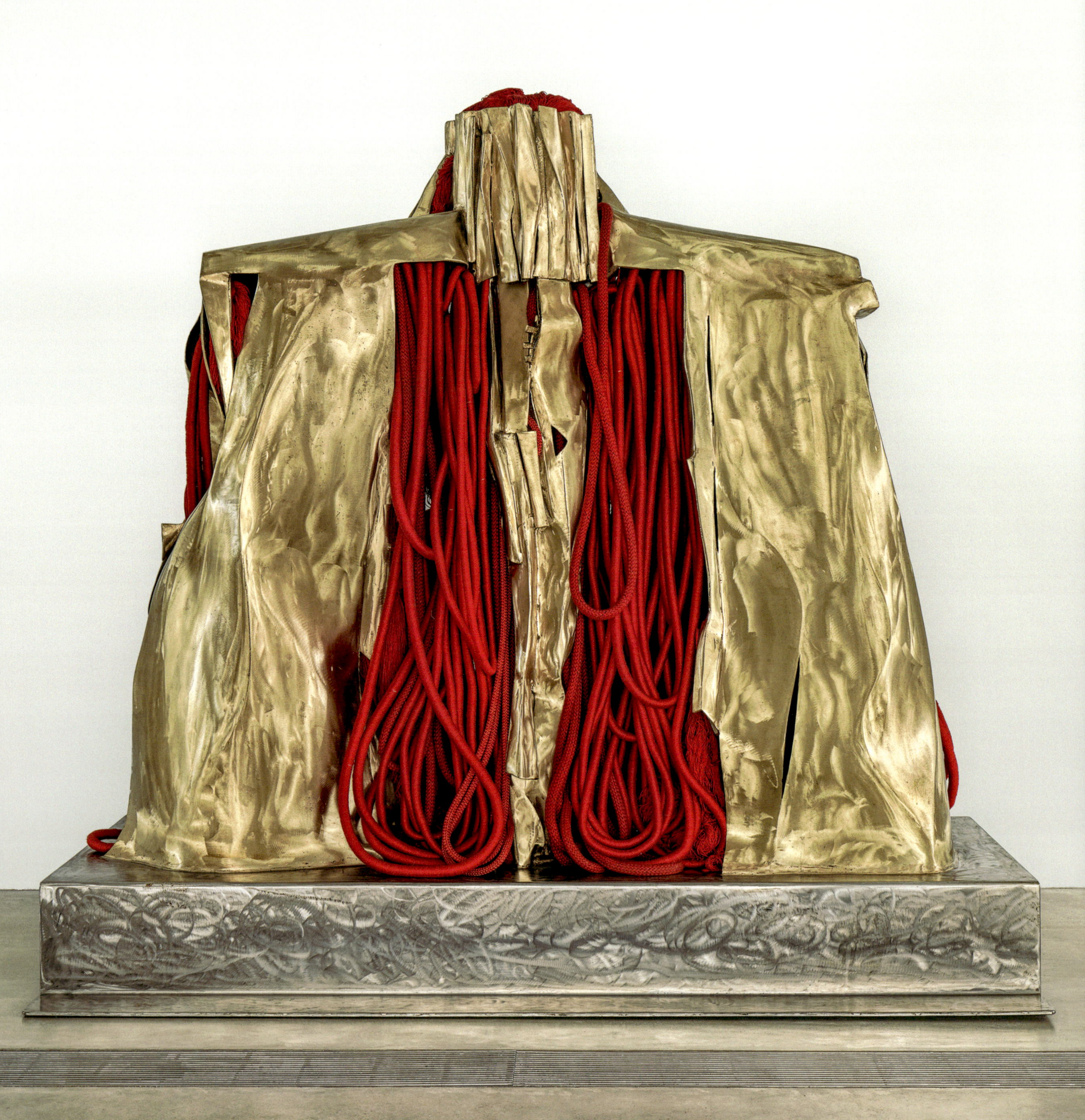

Mao Waved to the People

Mao waved to the People,
That curious ripple from
Little finger to
Index finger
And back *again*,
And
The People
Waved
Back.

Mao's Organ, 2007 (detail)

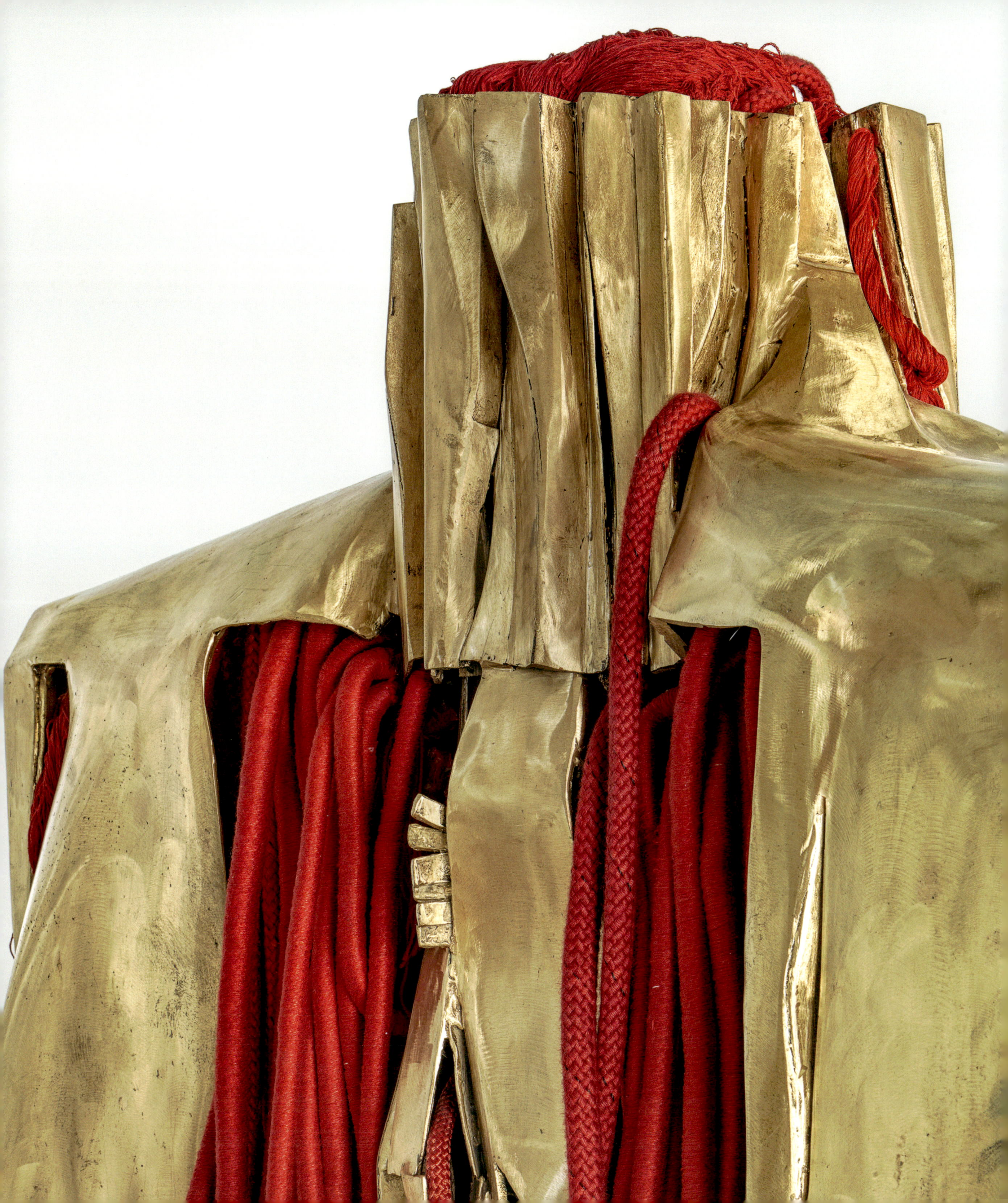

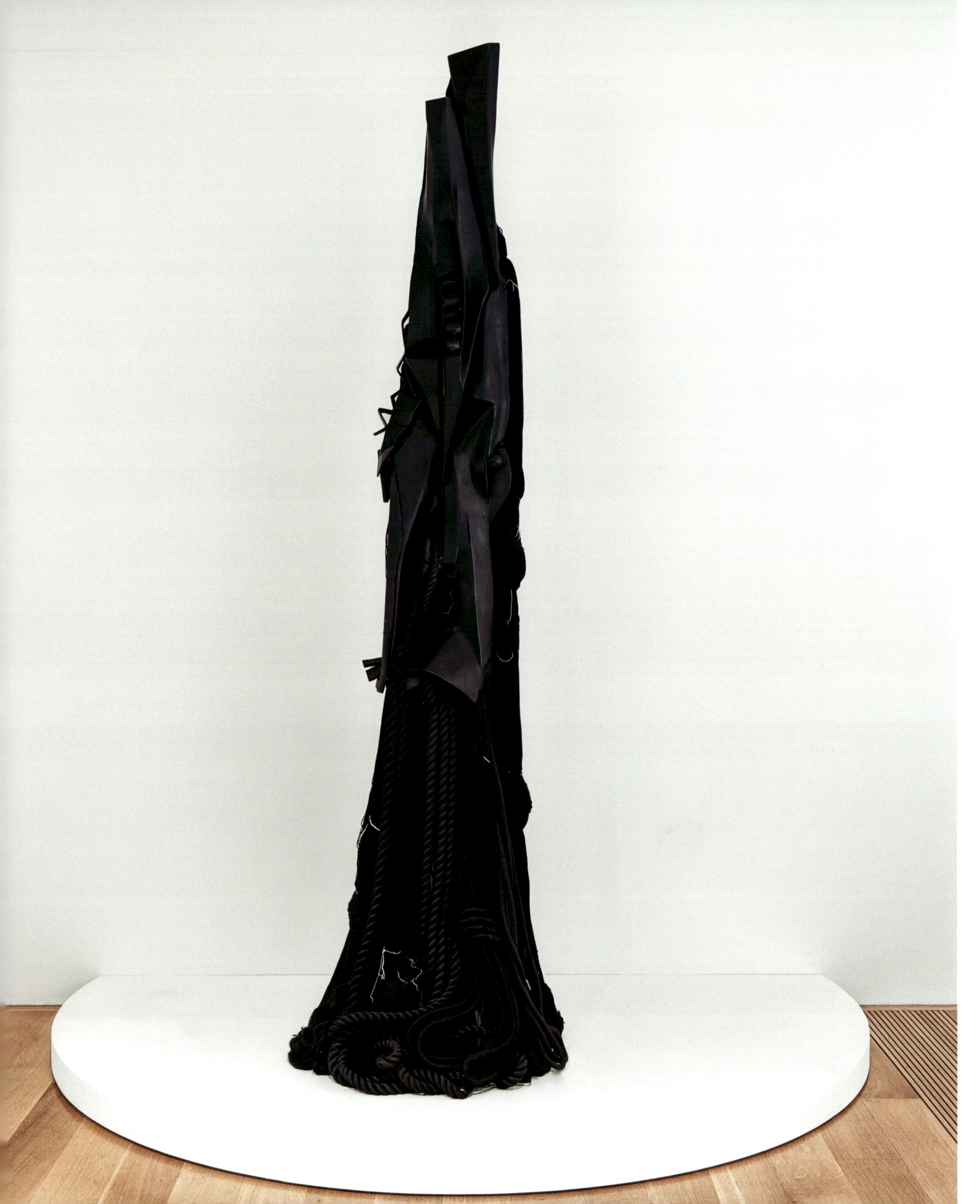

Black Obelisk #2, 2007. Bronze with black
patina, wool, and synthetic fibers with steel
support, 78 × 27 × 22 inches (198.1 × 68.6 ×
55.9 cm)

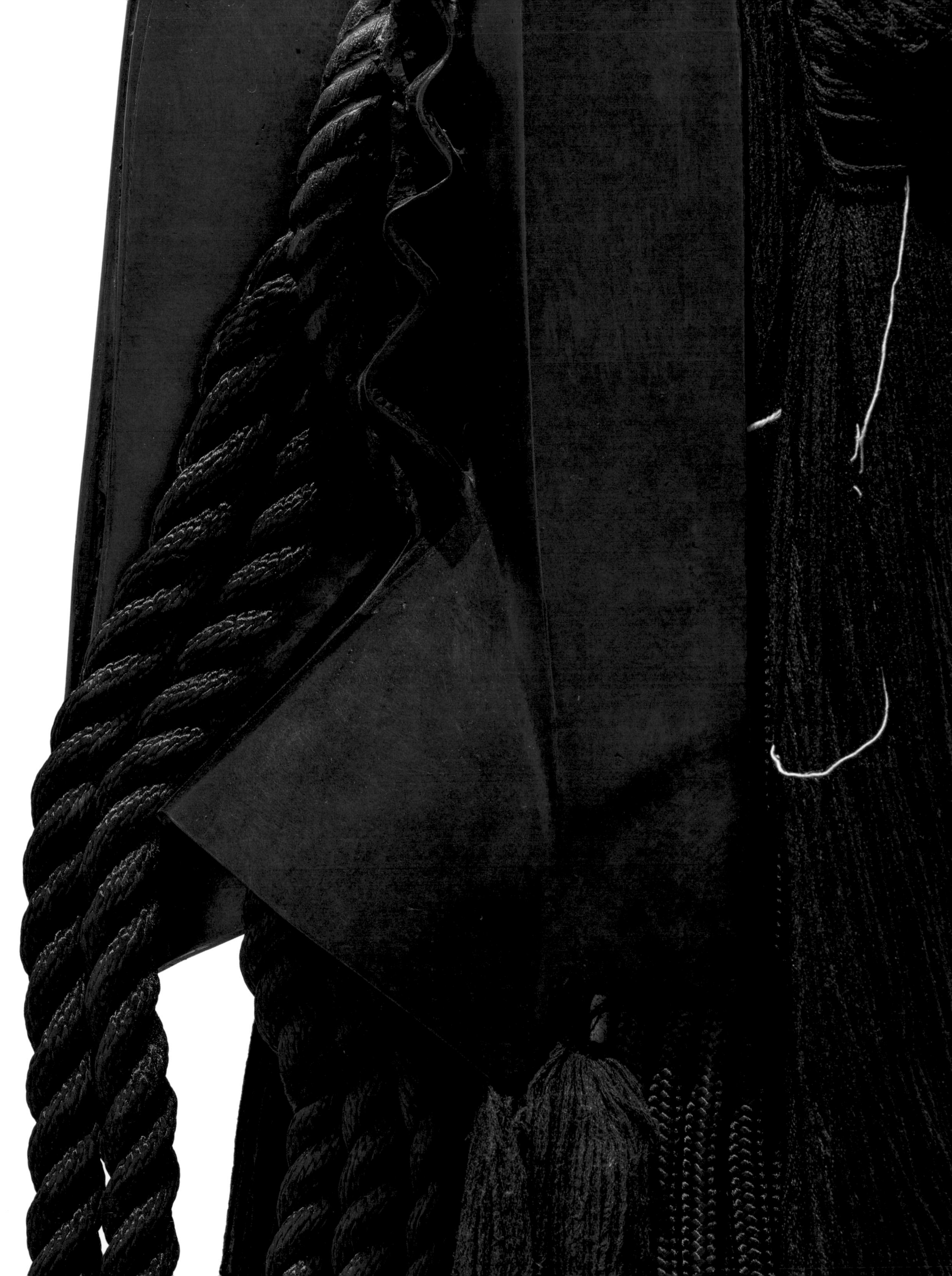

Suzette Spencer Why have silk and wool played such key roles in your sculpture? How do you imagine the relation between the two? I'm interested in how you come to use one instead of the other because there are several that use wool in lieu of silk, for example, *Malcolm X #2* (1970); *Malcolm X #4* (1970); *Black Obelisk* (1994); and *Confessions for Myself* (1972). Is there something about issues of masculinity, politics, or art that finds expression through the use of a rougher substance like wool?

Barbara Chase-Riboud It depends upon the structure of the sculpture, its literary theme, and the color of the patina. There are polished gold *Malcolms* and black patinated *Malcolms*. I usually decide which color the sculpture will be from the beginning and don't work in the same manner if it is gold rather than black or black rather than gold. The gold silk reflects light and takes a delicacy of form that the black wool can't achieve. It absorbs light rather than reflects it. It is somber, a bass or a cello rather than a viola or a violin or a harp. Wool is not only heavier, it falls differently; it sends a different message. Sometimes I combine black silk and black wool together like a duet. I don't think it has much to do with politics. It is what the viewer brings to the piece and his interpretation that makes the difference, although I am not denying the difference.

Suzette Spencer There is something to be said about verticality and the kinds of things that find meaning in verticality in your sculpture, especially in the downward progression from polished bronze to knotted silk.

Barbara Chase-Riboud This is the magic part, when the bronze becomes silk solidifying into the material that supports the weight of the metal despite the fact that you know this cannot be.

Excerpt from "On Her Own Terms: An Interview with Barbara Chase-Riboud" by Suzette A. Spencer, *Callaloo* 32, no. 3 (Summer 2009): 746–47.

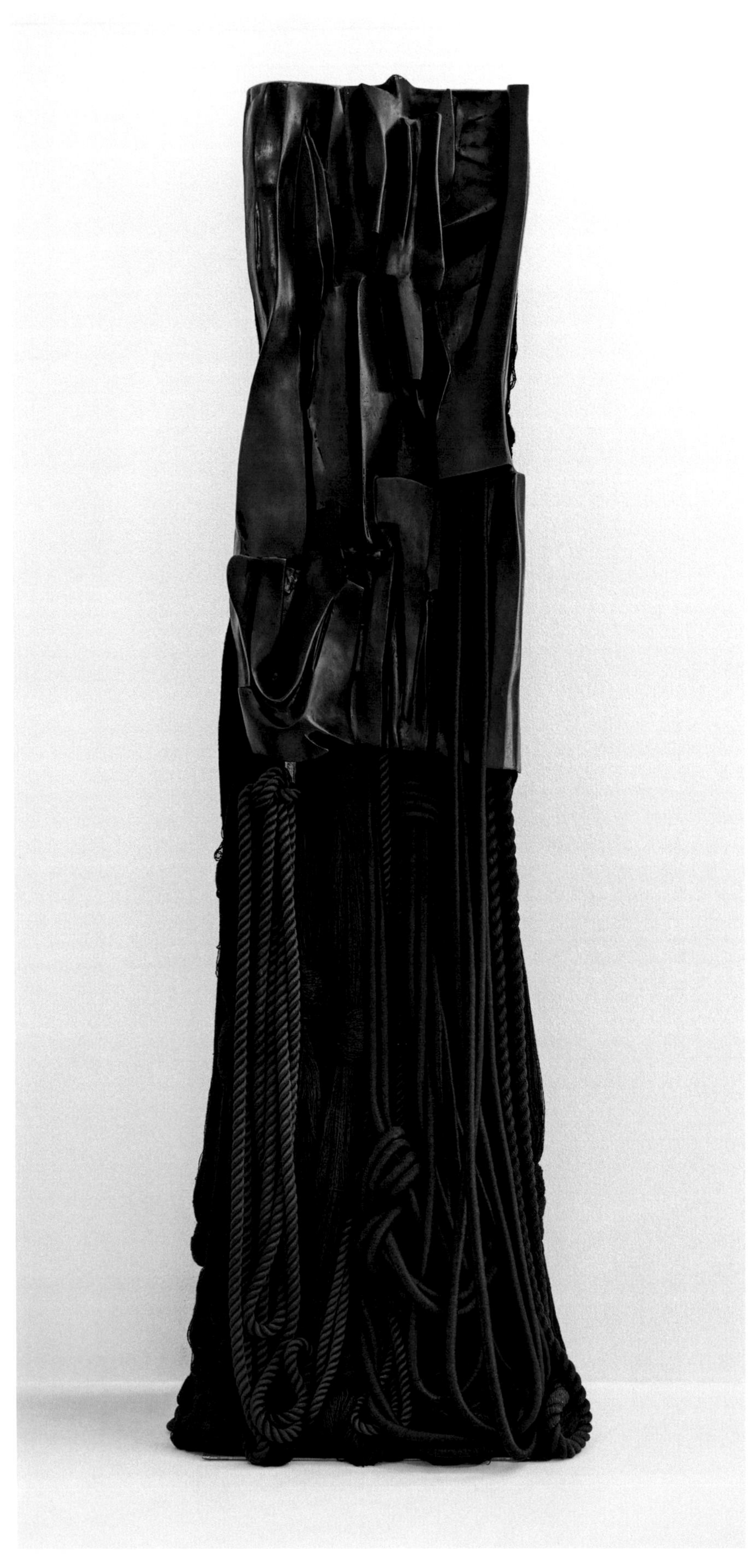

Malcolm X #9, 2007. Bronze with black patina, silk, wool, and synthetic fibers with steel support, 83½ × 27½ × 33 inches (212.2 × 69.8 × 58.4 cm)

Malcolm X #13, 2008. Bronze with black patina, silk, wool, and synthetic fibers with steel support, 86¾ × 45 × 34½ inches (220.3 × 114.3 × 87.6 cm)

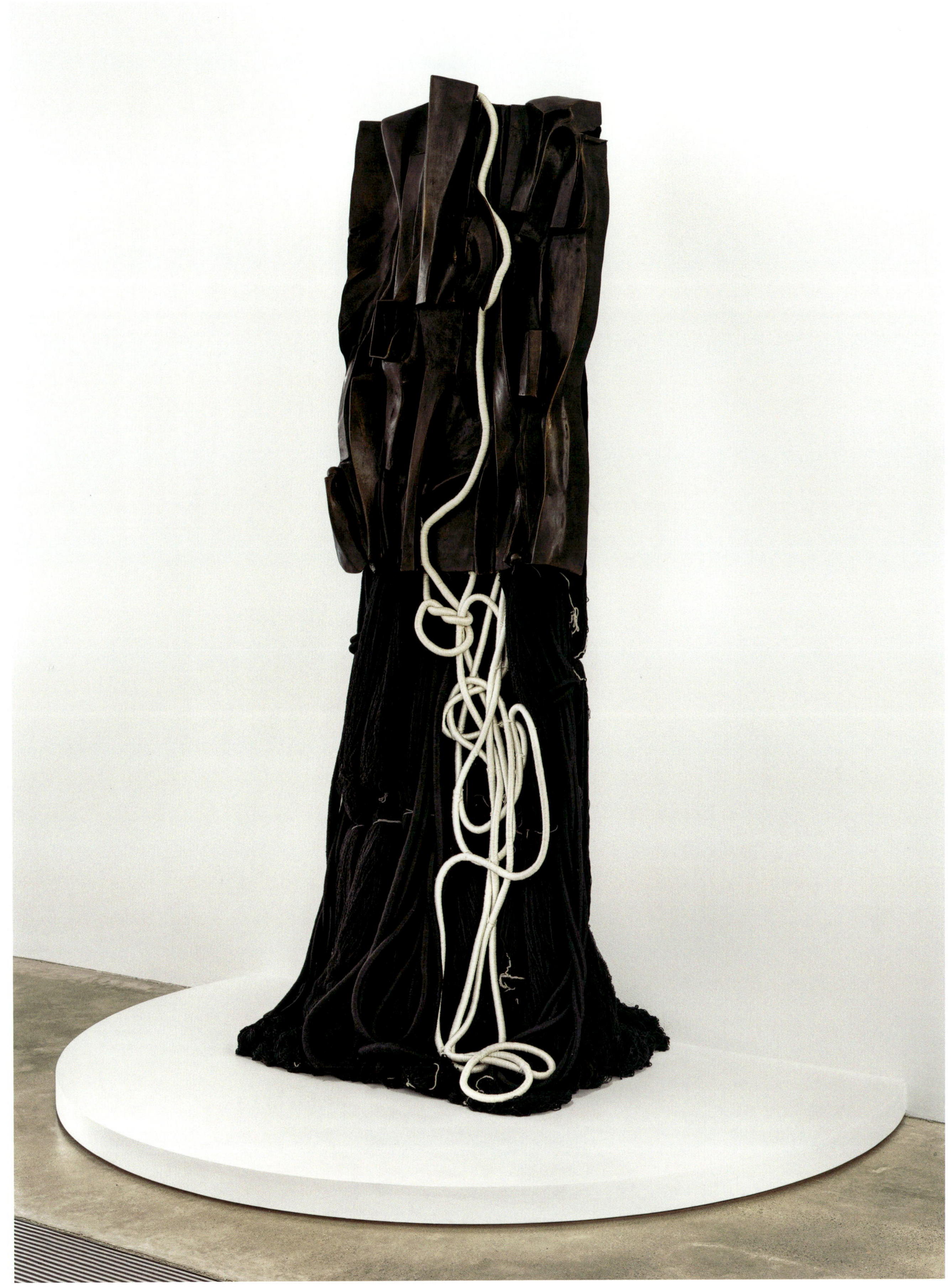

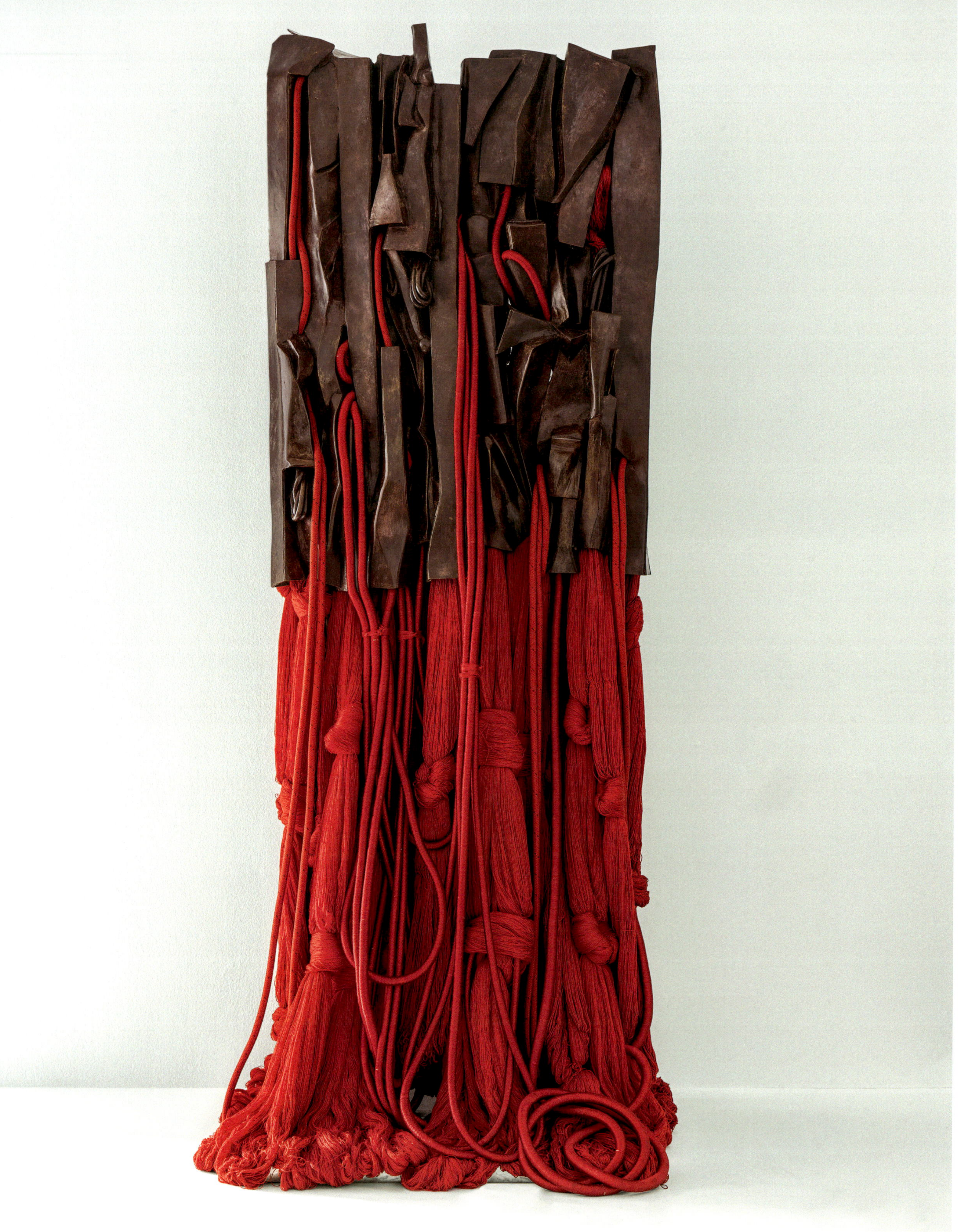

Malcolm X #16, 2016. Bronze with red
patina, silk, wool, and polished cotton and
synthetic fibers with steel support, 92 × 32 ×
30 inches (233.7 × 81.3 × 76.2 cm)

The detailing of the interplay of forms in the bronze, the cracks
and tears, the openings and closings, the continuous vibrant
ripple of the metal was achieved by the lost wax process: the
sculptor first constructed large thin sheets of wax, which were
then bent, slashed, and twisted, knotted, pleated, and carved.
Wooden copper pins were then used to connect different
parts before the wax model was encased in plaster and clay
molds to make the negative mold. The molten metal was then
poured to melt the wax. After this, the investment mold was
broken away and the cooled bronze removed from its casing.
Only a single, unique cast can be made by this process, but the
result had a precision not obtainable in other casting processes.

Excerpt from "Barbara Chase Riboud's Sculpture" by Peter Selz,
Callaloo 32, no. 3 (Summer 2009): 867.

Malcolm X #17, 2016 (detail)

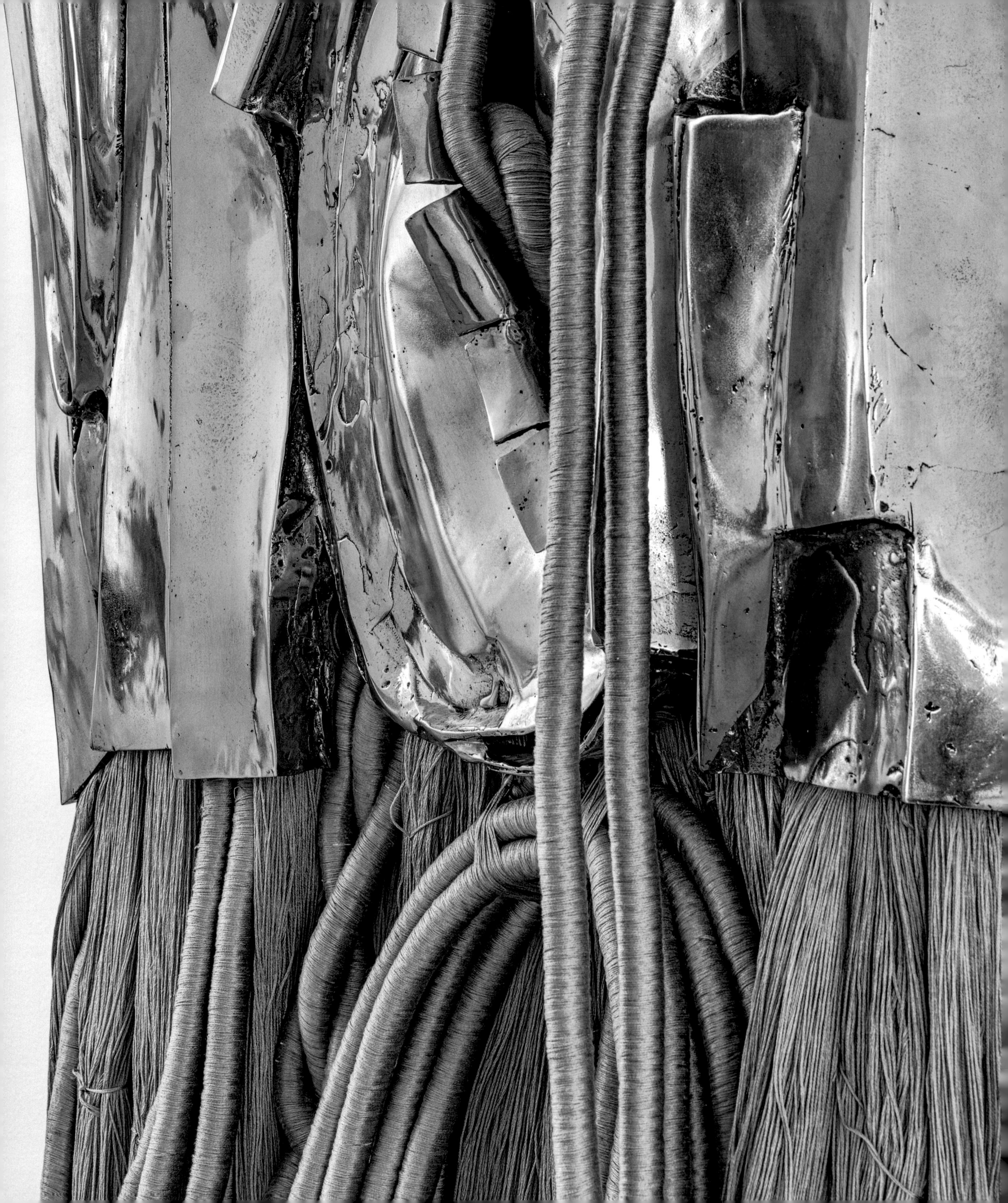

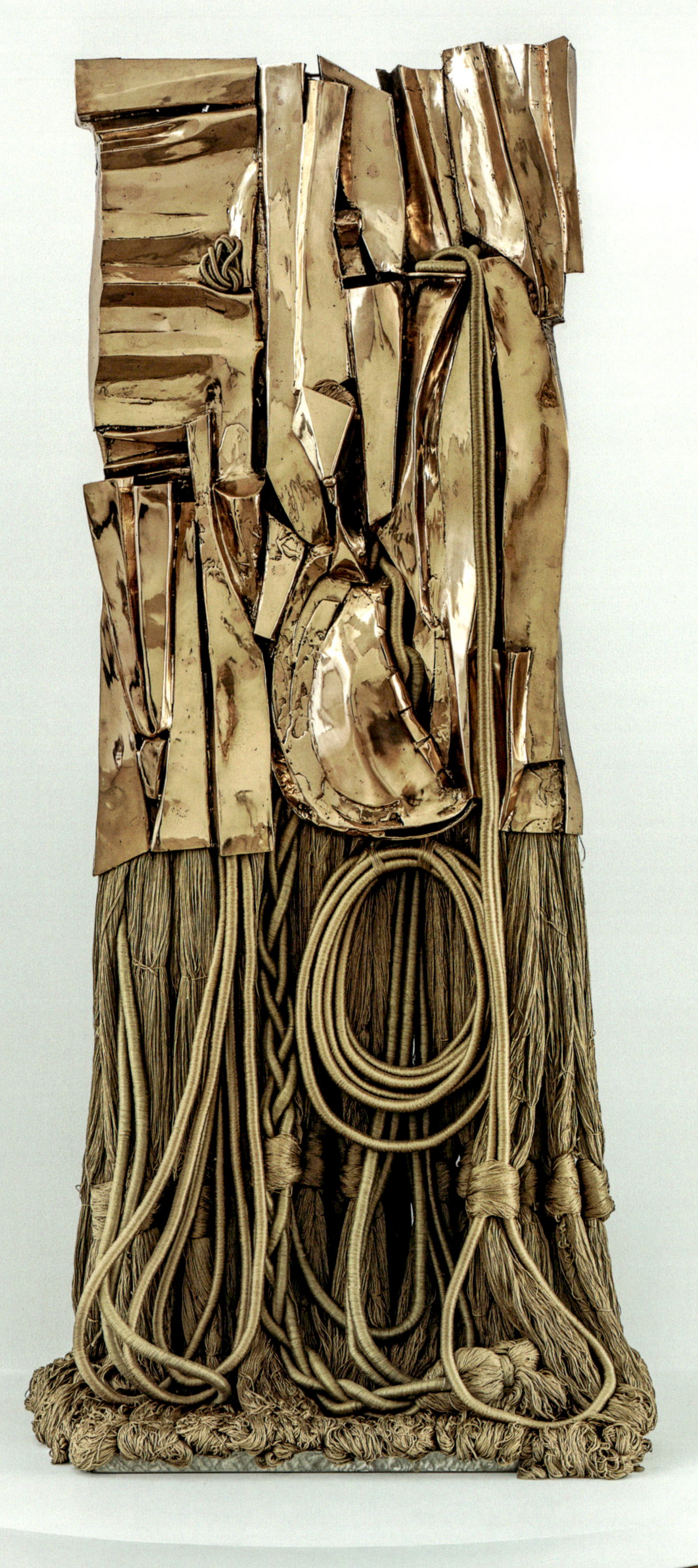

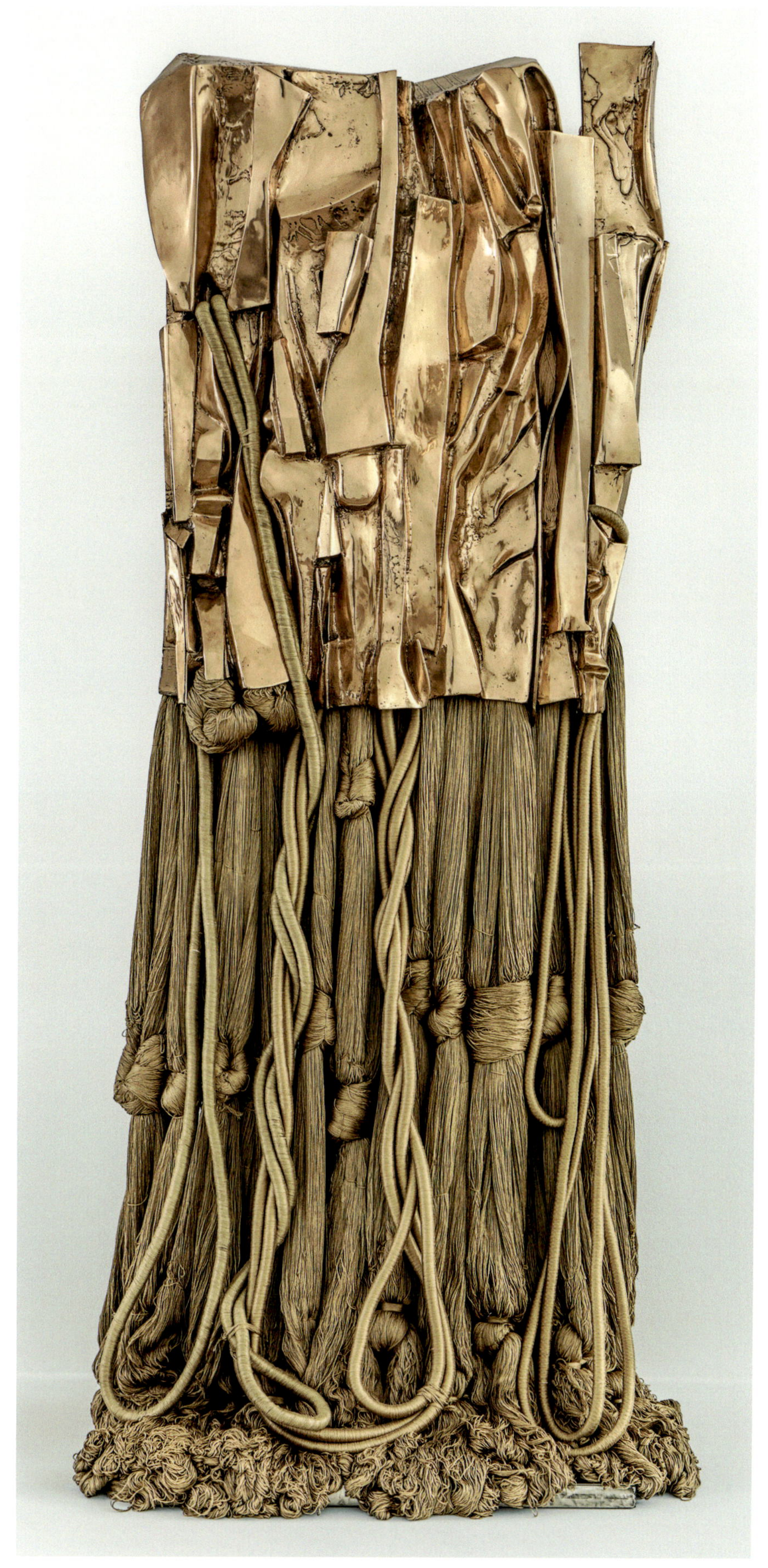

Malcolm X #17, 2016. Polished bronze and silk, 92 × 41 × 36 inches (233.7 × 104.1 × 91.4 cm)

Malcolm X #18, 2016. Polished bronze and silk with steel support, 92 × 32 × 30 inches (233.7 × 81.3 × 76.2 cm)

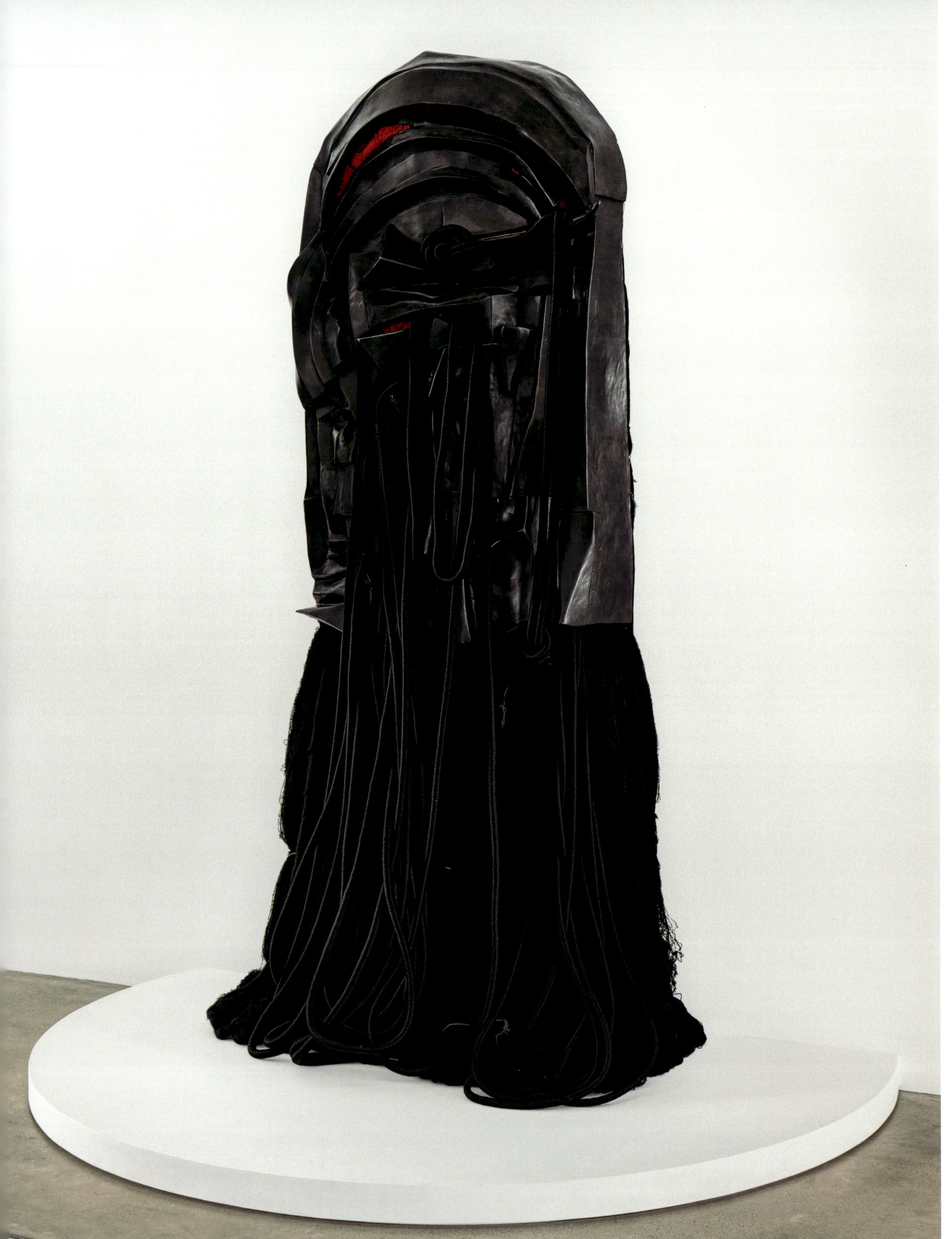

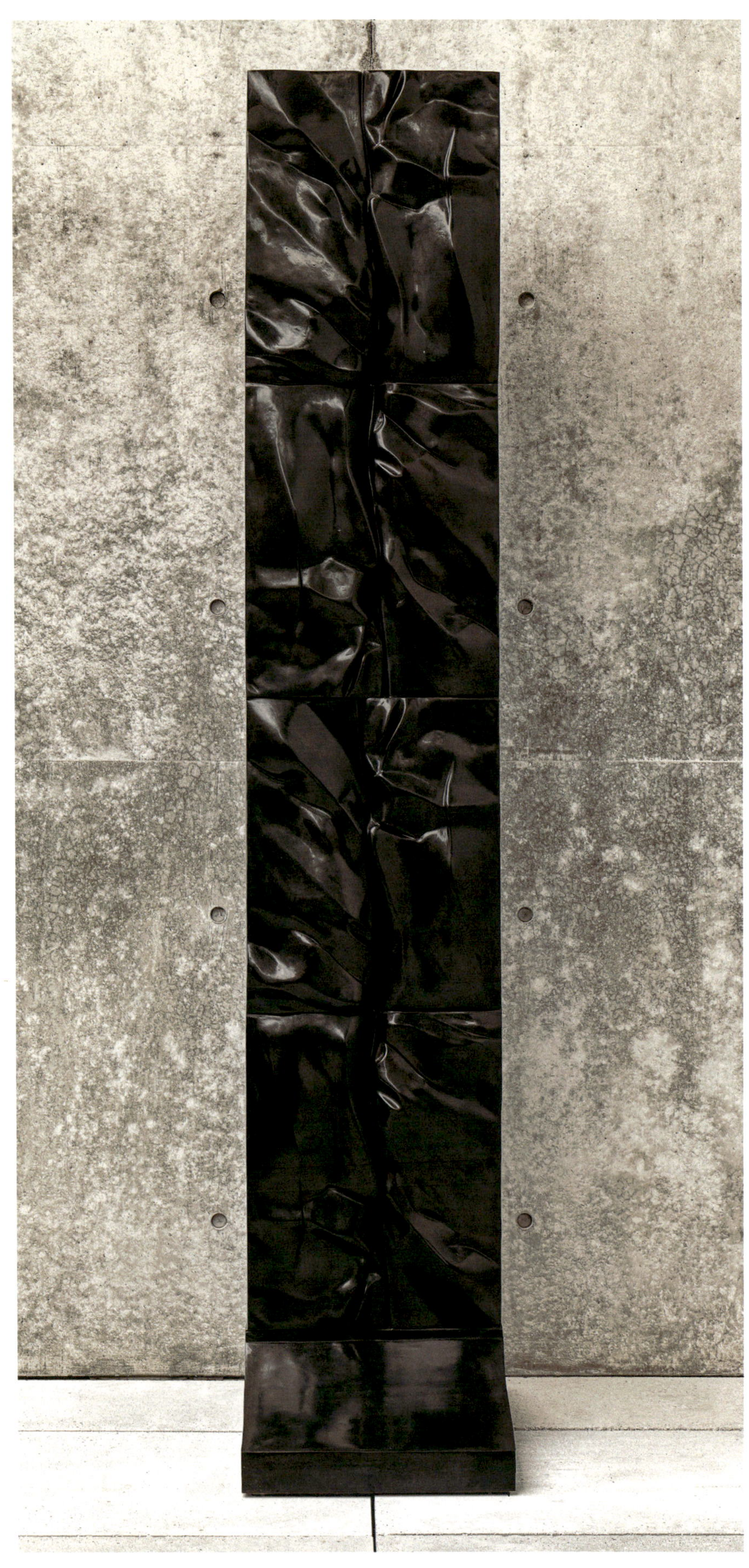

Standing Black Woman of Venice, 2021.
Black bronze, 96⅞ × 18⅛ × 27³⁄₁₆ inches (246 × 46 × 69 cm)

142

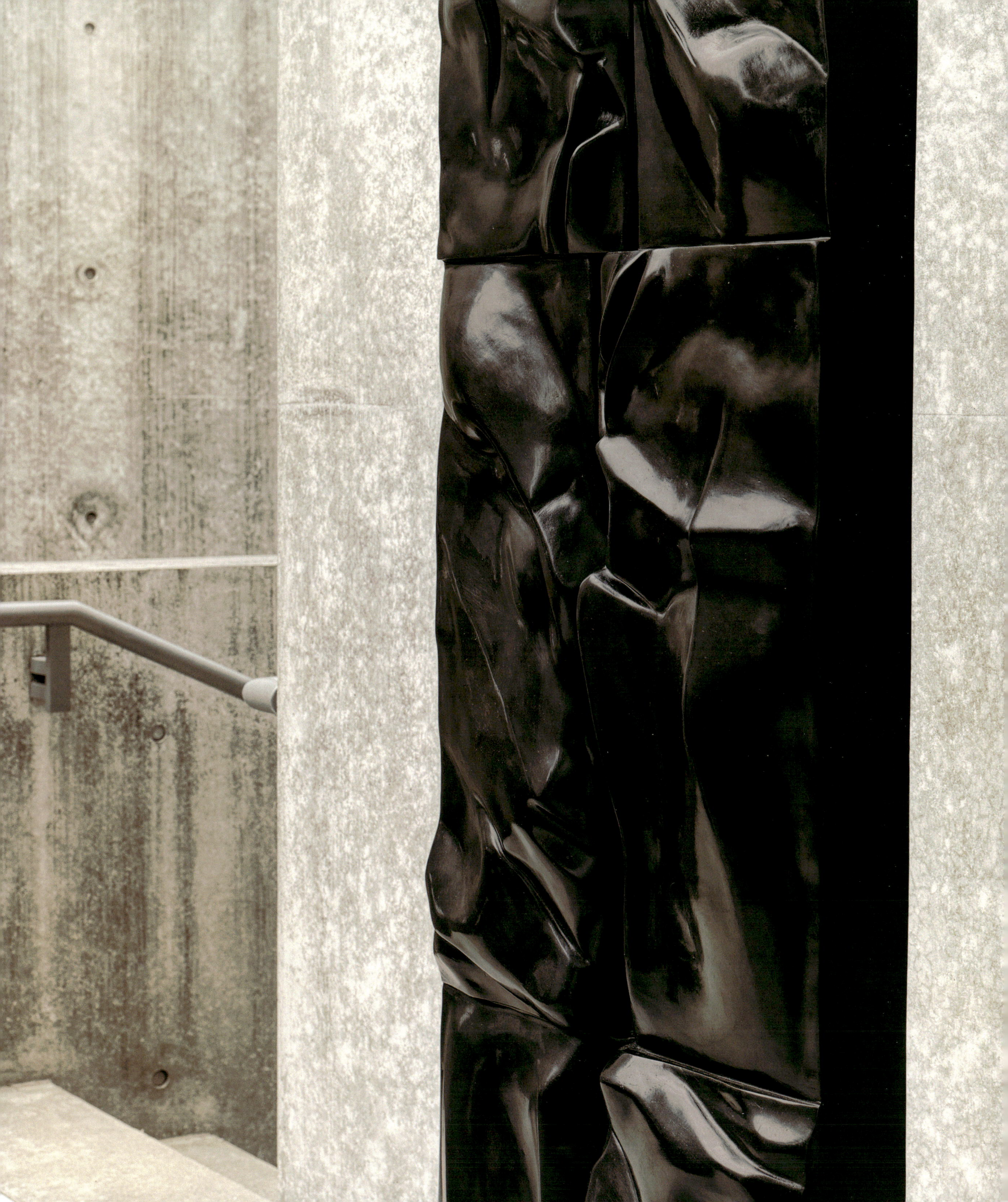

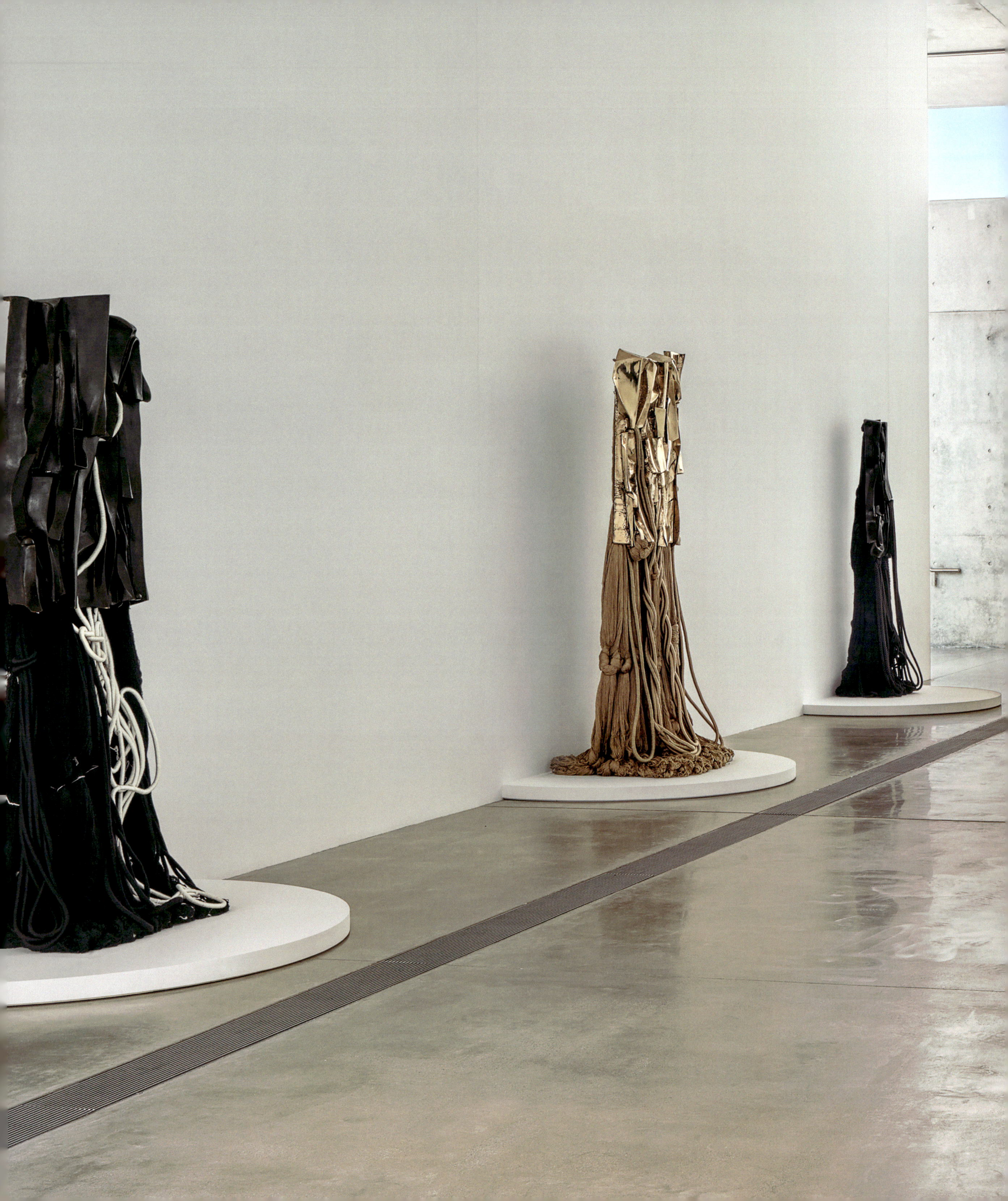

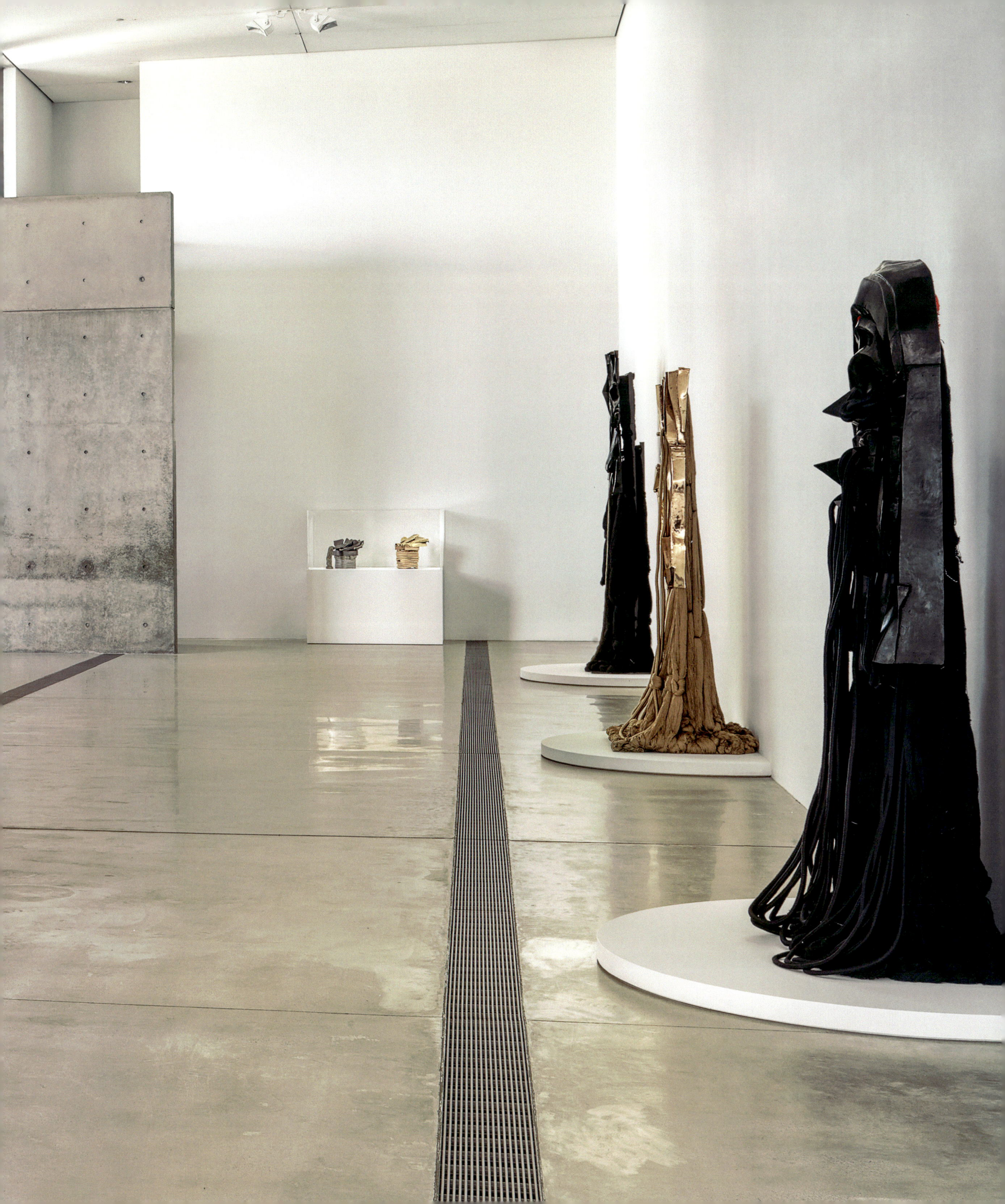

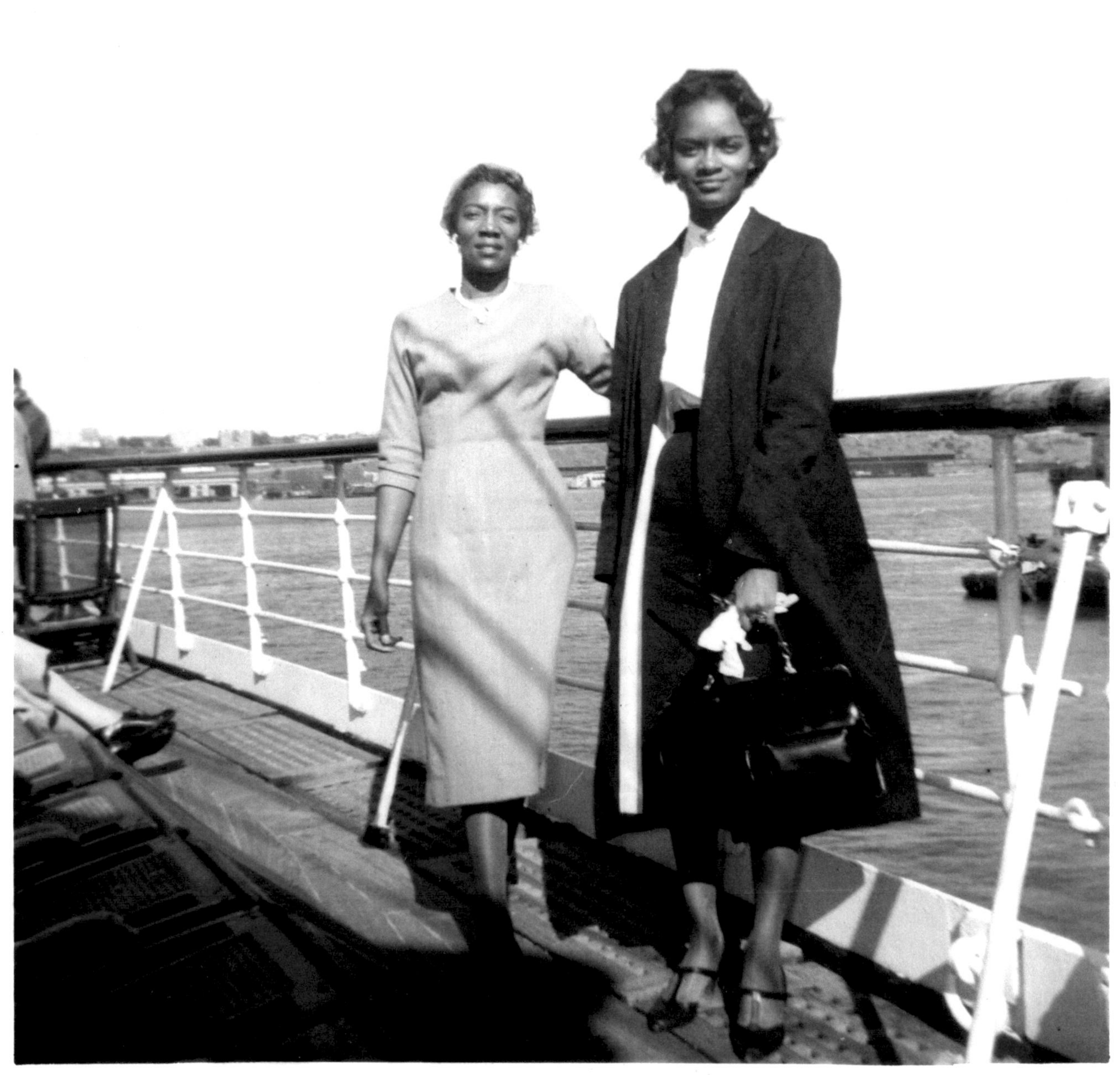

SEPT 1957

A CONVERSATION WITH THE ARTIST

Conducted by
Erin Jenoa Gilbert

This excerpt is taken from an oral history interview I conducted in 2019 with Barbara-Chase Riboud at her home in Paris, France, for the Smithsonian Archives of American Art. The conversation covers the artist's life from birth to the current moment, with a focus on her career as a sculptor. Chase-Riboud discusses the execution and exhibition of several of her most iconic series, including Malcolm X, Zanzibar, Cleopatra, Tantra, *and* La Musica, *which were created during the past five decades. Her descriptions illuminate her approaches to material and her engagement with memory and history.*

—*Erin Jenoa Gilbert*

Erin Jenoa Gilbert Take me back to your early memories of art-making and writing.

Barbara Chase-Riboud Well, there are no memories of writing, because I never considered myself a writer. I had a terrible experience when I was eleven, in middle school. I had written a poem, "In the Graveyard," about death, and autumn leaves, and all kinds of things. And my teacher accused me of copying it. She wanted me to go in front of the whole class and confess that I had plagiarized this poem. And I said I was not going to do that.

She sent me to the principal's office. The principal called my mother and my grandmother. They came to the school. They explained that they had seen me writing this poem on the kitchen table. So, to accuse me of plagiarism was really unfair.

And they said, "She doesn't have to apologize to you. You have to apologize to her, or we will take her out of school." And, of course,

Barbara Chase-Riboud and her mother, sendoff to Europe, *Le Flandre*, 1957

nobody did. So, my mother and grandmother took me out of school. But I never wrote another poem for forty years.

EG Prior to that moment, you were making art.

BCR I began art school when I was seven. I went to Fleisher Art Memorial's and the Philadelphia Museum of Art's classes for children. I remembered the first picture that fascinated me was a Degas, an enormous red ballerina. I would just stare at this picture every time I walked by it. I think this was the moment I decided that if I could make something as beautiful and as powerful as this painting, then I would be happy.

EG Let me ask you about when you were being home-schooled, and the transition from middle school to the Philadelphia High School for Girls.

BCR For me, it was normal that I was no longer in a public school. It was normal that I had tutors. My mother and grandmother supplemented my lessons until they got me into the elite high school of Philadelphia, which was girls only. I finished high school there and was valedictorian. I designed the yearbook. I was very happy there and I shone. It was all a matter of attitude. The school had only seven black girls. And they—I think began with me [laughs].

EG You enrolled in the Tyler School of Art in 1952. How did that experience shape your artistic practice?

BCR The dean was a man named Boris Blai, a Russian immigrant. The head professor of sculpture was a man named Sabatini, who was also an immigrant. And those two men sort of took me in and showed me that the United States of America was not the center of the world. They opened up the idea of Europe, and of travel.

And so, when I won this *Mademoiselle* contest— an editorship at *Mademoiselle* for the summer of 1956—they were the ones who pushed me to do it. I had interviewed Leo Lionni, the art director of *Fortune* magazine, who decided that I should go to Europe after Tyler. He recommended me for a John Hay Whitney Fellowship to Europe.

And because I was so young, they decided, "Well, she should go someplace that's institutional in Europe and it should be the American Academy in Rome." So, I ended up being the first black resident at the American Academy.

My mind was completely free of any kind of prejudice. I simply didn't know what was going to happen. My mother had just divorced my father, and at the same time had become a naturalized citizen. And I was leaving. I started writing letters home, from the boat, and mailed them in Paris. I continued to do so for the next fifty years.

In Rome, I got a letter from Yale University saying, "Would you like to come to Yale on a full fellowship for two years to the School of Architecture and Design?"

EG You met several other people while you were there, and you traveled. You left Rome and went to Egypt.

BCR I went to Egypt because my architectural colleagues said, "I dare you to come with us." I think there were twelve architects in the academy. I ran upstairs and packed my bag and I left with them that night for Brindisi, and we caught a Greek freighter for Alexandria the next morning. And as we were getting off the boat they left me standing on the wharf in Alexandria with no contacts whatsoever: no hotel, no nothing; not one name, not one address. They went off with an Egyptian colonel that had come to pick them up. And so, there I was.

EG What did you do?

Barbara Chase-Riboud in Karnak, Egypt, 1958

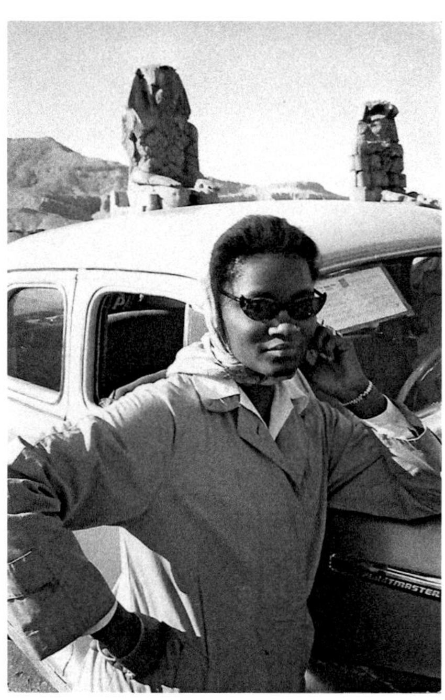

BCR I went up to the nearest policeman and said, "I need a hotel room.'

He said, "The Hilton hotel." And so, that's where I went, the most chic hotel in Alexandria. I walked into the lobby and I guess I really looked lost because I sat down, trying to think of what to do. I mean, I could have just turned around and got back on the boat. But I wasn't going to do that.

A very elegant, distinguished gentleman came over and said, "What are you doing in Egypt? Where is your nanny? Who's taking care of you?" He wanted to know where my mother was, and I said that my mother was in Philadelphia.

And he said, "Don't you know that you can get kidnapped and you'll end up in a harem somewhere? Egypt is dangerous for unescorted women." And so, he said, "Look, I am going to call the American embassy in Cairo and tell them you're on your way. I'm going to buy you a train ticket to Cairo. Do not talk to anybody on the train. Do not stop. My driver will take you to the station."

And I took the train from Cairo all the way up the Nile to Khartoum by myself. In the Valley of the Kings, I met a Magnum photographer who many years later introduced me to my first husband. There were two photographers—René Burri, who was Swiss, and a German photographer—and me.

René took a lot of pictures of me that day. I saw him later in Cairo and he became part of my life—I saw him several times in the States and then in Paris. And then he introduced me to Marc Riboud.

From Egypt, I went to Turkey, Istanbul, then Greece. I went to Delphi and finally wrote to my mother and told her where I was.

When I got back to the Academy, there was a rumor that MGM was making a movie called *Ben-Hur*. They were looking for actors, and since I didn't have any money, I decided this would be a good way to make some.

They took one look at me and said, "First of all, you're not Italian so we cannot hire you as an extra. But we can hire you as an actor. Here's the contract." I got something like twenty times what an extra would get. I got to meet Charlton Heston, who spent his time between scenes doing watercolors.

I was feeling very rich because I was making all this money. And that allowed me to make my first bronze castings—at least a dozen sculptures and one large sculpture, *Adam and Eve*, which was six feet tall. I learned the technique, which I still use today.

EG The lost-wax method.

BCR A small foundry in Rome introduced me to the lost-wax process, and I transferred that into a different technique using very thin sheets of wax, which is the basis of my technique, of my practice.

EG What stands out in your memory of traveling through Egypt, Istanbul, and to Delphi that influenced your practice and became a part of what we would see years later?

BCR All the Islamic art. I walked into the Santa Sophia and I burst into tears. I was at the top of Delphi and I burst into tears. I was in the middle of the Sahara Desert, looking up at the Sphinx, and I burst into tears. I mean, it was transformative. It had to be. This little girl from Philadelphia. It was absolutely transformative.

EG Looking at your work now, those influences are present. How did that experience provide you with the confidence to go into Yale's MFA program the next year?

BCR I thought the invitation from Yale was normal. I didn't know that I was going to be the first, and the only, black student in the entire architecture school. I graduated in 1960, and women didn't come to Yale until 1965, so I was there with two other women in the graduate school, period. One was a philosopher and the other a lawyer. And that was it. Sheila Hicks, who had had a Fulbright to Chile, was there, and there was me.

EG What professors stand out to you now as having influenced you deeply?

BCR Well, there was [Josef] Albers, Philip Johnson, Louis Kahn, and Paul Rand. I haven't made a list of them, but it was an ensemble of men—they were all men.

EG Did you have aspirations around architecture or public sculpture?

BCR I was in the architecture school, and then in my second year, I changed to sculpture. In my second year, one of the visiting critics and faculty was James Stirling, who was the poster boy for English architecture, a great architect. We fell in love, and he asked me to marry him, and I said, "Yes, but I have to graduate first." And so, when he left for London, I promised that in June, as soon as I graduated, I would meet him in London.

I had a commission from Jane Doggett, who had gotten me into Yale to begin with. She wanted a fountain for her mall in Washington, DC, and I said, okay, I would do it. So, I did it. It was eighteen feet tall; it weighed—I don't know, six tons. There was I don't know how many tons of travertine to make the pool. There was the waterworks; there were the molds for the stamping. There were all the architectural drawings to do; there was all the waterworks to do. There was the pool, and then there was the structure. And on top of all that, you know, when the water was turned on it made music. This was my thesis.

Three weeks before graduation the administration said that this was not acceptable as a thesis because it was not done under faculty supervision. So, I could not graduate because I didn't have a thesis. When the visiting faculty and all the visiting critics found out that my thesis had been rejected and that I was not going to graduate, they said, "Okay, if Ms. Chase doesn't graduate, then nobody graduates, because we're not rating anyone. You don't have a graduating class, period" [laughs].

EG They were willing to let the entire class not graduate if you didn't graduate?

BCR The administration gave in, but I would have to do another thesis in three weeks, a portfolio of etchings. I had not only to do the etchings, but I had to print and bind them with a text by Henri Peyre, who was the big French expert at Yale, on Rimbaud's *Season in Hell* in French. And so, I did, and I handed it in, and it has since disappeared.

EG And you became the first African American woman to earn an MFA from Yale.

BCR Yeah, in 1960. I regret that I didn't stay for commencement. I told them to send the diploma to my mother, and I left for London. Which means that my mother never saw me—my mother and my father, actually—never saw me graduate from Yale, walk down the aisle and get the diploma that my father was denied from the University of Pennsylvania. And if I had really thought about it, I would have stayed for commencement.

EG You mentioned your father having been denied a degree from the University of Pennsylvania.

BCR He had ambitions to be an architect, but he was not admitted to the University of Pennsylvania.

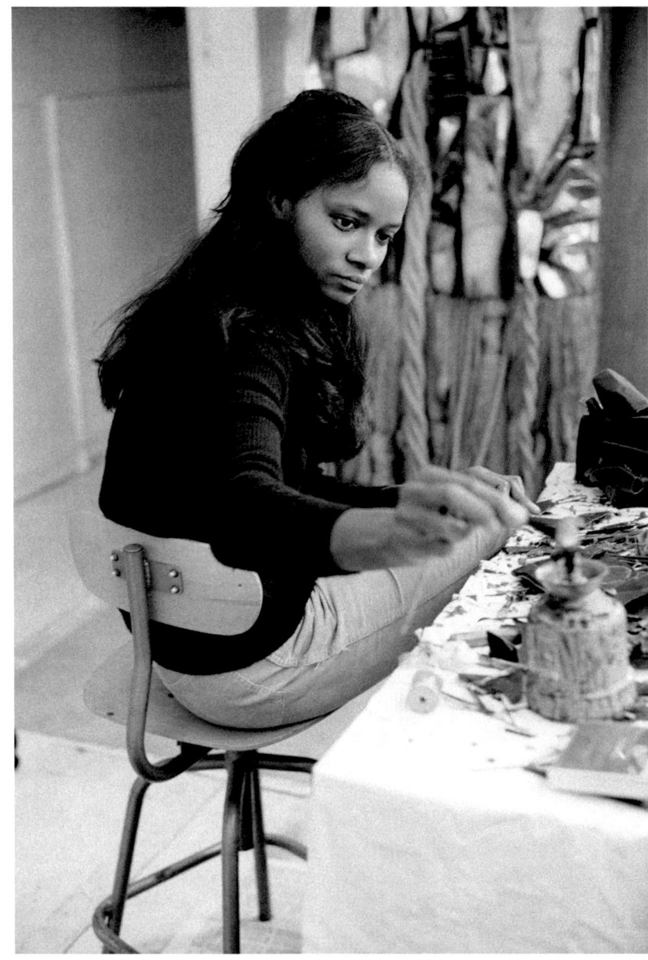

Barbara Chase-Riboud at her atelier at Rue Dutot, 1973

It was very simple. There were no blacks at University of Pennsylvania architecture school.

EG So, you went to London in June of 1960, and you're there with James. What happened then?

BCR It was wonderful. It was marvelous as far as I was concerned, and this went on until suddenly— and it really happened suddenly—one day I woke up in November, and I look out the window. It's pouring rain, and there are two Englishmen playing tennis in tennis whites back and forth, clunk, clunk, clunk. And I'm thinking, this country is crazy, you know [laughs]. "I've got to get out of here." So, I call a friend from Yale who's now an architect in Paris and I say, "Remember you said that I could come for the weekend anytime I wanted to? Well, I would like to—I'd like to get away for just a weekend, okay?"

René Burri was in Paris, and he says, "I've got to stop by the Magnum office to pick up some stuff," and so we passed by Magnum, which is on rue

Saint-Honoré on the other side of the river. And who was there but Marc Riboud, editing. And so, we come in; we go out. There are no introductions.

And a few days later, we go to an opening of Yves Klein and the new director of the *New York Times*, whose name was Taubman, says, "We're looking for an art director for the *New York Times* in Paris."

And so, I say, "Well, I'm very expensive, you know," and he says, "Well, I think that the *New York Times* can afford you [laughs]." I mean, I said it as a kind of joke, and he said it as a kind of joke. And before I knew it, I had this job, and so I was sort of half between Paris and London.

I began flying back and forth, or he [James] would come to Paris for the weekend, or I would go back home for the weekend, and this lasted until I went to the Magnum office to look for a photograph by Henri Cartier-Bresson, and Marc was there. And he said, "You know, I've been looking for you for months. René wouldn't give me your name. He wouldn't give me your telephone number." When I got home that night a messenger arrives at the door with my gloves that I left in the office of Magnum, with a note saying, "You're very forgetful, you know. Don't forget me because I'm leaving tonight for the Congo, and I will call you from the airport when I get back." And the rest is history.

EG At this moment, you've moved on with Marc Riboud and you're married, which situates you in Paris. This is another transition from working at the

Barbara Chase-Riboud in her Paris residence with bone sculpture *Nostradamus*, 1966

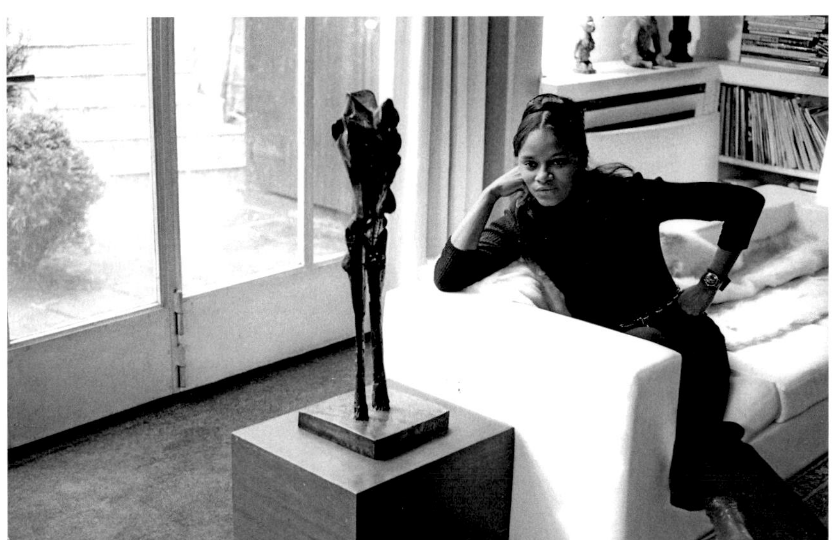

New York Times to your life as a practicing artist. So, you establish a studio in Paris in 1962.

BCR I kept my old foundry in Italy, which meant that I had to make these wax models and then somehow transport them to Italy, and I did this usually by train.

My second atelier was there, and I found just outside of Paris another foundry that did aluminum sandcasting, which I had never tried before. There I made the *Cleopatra* plaques, and they'd had this sort of secret method of combining aluminum and copper and iron, which produced a bronze which was iridescent, and nobody else in the world, as far as I can see, was able to do this.

So I began a series of straight aluminum sand-casting and then these plaques with which I made the capes, and the series is now six, I think. There's the cape, the chair, the bed, the door, and there's one other.

EG In 1963 you marched in Paris at the same time as the March on Washington. And then, in 1965, two things happen: Malcolm X dies and you go to China. How did Malcolm X's assassination affect you and your artistic practice?

BCR I was very upset. For me, it was this kind of sick rage. I decided to dedicate [the steles] to Malcolm X after the fact. They were untitled, as a matter of fact.

EG We'll revisit that idea, but I do want to talk a bit about China.

BCR It was mostly by airplane, but on the way back, the DC-7 propeller plane got caught in a storm and had to crash land. It was a local flight and all these little mechanics came and sort of glued this plane together, and then we were supposed to get back on it.

And I said, "I'm not getting on that plane [laughs]," and my guide, because I had a guide, said, "But you've got to get on that plane because that's the schedule, and you've got to get back to Peking by a certain date." And I said, "No way. Find me another way to get home, because I'm not getting on that plane again."

They finally found a train that was going to take three days to get back to Peking, and I said, "Okay, I'll take it." And so, they put me on the train without a guide, without an interpreter, and for three days I was in seventh heaven because I traveled the whole breadth of China all by myself in a compartment all by myself.

EG In 1966, you also participated in the first World Festival of Negro Arts in Dakar [now FESMAN]. Do you remember which sculptures you took?

BCR I sent two small bone sculptures. It was in the period where I was using real bones to make sculptures that I would then cast in bronze.

EG Where did the bones come from?

BCR I bought them on rue du Bac in the most famous taxidermy shop. They have to take the bones out of the skin in order to stuff the animals, and there was always a kind of reserve in their cellar.

EG And then in 1969, you move the studio from rue Blomet to the larger space in rue du [château] d'Eau. Is that because the works had already started to increase significantly in size?

BCR The rue du d'Eau studio was much larger. It was in an old factory that made Christmas cards. There was a courtyard and that's where I made all the aluminum sculptures and casts.

EG Sand casting?

BCR Yeah. And they were just getting bigger and bigger. I had to have a bigger studio.

EG That spring you were in *Seven Americans in Paris*, at Galerie Air France in New York.

BCR The Air France gallery sculptures were half bone, half futurist. If you could imagine that. And that was a decisive moment. And it was decisive also because I had not bothered to exhibit in the USA because I was just not interested. And this was kind of serendipity because Air France organized all this, and of course it was called *Americans in Paris*. And the funny thing is that the next show that I'm in, at New York University, is called *Americans in Paris*.

EG In 1969 you also attended the Pan-African Cultural Festival in Algiers. This may have been another moment where you had a set of interactions and conversations about Malcolm X. Is that true? What happened in Algiers?

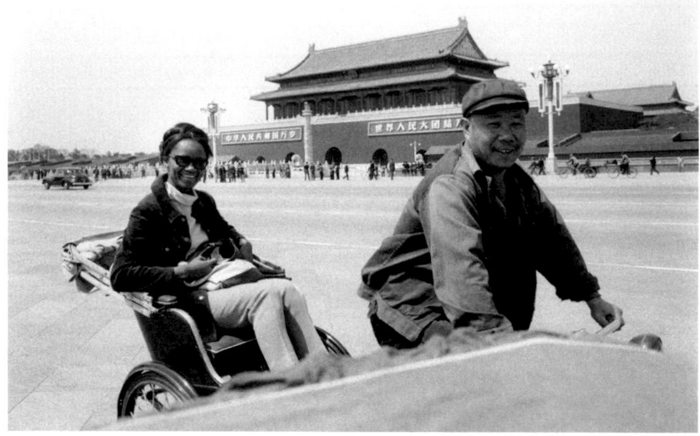

Barbara Chase-Riboud in Beijing, May 1965

BCR It was a festival and everybody who was anybody in the civil rights movement was there. You had to be there. It was three or four days of intense lectures, manifestos. One after the other about what was going on. And for the first time, it was international. It was not just Americans—Algerians, Nigerians, Ghanaians, Guineans, Sudanese, they were all there.

EG And that was this immediate postcolonial movement in Africa. So, at the same time, you have Jomo Kenyatta and Léopold Senghor and that wave of liberation.

BCR Exactly. And then the Africans taught the Americans how to do it. The whole discourse of colonialization, decolonialization, war, political war. The Americans didn't know all this stuff—what did they have as a reference? Africa had six hundred years and America had two hundred.

EG We're back in New York in that European context. And you have a show with Bertha Schaefer, who passes away the next year, and then you begin showing with Betty Parsons. Shortly thereafter, you and Betye Saar become the first African American women to exhibit at the Whitney. Your work is entitled *Ultimate Ground* and is included in the exhibition *Contemporary American Sculpture*.

And then in 1971, you are featured in the exhibition *Contemporary Black Artists in America* at the Whitney. And *Malcolm X #3* is the piece that's shown.

The film *Five*, for that segment that they shot, you said the studio was du d'Eau?

BCR That segment of the film was shot by René Burri. We've been friends ever since Egypt. And he was Marc's best friend, so of course, we were friends until he passed.

EG That segment for the film seems really intimate because it was really intimate. And when I first saw it, I thought how special it was to see you in Paris in your natural element. It seemed as though they shot you over the course of two days in the studio, in a foundry, and then picking up your sons and putting them in the car, and carrying out daily activities. So, it makes sense that it was someone who you'd known so closely.

That initial shot in the film is from your 1972 solo exhibition at Betty Parsons's gallery. Do you want to talk a little bit about that show?

BCR The Betty Parsons Gallery meant that I was in the front ranks of Postmodernism. I was showing with everybody—Cy Twombly, Ellsworth Kelly, [Mark] Rothko, Agnes Martin. She had three women artists.

EG Shortly thereafter MoMA acquires two drawings. So, in the context of these exhibitions, you're not just showing sculpture, you're also showing drawings.

And then you have a solo exhibition in 1973 at the University of California, Berkeley Art Museum.

BCR Yes, and it was only the second exhibition of a woman in the United States at a major American museum. The first being Georgia O'Keeffe [laughs].

EG And in that exhibition, *Confessions for Myself*, a large sculpture, is shown, which was then acquired by the Berkeley Art Museum. So that exhibition had weight—not just in the size and scope, but the acquisition of a major work. That black bronze has the character that you follow with in the *Malcolm X* steles, in that it is vertical and stands . . . how many feet high?

BCR It's enormous. Kind of monumental.

EG I'm thinking about the wool and the way in which this skirt is full, and you have the knots—this is what will be your signature style—in 1972.

BCR That's it. I will not change.

EG Another curator who I think had meaning for you at that time, and who you must have met

Barbara Chase-Riboud and *Bathers*, at her La Chenelière studio, 1969

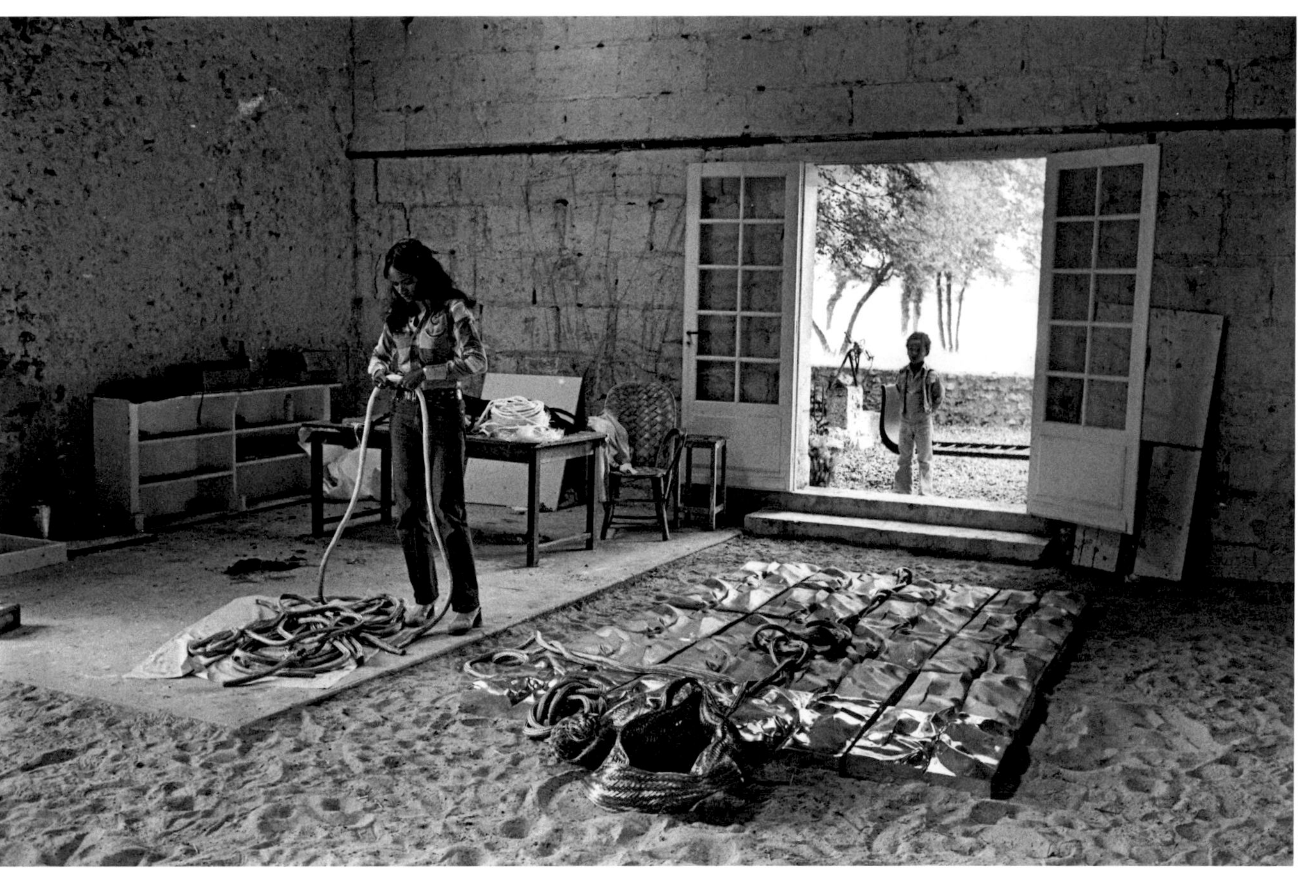

immediately after the exhibition, was Lowery Stokes Sims [the first African American woman curator at the Metropolitan Museum of Art]. She acquired a drawing.

BCR Yes. The funny story about that is that she has this letter where I'm thanking her for having acquired the drawing, and I call her, "Dear Mr. Sims" [laughs]. I assumed that Lowery Sims was a white male.

The same William Lieberman who had bought my first print for MoMA was now the head of twentieth century [art] at the Met, and he decided he was going to do my drawing show. He asked Lowery to do it, I mean, as her boss. Well, the Metropolitan staff gave her such a hard time. Lowery suffered for many years from asthma, and I told her that if she wanted her asthma to stop, she ought to leave the Met because that was what was wrong with her. There was nothing wrong with her [laughs].

EG Stress.

BCR She didn't have asthma, she wasn't sick. It was the Met that was sick, and as long as she was in that atmosphere, her body was going to do that to her. And it was so petty what they did—we knew that it was going to be a summer show, but we were happy enough, the show was from June until September, so it was long.

And people were so incensed that they did everything they could to sabotage this show. They didn't want it. They refused to do any kind of public-ity or communications for it. They refused a regular opening. They did a poster, but the catalog was a catalog from the Cameron Museum, which they just put a new cover on. Or, actually, I put a new cover on so that there would be a record of the exhibition. The only thing I asked them for besides the opening was the banner on the façade, because I just wanted the banner on the façade.

EG What year was this?

BCR This was 1999.

EG I'm just thinking now about how long it took for the museum to make an acquisition in 1973, but then to do an exhibition in 1999, and that exhibition actually having been an exhibition that was traveling from another venue first.

BCR It would never have happened if it hadn't been, because it would never have been organized in the first place.

EG I want to go back briefly to 1973, because in the same way that you have solidified a style and a signature in *Confessions for Myself*, the *Cleopatra* series is emerging. And *Cleopatra's Cape* is what we have on record as having been made and conceived of first in that year.

BCR The first one was *Cleopatra's Cape*, and it was because I found this foundry outside of Paris that could do this iridescent bronze. The reason I started the plaques was because Marc had written me from China that he had seen these extraordinary Han shrouds, which were made of plaques of jade pieces with gold. He didn't send me a photograph, so all I had was his description of these extraordinary objects and this bronze which glowed, which was luminous and iridescent. I put the two together and produced the first Cleopatra, which was not called *Cleopatra's Cape*, but simply *The Cape*. I changed the name when it became a series of six sculptures.

EG What's so interesting is that it seems like one fully constructed object. In your construction of the bed, each tiny tile is held together by wire and is hand-constructed.

In 1974, you have an exhibition at the Musée d'Art Moderne in Paris, and then you go to the Greek island of Skorpios to visit Jacqueline Kennedy Onassis. What do you remember most about that year?

BCR The exhibition in Paris was the first of an American female, period, and so it was a kind of landmark exhibition for them. It was a very beautiful catalog, and I exhibited *The Albino* for the first time. So, this sculpture has really traveled the globe under two different titles, *The Albino* and *All That Rises Must Converge*. And the reason for that is that it can be installed two different ways—closed and it's *All That Rises*, or open, and it's *Albino*. From now on probably, it will be referred to only as *The Albino*. It goes with a poem that was written—actually I don't know which came first, the sculpture or the poem. And I'm thinking the poem came first, and then the sculpture.

As far as Jacqueline was concerned, it was our summer vacation to go every year with friends from Paris to Spetses, which is a small Greek island near Athens, off the coast, and then in 1974, we flew over to Skorpios, which is 10 minutes from where we were, and the Onassises were there to greet us. And in the middle of the weekend, for one reason or another, we were sitting on the beach, and I suddenly start telling Jacqueline about Sally Hemings and my problems and why I should or shouldn't write this book, and that Toni Morrison can't do it at Random House. Random House doesn't want it; nobody wants this book.

Suddenly she turned to me and said, "Barbara, you've got to write this book. It's too important for you to just let it go." When [Aristotle] Onassis had died, she had a friend at Viking who offered her a job just to get her out of her grief and keep her busy, and she started calling my agent, saying, "Has Barbara handed in the manuscript yet?" No one else saw it; no one else knew what was in it or what was going on. And it went into Viking production.

So, we had no idea what a controversy was going to come out of this, because we thought we had a great historical story that everybody would be interested in, but we didn't know that it was going to be contested by the Jeffersonians, which made it famous, you know, without even trying, because no—it was my first book. It was my first novel, nobody had ever heard of me.

If they had just ignored the book, nothing would have happened. Nobody knew who I was. I was not a historical writer. I wasn't even a writer. This was my first book and there was a front-page *New York Times* review—a glowing review—and people went bananas.

EG And just for the sake of understanding the context of the novel, Sally Hemings is the mistress of Thomas Jefferson who bears seven children for him and who lives at Monticello.

BCR But she was his enslaved woman, who was also his wife's sister—his wife's half-sister—and with whom he had lived for thirty-eight years and had seven children. And nobody knows what she looked like, but she probably looked like his dead wife. They were half-sisters.

EG And, again, for the context of the discussion around how this impacted you and how this impacted your career, this novel was highly contested, and then years later DNA evidence proved that your hypothesis . . .

BCR That I was right.

EG So, you endured a great deal.

BCR I endured thirty-eight years of contestation and defamation and whatever else you want to add to that because people were swearing on the heads of their children that this was not true, that this had never happened.

EG So, in the coming years, you also showed at the Tehran Museum of Contemporary Art, a set of drawings, and then you showed in Freiburg, Germany, and then your work was included in Documenta at Kassel.

BCR It was interesting to sort of situate myself on the international scene.

EG Then you were included in exhibitions at the Pompidou and the Smithsonian, and here we are now at 1979, and the Sally Hemings novel is published. In 1980, you're in an exhibition at MoMA PS1, the *Afro-American Abstraction* exhibition. What's happening for you personally in this moment? How are you changing?

BCR Well, there was a seismic change in my personal life simply because I divorced Marc Riboud. There was no kind of transition period between a complete change of existence really. I came out of my agent's office in New York; I was walking down 57th Street, and I met Sergio Tosi for the third time, and my life changed overnight.

We went out that evening to see *Evita*, which he had already seen, but he lied. And coming out of *Evita*, we were walking down Broadway, and we didn't want to go home, we didn't want to go to a hotel—but we didn't want to separate either. And so, we went to an all-night movie that was playing *Fame*.

EG And you married the next year, in 1981?

BCR As soon as my divorce was final, we got married. I went from being alone, in that Marc's photography had been the central part of our lives, and the rest of our lives circulating around that, and then by marrying an art professional, suddenly all that energy and all that circulation was around me.

Sergio has one of the best eyes in the world, and he never judged what I was doing, but I could judge what I was doing by looking at him. He didn't have to say anything [laughs]. And so, this was the beginning of a whole new attitude toward my work and a new

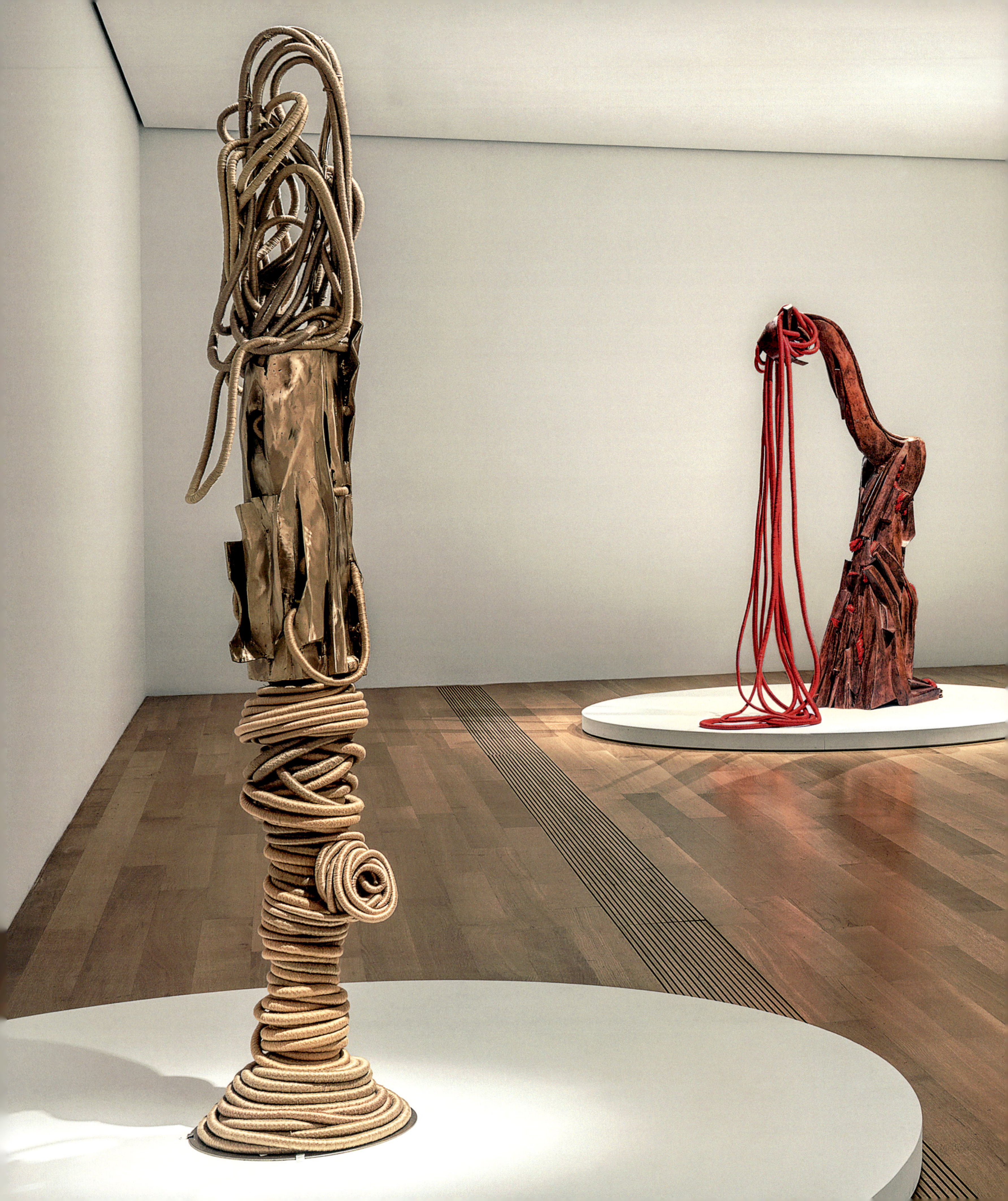

eye on what I was doing, and a kind of ambition that I didn't have before, because, of course, for my family and my in-laws, this was a hobby—"this is what Barbara did in her spare time" changed to "this is what Barbara does, and you better stay out of her way."

EG Which studio space were you in at this moment?

BCR Rue des Plantes. This was when Sergio was running the cultural center in Paris, and one of the perks was I had a magnificent atelier, 1930s atelier, on rue des Plantes which was really gorgeous.

EG Betty Parsons dies the next year [1982], so you lose your gallerist.

BCR I did—after she died, everybody got a gallery but me and the other two women.

EG So, you were without representation for at least twenty years?

BCR Yeah, which, in a way, might have been beneficial, because I worked directly with museums. The one thing I lost were gallery exhibitions, because all the exhibitions after that were in museums.

EG You have a series of ongoing museum exhibitions beginning with Paris. The next year, 1984, is *East/West Contemporary American Art* at the California Afro-American Museum, and you just continued to have exhibitions with institutions. You have these exhibitions without representation, but sometimes works are being acquired as a result of the exhibitions, so you did this yourself. In 1985 you establish a space in Rome.

BCR Sergio had decided that somebody ought to live in the country they were born in so we found this palazzo which is extraordinary, historically. Cy Twombly lived next door.

EG So, this is a homecoming of sorts, to be back in Rome. And you go regularly to the same space every summer. Do you have a studio there?

BCR There is no studio. I don't work there because my foundry is in Milan. I write there sometimes.

EG In 1990, you begin a series called *La Musica*. How did that came about?

BCR It's one of my longest series—there are sixteen or seventeen *La Musicas*—and it's ongoing. They all go back to the idea of musical instruments and the combination of the silk and the bronze. There are a lot of small sculptures, a foot or a foot and a half, and then there are enormous sculptures, which are the *Parkway/Marian* sculptures and a couple of *Marian Anderson* sculptures that are as tall as the ceiling. The name is simply Italian for music. So, they could very easily be called *Music*.

EG So, at this moment you are still without representation, but you have acquisitions by museum institutions. The Metropolitan Museum of Art purchases *All That Rises Must Converge*. You were presenting the *Shelf Sculptures* in new spaces. And you are also proposing the *Middle Passage Monument*. So, what was the *Middle Passage Monument*, and to whom did you make that proposal?

BCR It's a scale model for an enormous double obelisk with a kind of bridge and a long chain that goes around a bridge. The proposal was made to the White House, but [President Bill] Clinton wasn't interested.

EG The proposal dated April 1994 reads "The Middle Passage memorial honors the 11 million victims and the 30 million deportees of the African diaspora, 1492, 1865, and 1888." Where did you envision it being placed?

BCR My first idea was that there would be more than one, and that they would be placed in cities across the United States. Anybody who wanted one and had the money to build it could have it.

EG It's very interesting to think about the removal of Confederate monuments, particularly in the South, at this moment in American history and what those should be replaced with or whether or not they should be replaced, and this proposal to have built something that, in size and in presence, would eliminate the need to remove anything else, but simply hold accountable both sides of the history.

BCR And the interesting thing is I was sure that somebody else would build something similar by now. You know, in 1994, that's thirty years ago.

EG We've established that you're at least thirty years ahead of your time. In 1995 you won a commission for a monument that has been realized, the *Africa Rising* sculpture in the US General Services Administration building.

BCR *Africa Rising* was a commission from the US General Services Administration. A competition for the federal building at Foley Square, which they were building on the grave of the slave population cemetery, on the other side of Wall Street in New York. It's 18 feet tall, in cast bronze with a silver patina. I had used Sarah Baartman's[1] body in abstraction as the Nike on the top of *Africa Rising*. She had a face which was half Naomi Campbell and half Sarah Baartman in abstraction.

Now it's in a place that is closed to the public, and she's guarded by two or three armed guards, policemen. She has an electronic door all around her, and nobody can get into or out of the space that she was designed for. So, what we are trying to do at this point is to move her out of the federal building and onto a public space where she will be seen by the public. And this will probably be one of the last things I will do art-wise, is to make sure that she has a place somewhere on public view before I quit this planet.

EG In 1996, you do the *Monument* drawings, twenty-four charcoal-and-ink drawings. Do you want to talk about that set of drawings and how even Foley Square plays out in many of the sites you've chosen for those drawings?

BCR It was for a show that Anthony Janson organized; he wrote the classic art textbook that's used in all colleges. The drawings have automatic writing, which is also poetry, that's untranslatable because it's in a language that no one understands except me. There's a combination of the etchings, of the writing, of the poetry, and of the draftsmanship all on one sheet of paper. The invisible monuments, I call them. You know, the invisible people that pass through history, making history, but never being noted as such.

EG In 1996, you have a few major exhibitions, *Explorations in the City of Light*, which looks at African American artists in Paris, at The Studio Museum in Harlem, among other venues. *Three Generations of African American Women Sculptors: A Study in Paradox*; *Bearing Witness: Contemporary African American Women Artists*. You also are receiving a third honorary doctorate, and you are at this point knighted by the French government as a

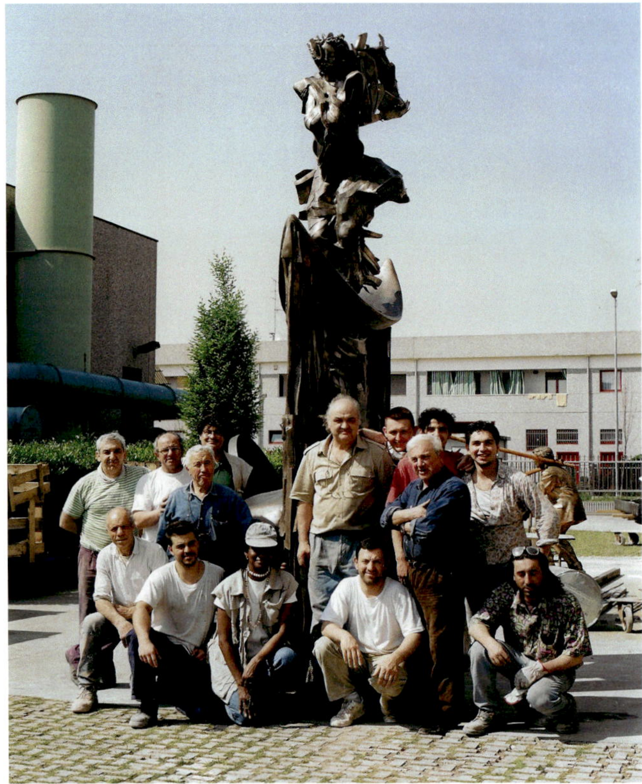

Barbara Chase-Riboud and foundry workers with *Africa Rising*, 1997

Chevalier des Arts et des Lettres. Can we talk about how that felt?

BCR There is no other woman artist who has been knighted by the French government, and no American-born woman living in France who's been knighted in this way.

EG And then you have an exhibition at Moeller Fine Art in New York. And then in terms of your European presence, this series, *Cleopatra*—the *Cleopatra's Marriage Contract*—is acquired by the British Museum.

BCR That was an enormous honor, and a surprise, because it was their big Cleopatra exhibit, enormous exhibit. My work was the only contemporary thing in it; drawing, sculpture, whatever. And, of course, it was the same year or the year after that they found a real Cleopatra's marriage contract, which I have—which has her signature on it. And so, it's almost like, you know, a Sally Hemings story because you imagine it, you make it, and then it comes true.

EG So, the next year—perhaps you were in Milan, because the next set of *Malcolm X* sculptures are

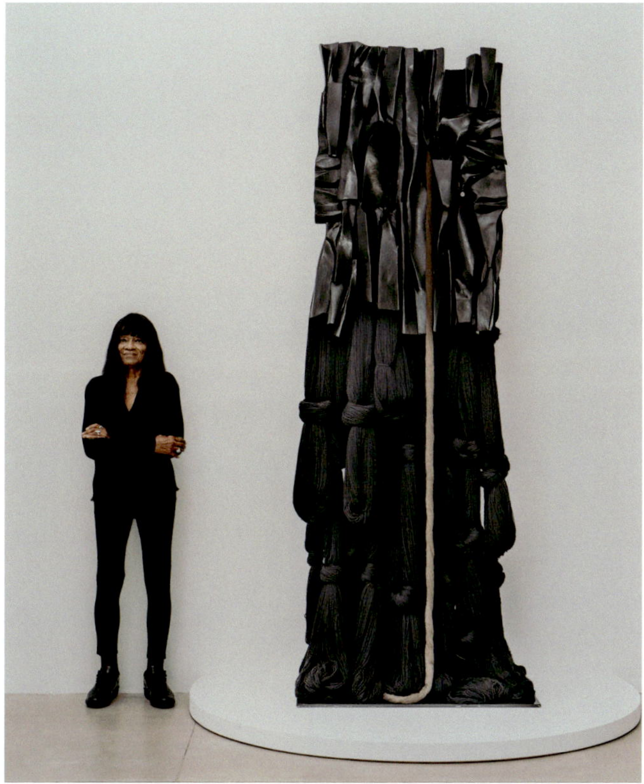

Barbara Chase-Riboud with *Zanzibar*, 1974

being cast at this moment. Do you remember what was the impetus to make them now? Why, in 2003, did you decide to make another four?

BCR I think it was simply because they were evolving into more Brutalist forms. A little bit more futuristic in their configurations, and I had sort of evolved the technique to such perfection that I thought, "I will take these steles as far as they will go to the extremities of undercutting and baroqueism."

EG In the end of 2013, you have an exhibition at the Philadelphia Museum of Art featuring the *Malcolm X* steles, and at this point there are even more than there were in the beginning.

BCR The total now is twenty.

EG So, you went from an original four to twenty over a period of about thirty years. What happened for you in this moment? Because in thinking about the few things that have happened since, there was, I think, an expanded understanding of—in this context.

BCR That it was a kind of apex of my sculptural practice. The *Malcolms* that came before are very

beautiful. They were softer, they were more manageable than the last five, which came into being in the same way that "Helicopter" is probably the last poem I'm going to write, or—it's not the last poem I'm going to write, but it's the last poem I'm going to publish. And there's a kind of realization in the last five, and a kind of definitiveness about them, that makes me think that there will never be number twenty-one.

EG So, in this moment after the *Malcolm X* steles are realized as a group of twenty, there are exhibitions in which you are included that are concurrent with our collective thinking around the impact of the '60s on the contemporary moment. There's *Witness: Art and Civil Rights in the Sixties* at the Brooklyn Museum; there's *The Color Line: African-American Artists and the Civil Rights in the United States*, at the Musée du quai Branly. There's *Circa 1970* at The Studio Museum in Harlem in 2016, and then in 2017, concurrent with the gallery show at Michael Rosenfeld, you have *We Wanted a Revolution: Black Radical Women, 1965–85*, which is really a culminating view on how the relationship between artistic practice and activism manifested itself in film and photography and performance and sculpture and drawing.

And how does it feel to have been positioned at this moment as not just a feminist but a civil rights activist and as one who has, though the works themselves are not politicized, a statement within this larger political moment?

BCR I am not radical, I am not a revolutionary, and I am not a woman. And I am not black; I am born in America.

As far as I'm concerned, my reputation as a great abstractionist is quite enough for me, and what else would I like? The Nobel Prize [laughs]? But other than that—well, I would settle for a Pulitzer in poetry. I think that I've done my job and left a body of work that's interesting enough for other people to follow, and you can't ask for anything more than that. And as I said, been there, done that, because the places I've seen and the places I've been have been unforgettable.

Note

1. Sarah Baartman was a Khoisan woman who was exhibited as a freak show attraction in nineteenth-century Europe under the name Hottentot Venus.

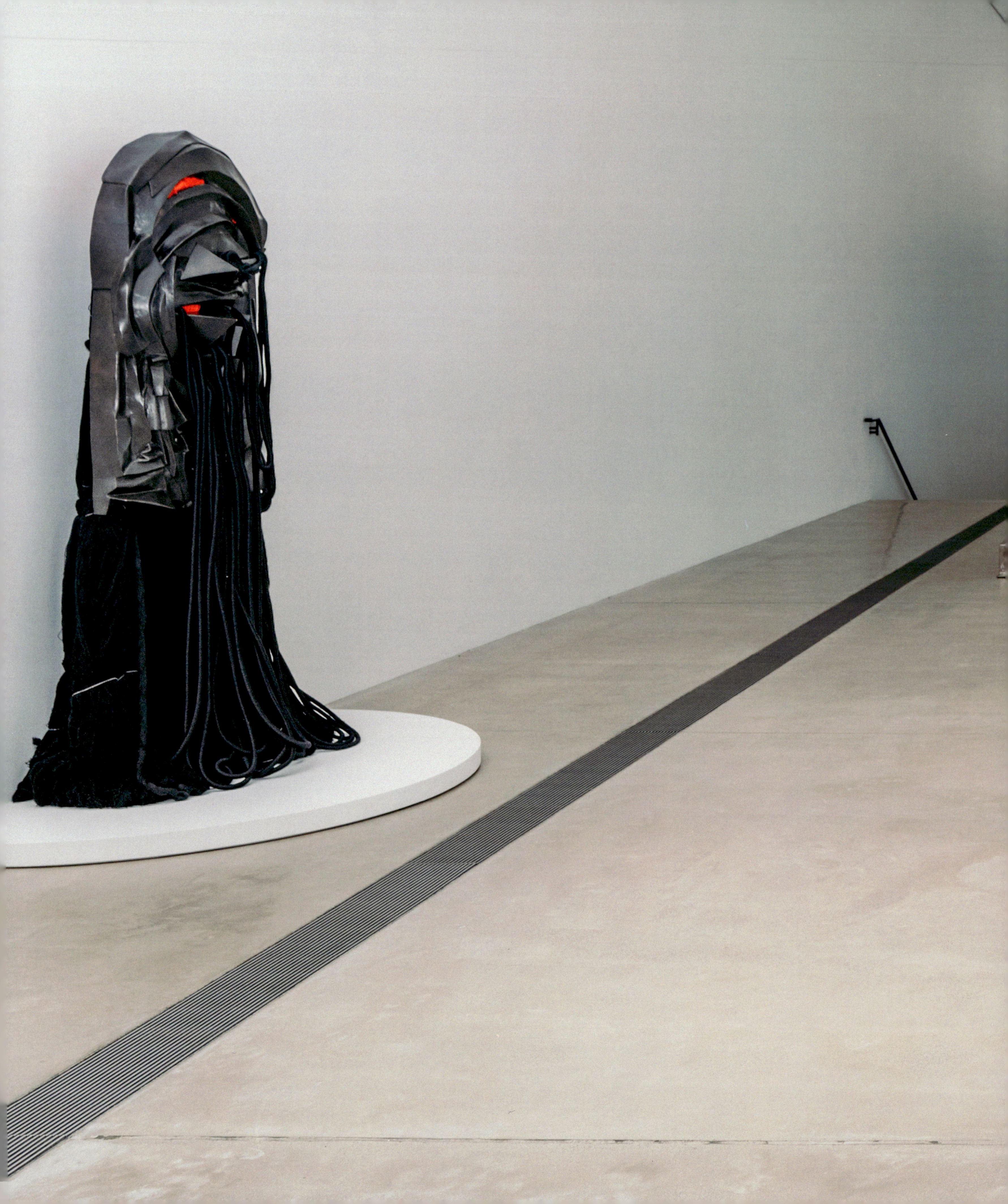

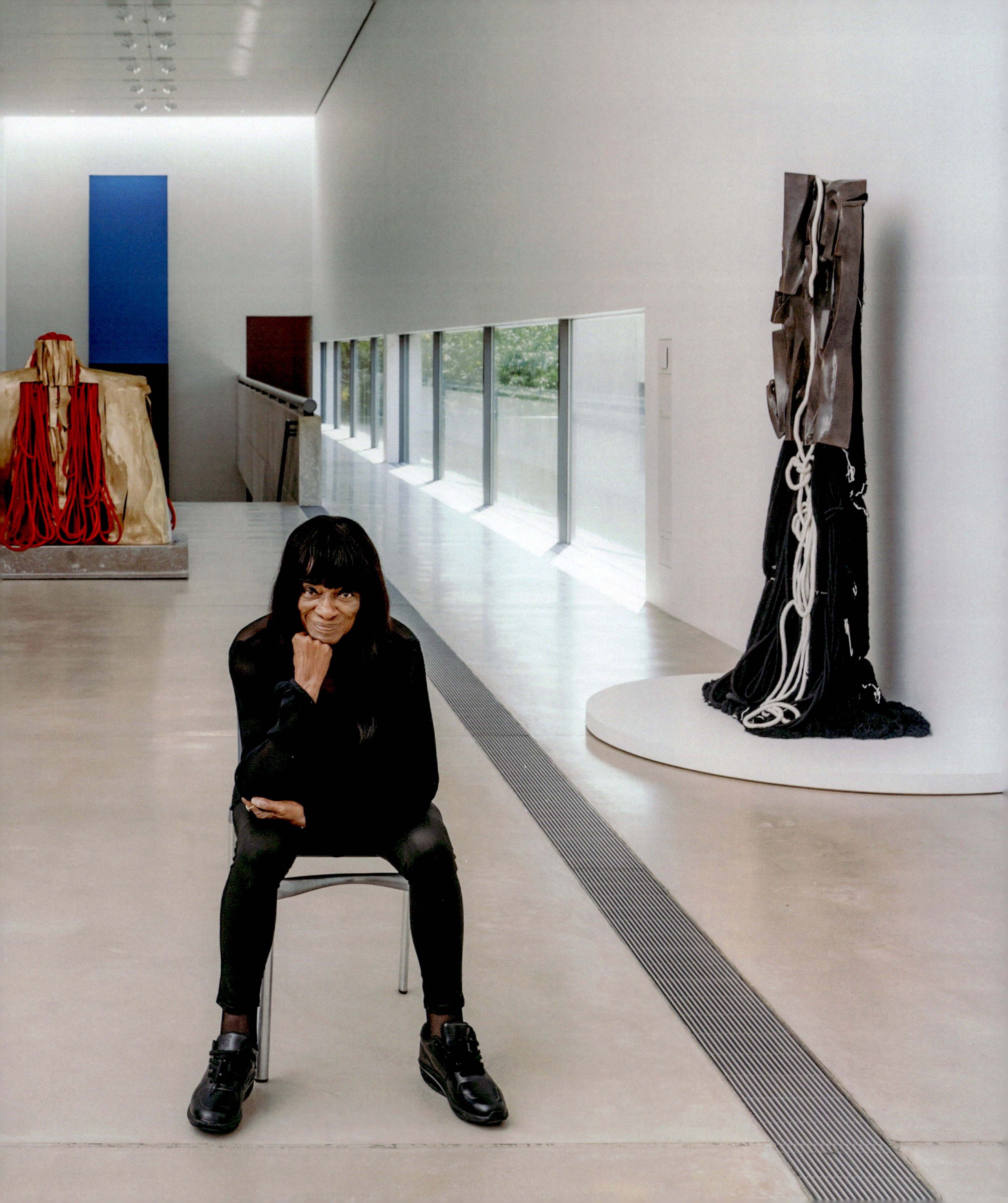

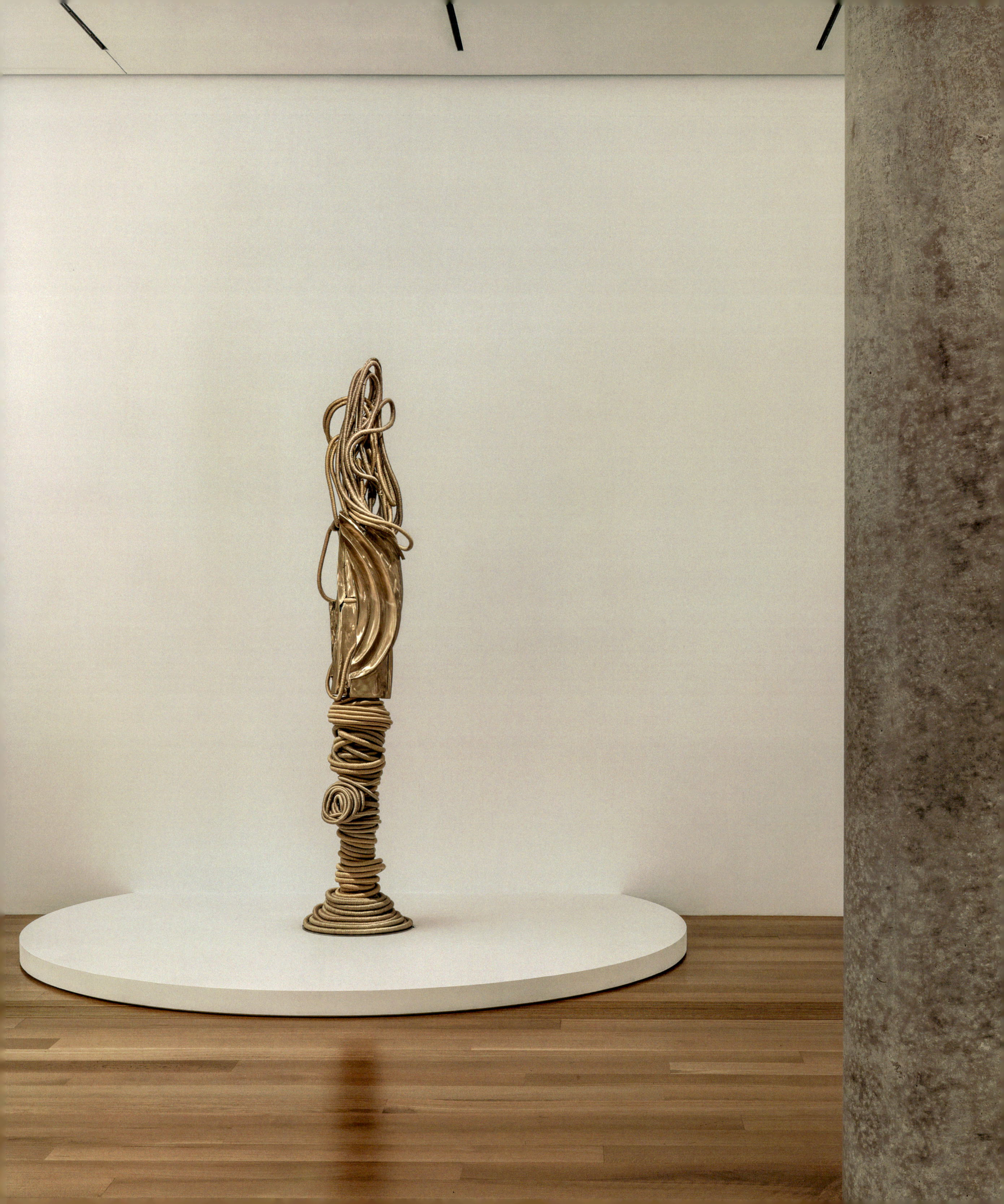

CHECKLIST

Le Lit, 1966
Charcoal, charcoal pencil, and ink with engraving and aquatint on paper
31½ × 23⅞ inches (80 × 60.6 cm)
Private collection
Pages 35, 51

Le Lit, 1966
Charcoal and charcoal pencil on paper
30 × 22⅛ inches (76.2 × 56.2 cm)
Private collection
Page 52

Le Lit, 1966
Charcoal, charcoal pencil, and ink with engraving and aquatint on paper
31½ × 23⅞ inches (80 × 60.6 cm)
Private collection
Page 53

Nostradamus, 1966
Bronze
30⅝ × 10 × 10 inches (77.8 × 25.4 × 25.4 cm)
Collection of Stella Jones
Page 50

Untitled, 1966
Charcoal on paper
30 × 21⅞ inches (76.3 × 55.7 cm)
The Museum of Modern Art, New York.
Gift of Betty Parsons Gallery, 1972
Page 56

Untitled, 1966
Charcoal, charcoal pencil, and ink with engraving and aquatint on paper
31½ × 23⅞ inches (80 × 60.6 cm)
Private collection
Page 57

Le Lit, 1966–73
Charcoal, charcoal pencil, and ink with engraving and aquatint on paper
31½ × 23⅞ inches (80 × 60.6 cm)
Private collection
Page 54

Homage to Gustave Courbet, 1967
Polished bronze and silk
29 × 30 × 5½ inches (73.7 × 76.2 × 14 cm)
Private collection
Page 60

Untitled, 1967
Pencil and charcoal on paper
11⅛ × 10¼ inches (28 × 26 cm)
The Museum of Modern Art, New York.
Gift of The Grace M. Mayer Collection, 1999
Pages 37, 61

Well of the Concubine Pearl, 1967
Polished aluminum, silk, wool, linen, synthetic fibers, and steel chain on painted steel base
81 × 30 × 30 inches (205.7 × 76.2 × 76.2 cm)
Private collection
Page 65

Time Womb Jacqueline, 1970
Polished aluminum
61⅛ × 50⅝ × 4⅞ inches
(155.3 × 128.6 × 12.4 cm)
Private collection
Page 58

Untitled, 1971
Charcoal and pencil on paper
29⅞ × 22⅛ inches (76 × 56.4 cm)
The Museum of Modern Art, New York.
David Rockefeller Latin American
Fund, 1972
Page 62

Zanzibar Table Black #2, 1972
Bronze with black patina, silk, linen, and
synthetic fibers
13½ × 12½ × 17 inches (34.3 × 31.8 ×
43.2 cm)
Private collection
Page 74

Zanzibar Table Gold, 1972
Polished bronze and silk
15¼ × 13 × 12¾ inches (38.7 × 33 ×
32.4 cm)
Collection of Beth Rudin DeWoody
Page 75

Landscape and Cords, 1973
Charcoal and charcoal pencil on paper
22¼ × 19¾ inches (56.5 × 50.2 cm)
Private collection
Page 63

Le Manteau (The Cape), or *Cleopatra's
Cape*, 1973
Bronze, hemp rope, and copper
83⅛ × 70⅛ × 66⅝ inches (211.1 ×
178.1 × 169.2 cm)
The Studio Museum in Harlem; gift of
the Lannan Foundation
Pages 83, 84

Zanzibar, 1974
Polished bronze with black patina,
silk, wool, and synthetic fibers with
steel support
108¼ × 34⅝ inches (275 × 88 cm)
Private collection
Page 70

L'Architectura, 1984/2021
Bronze with black patina, wool,
and other fibers
124 × 135 ½ × 15⅛ inches (315 × 344.2 ×
38.4 cm)
Private collection
Page 66

Cleopatra's Door, 1984
Multicolored cast-bronze plaques
over oak
98½ × 59 × 19¾ inches (250 × 150 ×
50 cm)
Private collection
Page 87

Cleopatra's Chair, 1994
Multicolored cast-bronze plaques
over oak
39⅜ × 49⅝ × 43¼ inches (100 × 126 ×
110 cm)
Private collection
Pages 40, 88

*Peter Paul Rubens' Mother's Monument,
Antwerp*, 1996
Charcoal, charcoal pencil, and ink with
engraving and aquatint on paper
31½ × 23⅞ inches (80 × 60.6 cm)
Private collection
Page 98

Zola's Monument, Paris, 1996
Charcoal, charcoal pencil, and ink with
engraving and aquatint on paper
31½ × 23⅞ inches (80 × 60.6 cm)
Private collection
Page 100

*The Precious Concubine Pearl's
Monument, Beijing*, 1997
Charcoal, charcoal pencil, and ink with
engraving and aquatint on paper
31½ × 23⅞ inches (80 × 60.6 cm)
Private collection
Page 99

Sarah Baartman Red Drawing #4, 1997
Pastel and graphite on paper
28 × 20 inches (71.1 × 50.8 cm)
Private collection
Page 94

Africa Rising Bust Overcast #1, 1998
Bronze with silver patina
25⅜ × 17 × 18½ inches (64.5 × 43.2 ×
47 cm)
Private collection
Page 97

La Musica Alabaster, 1998
Bronze and alabaster
40½ × 35 × 12 inches (102.9 × 88.9 ×
30.5 cm)
Private collection
Page 109

La Musica Black #1, 1998
Bronze with black patina and silk
23⅞ × 21¼ × 9⅝ inches (60.6 × 54 ×
24.4 cm)
Gardy St. Fleur Collection
Page 106

Woman's Monument, 1998
Bronze
31 × 30¼ × 18½ inches (78.7 × 76.8 ×
47 cm)
Private collection
Page 103

Cleopatra's Marriage Contract, 2000
Handmade paper, graphite, ink, wax,
and cord
39 × 42 × 1 inches (99.1 × 106.7 × 2.5 cm)
Private collection
Pages 90, 91

La Musica Archaeological, 2003
Bronze and silk cord
21 × 26¾ × 11 inches (53.3 × 67.9 ×
27.9 cm)
Private collection
Page 107

La Musica Marian Anderson, 2003
Bronze, silk, and synthetic fibers
45¼ × 25⁵⁄₁₆ × 10⅝ inches (115 × 65 ×
27 cm)
Collection of Nigel and Ayodele Hart
Page 111

La Musica Red #4, 2003
Bronze with red patina and silk
29½ × 28¼ × 12¼ inches (74.9 × 71.8 ×
31.1 cm)
Private collection
Page 112

Black Obelisk #2, 2007
Bronze with black patina, wool, and
synthetic fibers with steel support
78 × 27 × 22 inches (198.1 × 68.6 ×
55.9 cm)
Private collection
Pages 128, 130

Malcolm X #9, 2007
Bronze with black patina, silk, wool, and
synthetic fibers with steel support
83½ × 27½ × 33 inches (212.2 × 69.8 ×
58.4 cm)
Private collection
Page 132

Mao's Organ, 2007
Polished bronze and silk with steel base
64½ × 71 × 43½ inches (163.8 × 180.3 ×
110.5 cm)
Private collection
Pages 124, 127

La Musica Red Parkway, Josephine, 2007
Bronze with red patina and silk
72⅞ × 49 × 19 inches (185.1 × 124.5 × 48.3 cm)
Private collection
Pages 119, 121, 123

Nursery #3, 2007
Black bronze, silk, and rope
189 × 36⅛ × 24¼ inches (480.1 × 91.8 × 61.6 cm)
Private collection
Page 67

Shaka Zulu Monument, Capetown, 2007
Charcoal, charcoal pencil, and ink with engraving and aquatint on paper
31½ × 23⅞ inches (80 × 60.6 cm)
Private collection
Page 101

Twin Towers, 2007
Polished bronze and silk with steel base
65¾ × 36⅜ × 25¾ inches (167 × 92.4 × 65.4 cm)
Private collection
Page 114

Anne d'H, 2008
Bronze and silk
73 × 13½ inches (185.4 × 34.3 cm)
Philadelphia Museum of Art: Gift of the artist in memory of Anne d'Harnoncourt, 2013
Pages 115, 117, 162

Malcolm X #13, 2008
Bronze with black patina, silk, wool, and synthetic fibers with steel support
86¾ × 45 × 34½ inches (220.3 × 114.3 × 87.6 cm)
Collection of the Kemper Museum of Contemporary Art, Kansas City, Missouri, Bebe and Crosby Kemper Collection, Museum purchase made possible by a gift from Bebe and Crosby Kemper Foundation, 2018.01.01
Page 133

Malcolm X #16, 2016
Bronze with red patina, silk, wool, and polished cotton and synthetic fibers with steel support
92 × 32 × 30 inches (233.7 × 81.3 × 76.2 cm)
Yale University Art Gallery, Janet and Simeon Braguin Fund
Pages 4, 134

Malcolm X #17, 2016
Polished bronze and silk
92 × 41 × 36 inches (233.7 × 104.1 × 91.4 cm)
Shah Garg Collection
Pages 137, 138

Malcolm X #18, 2016
Polished bronze and silk with steel support
92 × 32 × 30 inches (233.7 × 81.3 × 76.2 cm)
Private collection
Page 139

Malcolm X #19, 2017
Bronze with black patina, silk, wool, polished cotton, and synthetic fibers with steel support
89¼ × 44 × 27 inches (226.7 × 111.8 × 68.6 cm)
Private collection
Pages 12, 140

His Phallus in Hand (White Drawing), 2020
Silk on Arches paper
29½ × 21⅝ inches (75 × 55 cm)
Private collection
Page 79

Jeanne Amoor (White Drawing), 2021
Silk on Arches paper
29½ × 21⅝ inches (75 × 55 cm)
Private collection
Page 78

Rue des Plantes (White Drawing), 2021
Synthetic white silk on Arches paper
25½ × 19⅝ inches (64.8 × 49.8 cm)
Private collection
Page 76

Standing Black Woman of Venice, 2021
Black bronze
96⅞ × 18⅛ × 27³⁄₁₆ inches (246 × 46 × 69 cm)
Private collection
Pages 142, 143

BIBLIOGRAPHY

Select Monographs and Solo Exhibition Catalogues

Cachin, Françoise, and Barbara Chase-Riboud. *Chase Riboud*. Paris: Musée d'art moderne de la ville de Paris, 1974.

Chase-Riboud, Barbara. *Barbara Chase-Riboud: Dessins et sculptures: Couples mythologiques*. Paris: Cadran Solaire, 1966.

Chase-Riboud, Barbara. *Barbara Chase Riboud: Four Monuments to Malcolm X—Sculptures*. New York: Bertha Schaefer Gallery, 1970.

Chase-Riboud, Barbara. *Barbara Chase-Riboud*. Paris: Kiron, 1994.

Chase-Riboud, Barbara. *Barbara Chase Riboud: The Monument Drawings*. Wilmington, NC: St. John's Museum of Art; Baltimore, MD: Walters Art Museum, 1997 and 2000.

Chase-Riboud, Barbara, and W. Hülsen. *Chase Riboud: Skulpturen, Zeichnungen*. Freiburg: Kunstverein, 1976.

Chase-Riboud, Barbara, and Wend von Kalnein. *Chase Riboud: Zeichnungen*. Düsseldorf: Das Kunstmuseum, 1974.

Chase-Riboud, Barbara, Friederich Wilheim Heckmanns, and Antonio Calderara. *Chase-Riboud, Calderara*. Krefeld: Galerie & Edition Merian, 1973.

Chase-Riboud, Barbara, Carlos Basualdo, Françoise Nora-Cachin, and John Vick. *Barbara Chase-Riboud: Malcolm X—Complete*. New York: Michael Rosenfeld Gallery, 2017.

Chase-Riboud, Barbara, Carlos Basualdo, Timothy Rub, Gwendolyn DuBois Shaw, Ellen Handler Spitz, and John Vick. *Barbara Chase-Riboud: The Malcolm X Steles*. Philadelphia: Philadelphia Museum of Art; New Haven and London: Yale University Press, 2013.

Désanges, Guillaume. "Barbara Chase-Riboud: Avatars." *Le Journal de la Verrière* 24 (2020): 1–23. Exhibition pamphlet published by the Fondation d'Entreprise Hermès.

Heckmanns, Friedrich Wilhelm, Françoise Nora-Cachin, Geneviève Monnier, and Barbara Chase-Riboud. *Chase-Riboud*. Berkeley, CA: University Art Museum, 1973.

Selz, Peter. *The Work of Chase-Riboud*. Berkeley: University Art Museum at Berkeley, 1972.

Selz, Peter, and Anthony F. Janson. *Barbara Chase-Riboud, Sculptor*. New York: Harry N. Abrams, 1999.

Select Essays, Articles, and Interviews

1959: "Barbara Chase Studies in Rome." *Ebony Magazine*. April: cover.

1970: Kramer, Hilton. "Black Experience and Modernist Art." *New York Times*, 14 February, 23.

1970: Grillo, Jean Bergantini. "Malcolm: Monuments in Bronze and Braid." *The Phoenix*, 16 April, 18.

1970: Kibby, David. "MIT Press Release Bulletin." *Malcolm X Exhibit*, Hayden Gallery, 8 April.

1970: Rose, Barbara. "Black Art in America." *Art in America*, July–December: 54–67.

1972: Cachin, Françoise. "From Another Country." *ARTnews*, March: 28–29.

1972: Mallow, James R. "Barbara Chase-Riboud." *New York Times*, 1 April, 19.

1973: Hershman, Lynn Lester. "Sculpture as Beauty." *Art Week*, 10 February, 1 and 12.

1973: Russell, John. "Barbara Chase-Riboud, Betty Parsons Gallery." *New York Times*, 12 April.

1974: Dallier, Aline. "Women and Soft Art." *Opus International*, September: 49–53.

1974: Gandouet, Marielle. "Barbara Chase-Riboud." *Le Monde*, 17 May, 23.

1974: Terrell, Angela. "From Sculpture to Poetry." *Washington Post*, 7 July, H1 and H15.

1975: Bierre, J.F. "Dakar." *L'Ouest African*, 28 March.

1977: McFadden, Jerome. "B.C.R." *Sepia Magazine*, July.

1977: Hess, Thomas. "For Each Man Kilns The Thing He Loves." *New York Magazine*, 1 August: 56–59.

1980: Hughes, Robert. "Art: Going Back to Africa." *Time Magazine*, 31 March: 72.

1980: Henry, Susan. "Profile: Chase-Riboud." *Ms. Magazine*, October: 35–40.

1986: "The 100 Most Influential Black Americans." *Ebony Magazine*, May: 47.

1988: Reavis, Edward. "Tribute to an Artist." *Stars and Stripes*, 29 July.

1990: Newton, Edmund. "The Artist at Work." *Los Angeles Times*, 3 May, J1 and J9.

1995: Kimmelman, Michael. "Harlem Sculpture Garden, Turning an Alley into a Showcase for Sculpture." *New York Times*, 22 September.

1995: Smith, Elmer. "Triumphant Return for Author-Artist." *Philadelphia Daily News*, 22 September.

1996: Kimmelman, Michael. "Black Artists at Home in Postwar Paris." *New York Times*, 18 February, 39.

1998: Brown, M. "Sculptor Barbara Chase-Riboud." *The New Orleans Tribune*, March.

1998: Crushshon, Theresa. "Barbara Chase-Riboud." *The New Orleans Tribune*, February.

1999: Cannon, Steve. "An interview w. Barbara Chase-Riboud." *A Gathering of the Tribes 9* (2000): 32–35.

1999: Jones, Lisa. "A Most Dangerous Woman." *Village Voice*, 9 February.

2006: Armand, Claudine. "Interview with Barbara Chase-Riboud." In *Ancrages/Passages*. Edited by Claudine Armand, André Kaenel, and Claire Omhovère, 15–37. Nancy: Presses Universities de Nancy.

2006: Braxton, Joanne M. "The Spiritual, the Sexual, and the Sublime: Approaches to Barbara Chase-Riboud's *Tantra* Series." *International Review of African American Art* 21, no. 3: 16–19.

2009: Spencer, Suzette A., and Carlos A. Miranda. "Barbara Chase-Riboud." *Callaloo* 32, no. 3 (Summer).

2013: Daugherty, Gregory N. "Barbara Chase-Riboud's Multimedia Receptions of Cleopatra." *New Voices in Classical Reception Studies* 8: 48–64.

2017: Chase-Riboud, Barbara, and Hans Ulrich Obrist. "Memory Is Everything: Barbara Chase-Riboud." *Mousse Magazine* 60 (October–November): 101–13.

2019: Oral history interview with Barbara Chase-Riboud, June 7–11. Archives of American Art, Smithsonian Institution, Washington, DC.

2020: Vidal, Pauline. "Barbara Chase-Riboud." *L'Oeil* 738 (November): 36–37.

Select Group Show Catalogues

3rd Biennale of Sydney: European Dialogue. Sydney: Art Gallery of New South Wales, 1979.

Afro-American Artists: New York and Boston. Roxbury, CT: Museum of the National Center of Afro-American Artists, 1970.

Black Artists: Two Generations. Newark, NJ: Newark Museum, 1971.

Bowling, Frank, and Kellie Jones. *Energy/Experimentation: Black Artists and Abstraction 1964–1980*. New York: Studio Museum in Harlem, 2006.

Buffalo, Andreen. *Explorations in the City of Light: African-American Artists in Paris, 1945–1965*. New York: Studio Museum in Harlem, 1996.

Carbone, Teresa A., and Kellie Jones. *Witness: Art and Civil Rights in the Sixties*. New York: Monacelli Press, 2014.

Dix Artistes Nègres des États-Unis; Premier Festival Mondial des Arts Nègres, Dakar, Sénégal, 1966. Ten Negro Artists from the United States; First World Festival of Negro Arts, Dakar, Senegal,

1966. New York: US Committee for the First
World Festival of Negro Arts, New York.

Doty, Robert M. *Contemporary Black Artists in
America.* New York: Whitney Museum of American Art, 1971.

Dziedzic, Erin, and Melissa Messina. *Magnetic Fields:
Expanding American Abstraction, 1960s to Today.*
Kansas City, MO: Kemper Museum of Contemporary Art, 2017.

Figura, Starr. *Making Space: Women Artists and
Abstraction 1945–1970.* New York: Museum of
Modern Art, 2017.

Fonvielle-Bontemps, Jacqueline, and David C.
Driskell. *Forever Free: Art by African-American
Women, 1862–1980.* College Park: University of
Maryland Art Gallery, 1981.

Godfrey, Mark, and Zoé Whitley. *Soul of a Nation: Art
in the Age of Black Power.* London: Tate Publishing, 2017.

Keith, Naima J., and Diana Nawi. *Prospect.5 New
Orleans: Yesterday We Said Tomorrow.* New York:
Rizzoli Electa, 2021.

King-Hammond, Leslie, Tritobia H. Benjamin, Carolyn
Elizabeth Shuttlesworth-Davidson, and Roslyn A.
Walker. *3 Generations of African American
Women Sculptors: A Study in Paradox.* Philadelphia: Afro-American Historical and Cultural
Museum, 1996.

Kingsley, April. *Afro-American Abstraction: An
Exhibition of Contemporary Painting and Sculpture by Nineteen Black American Artists.* New
York: PS 1, 1981.

Krattenmaker, Kathleen, and Richard J. Powell.
*Represent: 200 Years of African American Art in
the Philadelphia Museum of Art.* New Haven, CT:
Yale University Press, 2014.

Kuspit, Donald, and Tricia Laughlin Bloom. *Seeing
America: The Arc of Abstraction.* Newark, NJ:
Newark Museum, 2019.

Morris, Catherine, and Rujeko Hockley. *We Wanted a
Revolution: Black Radical Women, 1965–85: New
Perspectives.* New York: Brooklyn Museum, 2018.

Sims, Lowery Stokes, Kathleen Hulser, and Cynthia R.
Copeland. *Legacies: Contemporary Artists
Reflect on Slavery.* New York: New-York Historical
Society, 2006.

Soutif, Daniel. *The Color Line: Les artistes Africains-
Américains et la ségrégation, 1865–2016.* Paris:
Musée du quai Branly-Jacques Chirac, 2016.

Renwick Gallery. *The Object as Poet.* Washington,
DC: Smithsonian Institution Press, 1977.

Walker, Susan, and Peter Higgs. *Cleopatra of Egypt:
From History to Myth.* London: The British
Museum Press, 2001.

Literary Works of Barbara Chase-Riboud, 1974–2022

Novels

Chase-Riboud, Barbara. *Sally Hemings.* New York:
Viking Press, 1979.

Chase-Riboud, Barbara. *Valide: A Novel of the Harem.*
New York: Morrow, 1986.

Chase-Riboud, Barbara. *Echo of Lions.* New York:
Morrow, 1989.

Chase-Riboud, Barbara. *The President's Daughter.*
New York: Drown Publishers, 1994.

Chase-Riboud, Barbara. *Roman égyptien.* Paris:
Editions du Felin, 1994.

Chase-Riboud, Barbara. *Hottentot Venus.* New York:
Anchor Books, 2004.

Chase-Riboud, Barbara. *The Great Mrs. Elias.* New
York: Amistad, 2022.

Books of Poetry

Chase-Riboud, Barbara. *From Memphis and Peking:
Poems.* New York: Random House, 1974.

Chase-Riboud, Barbara. *Portrait of a Nude Woman as
Cleopatra.* New York: Morrow, 1987.

Chase-Riboud, Barbara. *Everytime a Knot Is Undone,
a God Is Released: Collected and New Poems,
1974–2011.* New York and Oakland: Seven Stories
Press, 2014.

Non-Fiction

Chase-Riboud, Barbara. *I Always Knew: A Memoir.*
Princeton: Princeton University Press, 2022.

Librettos

Cleopatra: A Melologue, 1987. Music by
Anthony Vores.

Egypt's Nights: An Opera, 2008. Music by
Leslie Burrs.

DEGREES AND AWARDS

Education

1956 BFA, Tyler School at Temple University, Philadelphia

1960 MFA, Yale University School of Design and Architecture, New Haven, CT

Awards and Honors

1957 John Hay Whitney Fellowship, American Academy in Rome

1979 Janet Heidinger Kafka Prize, *Sally Hemings* (Viking Press, 1979)

1981 Honorary Doctorate of Fine Arts, Temple University, Philadelphia

1987 Carl Sandburg Award, *Portrait of a Nude Woman as Cleopatra* (Willam Morrow, 1987)

1993 Honorary Doctorate of Letters, Muhlenberg College, Allentown, PA

1995 Brandywine Lifetime Achievement Award, Philadelphia

1996 Honorary Doctorate of Letters, University of Connecticut, Mansfield

1996 Knighthood, Ordre des Arts et des Lettres, France

2003 Black Caucus of the American Library Association Literary Award, *Hottentot Venus* (Doubleday, 2003)

2007 Women's Caucus for Art Lifetime Achievement Award
Alain Locke Award, Detroit Institute of Arts

2013 Tannie Award, Visual Art, Paris

2020 Anonymous Was a Woman Award, New York

2021 AWARE Outstanding Merit Prize, Prix d'Honneur, Paris
Grand Prix Artistique, Simone and Cino Del Duca Foundation, Paris

2022 Knighthood, The National Order of the Legion of Honour, France

Select Solo Exhibitions

1958 Galleria l'Obelisco, Rome
American Academy, Rome
Festival of Two Worlds, Spoleto, Italy

1966 Galerie Cadran Solaire, Paris

1970 Bertha Schaefer Gallery, New York
Monuments to Malcolm X, Massachusetts
Institute of Technology, Hayden Gallery,
Cambridge, MA

1972 *Barbara Chase-Riboud Exhibition*, Betty
Parsons Gallery, New York

1973 University Art Museum, Berkeley, CA; Detroit
Institute of Arts; Indianapolis Art Museum
Leslie Tonkonow Gallery, New York
Cleveland Museum of Art

1974 Musée d'Art Moderne de la Ville de Paris
Staatliche Kunsthalle, Baden-Baden,
Germany
Merian Gallery, Krefeld, Germany
Kunstmuseum, Düsseldorf, Germany

1975 Betty Parsons Gallery, New York
United States Cultural Center, Tunis, Tunisia;
Bamako, Mali; Freetown, Sierra Leone; Accra,
Ghana; Dakar, Senegal
Musée d'Art Contemporain, Tehran, Iran

1976 Kunstverein, Freiburg, Germany
Musée Reattu, Arles, France

1977 Documenta VI, Kassel, Germany

1980 Bronx Museum, NY

1981 Sergio Tosi Stampatore Gallery, New York

1990 Pasadena College Art Gallery and Sculpture
Garden, CA

1994 94 Espace Kiron, Paris

1997 Kenkeleba House Gallery, New York

1998 Stella Jones Gallery, New Orleans
*Barbara Chase-Riboud: The Monument
Drawings*, St. John's Museum of Art, Wilm-
ington, NC; Metropolitan Museum of Art,
New York; African American Museum,
Philadelphia; Walters Art Gallery, Baltimore;
Diggs Gallery, Winston-Salem, NC
Bianca Pilat Contemporary Art, Chicago

1999 Achim Moeller Gallery, New York

2001 Walter Gomez Gallery, Baltimore

2002 G.R. N'Namdi Gallery, Detroit; Chicago

2004 *Chase-Riboud*, Galleria Giulia, Rome

2008 *Chase-Riboud*, Galleria Giulia, Rome

2013 *Barbara Chase-Riboud: The Malcolm X
Steles*, Philadelphia Museum of Art; Berkeley
Art Museum and Pacific Film Archive, CA

2014 *Barbara Chase-Riboud: One Million Kilometers
of Silk*, Michael Rosenfeld Gallery, New York

2017 *Barbara Chase-Riboud—Malcolm X: Complete*, Michael Rosenfeld Gallery, New York

2020 *Barbara Chase-Riboud: Avatars, "Matters of
Concern | Matières à panser,"* La Verrière,
Fondation d'entreprise Hermès, Brussels

2022 *Barbara Chase-Riboud Monumentale: The Bronzes*, Pulitzer Arts Foundation, St. Louis
Infinite Folds, Serpentine Galleries, London

Select Group Exhibitions

1954 *Scholastic Art Awards*, ACA Gallery, New York

1958 *International Exhibition of Painting and Sculpture Biennale*, Carnegie Institute, Pittsburgh

1959 *National Painting and Drawing Exhibition*, Pennsylvania Academy of the Fine Arts, Philadelphia

1961 *Salon de Mai*, Musée National d'Art Moderne, Paris

1966 *Premier Festival Mondial des Arts Nègres: 10 Artists des États-Unis*, Dakar, Senegal

1969 *7 Américains de Paris*, Galerie Air France, New York
L'Oeil Écoute, Musée Réattu, Festival of Avignon, France

1970 *Afro-American Artists: New York and Boston*, The Museum of the National Center of Afro-American Artists, Boston; School of the Museum of Fine Arts at Tufts University, Boston; Museum of Fine Arts, Boston
Contemporary American Sculpture, Whitney Museum of American Art, New York
Sculpture—The Artists Plus Discoveries, Betty Parsons Gallery, New York

1971 *Salon des Nouvelles Réalités*, Galeries Nationales d'Exposition du Grand Palais, Paris
Black Artists: Two Generations, Newark Museum, NJ
Salon de la Jeune Sculpture, Musée National d'Art Moderne, Paris
Contemporary Black Artists in America, Whitney Museum of American Art, New York

1973 The Royal Ontario Art Museum, Montreal
Sources of Inspiration, Betty Parsons Gallery, New York

1974 *Masterworks of the Seventies*, Albright-Knox Gallery, Buffalo, NY
Woman's Work: American Art 1974, Museum of the Philadelphia Civic Center, Philadelphia

1976 *The Sydney Biennial*, Sydney, Australia

1977 *The Object as Poet*, National Museum of American Art, Smithsonian Institution, Washington, DC; American Craft Museum, New York

Les Mains Regardant, Centre Georges Pompidou, Paris
European Drawings, Art Gallery of Ontario, Toronto

1979 *3rd Biennale of Sydney: European Dialogue*, Sydney, Australia
Another Generation, The Studio Museum in Harlem, New York

1980 *European Drawings*, The Art Gallery of South Australia, Adelaide
Afro-American Abstraction: An Exhibition of Contemporary Painting and Sculpture by Nineteen Black American Artists, Institute for Art and Urban Resources (now MoMA PS1), New York; Everson Museum of Art, Syracuse, NY; Los Angeles Municipal Art Gallery, Barnsdall Park; Oakland Museum of California; Brooks Memorial Art Gallery (now Memphis Brooks Museum of Art), Memphis, TN; Warner Gallery, South Bend Art Center, IN; Toledo Museum of Art, OH; Bellevue Arts Museum, WA; Laguna Gloria Art Museum (now The Contemporary Austin), Austin, TX; Mississippi Museum of Art, Jackson, MS

1981 *Forever Free: Art by African-American Women 1862–1980*, Center for Visual Arts Gallery (now the University Galleries), Illinois State University, Normal

1983 *Noeuds et Ligatures*, F.N.A.P. Rothschild Museum, Paris

1984 *East/West Contemporary American Art*, California Afro-American Museum, Los Angeles

1995 *The Second Fujisankei Biennale: International Exhibition for Contemporary Sculpture*, Hakone, Japan
Artist's Choice: Elizabeth Murray, Modern Women, The Museum of Modern Art, New York
The Listening Sky, The Studio Museum in Harlem, New York

1996 *Three Generations of African American Women Sculptors: A Study in Paradox*, African American Historical and Cultural Museum, Philadelphia; The Equitable Gallery, New York; California African-American Museum, Los Angeles; Telfair Museum of Art, Savannah, GA; Smithsonian Institution, Washington, DC
Explorations in the City of Light: African-American Artists in Paris, 1915–1965, The Studio Museum in Harlem, New York;

Chicago Cultural Center; New Orleans Museum of Art

Bearing Witness: Contemporary African American Women Artists, Spelman College Museum of Fine Art, Atlanta; Tuskegee University Art Gallery, AL; Fort Wayne Museum of Art, IN; St. Paul Museum, MN; Museum of African American Culture, Fort Worth, TX; Portland Museum of Art, OR; The Museum of Fine Arts, Houston

1999   *Design Awards*, Smithsonian Institution, Washington, DC

2001   *Cleopatra: From History to Myth*, The British Museum, London

2006   *Abstraction, Energy Experimentation*, The Studio Museum in Harlem, New York
Legacies: Contemporary Artists Reflect on Slavery, New-York Historical Society Museum & Library

2008   *[un]common threads*, Michael Rosenfeld Gallery, New York

2012   *Art Festival of Two Worlds*, Dakar, Senegal

2014   *Witness: Art and Civil Rights in the Sixties*, Brooklyn Museum of Art, NY; Hood Museum of Art, Hanover, NH

2015   *Represent: 200 Years of African American Art*, Philadelphia Museum of Art
It's Never Just Black or White, Michael Rosenfeld Gallery, New York
Nero su Bianco, American Academy in Rome
We Speak: Black Artists in Philadelphia, 1920s–1970s, Woodmere Art Museum, Philadelphia

2016   *The Color Line: African-American Artists and the Civil Rights in the United States*, Musée du quai Branly, Paris
Circa 1970, The Studio Museum in Harlem, New York

2017   *We Wanted a Revolution: Black Radical Women, 1965–85*, Brooklyn Museum, NY; California African American Museum, Los Angeles; Albright-Knox Art Gallery, Buffalo, NY; Institute of Contemporary Art, Boston
Third Space: Shifting Conversations about Contemporary Art, Birmingham Museum of Art, AL
Magnetic Fields: Expanding American Abstraction, 1960s to Today, Kemper Museum of Contemporary Art, Kansas City, MO; National Museum of Women in the Arts, Washington, DC; Museum of Fine Arts, St. Petersburg, FL

20/20, The Studio Museum in Harlem, New York; and Carnegie Museum of Art, Carnegie Institute, Pittsburgh
Making Space: Women Artists and Postwar Abstraction, The Museum of Modern Art, New York

2018   *Out of Easy Reach*, Stony Island Arts Bank, Rebuild Foundation, Chicago
Taurus and the Awakener, David Kordansky Gallery, Los Angeles

2019   *Making Knowing: Craft in Art, 1950–2019*, Whitney Museum of American Art, New York
"New Monuments," Collection 1940s–1970s, The Museum of Modern Art, New York
Soul of a Nation: Art in the Age of Black Power, de Young Museum, Fine Arts Museums of San Francisco
Art of Defiance: Radical Materials, Michael Rosenfeld Gallery, New York
Generations: A History of Black Abstract Art, The Baltimore Museum of Art
Seeing America, Newark Museum, NJ
David Hammons, Ted Joans: Exquisite Corpse, Lumiar Cité, Maumaus, Lisbon, Portugal
Lexicon: The Language of Gesture in 25 Years at Kemper Museum, Kemper Museum of Contemporary Art, Kansas City, MO
Art Purposes: Object Lessons for the Liberal Arts, Bowdoin College Museum of Art, Brunswick, ME
Or Both, Moore College of Art & Design, Philadelphia

2020   *Riffs and Relations: African American Artists and the European Modernist Tradition*, The Phillips Collection, Washington, DC
"Awakened in You": The Collection of Dr. Constance E. Clayton, Pennsylvania Academy of the Fine Arts, Philadelphia
Mapping The Collection, Museum Ludwig, Cologne, Germany

2021   *Yesterday We Said Tomorrow*, Prospect.5, Newcomb Museum of Art at Tulane University, New Orleans
Dream Monuments, Menil Drawing Institute, Houston

2022   *Standing Black Woman in Venice*, Fondation Giacometti, Paris

SELECTED INSTITUTIONAL COLLECTIONS

Berkeley Art Museum and Pacific Film Archive, CA
Birmingham Museum of Art, AL
Bowdoin College Museum of Art, Brunswick, ME
Cameron Art Museum, Wilmington, NC
Centro de Arte Contemporaneo Wilfredo Lam, Havana, Cuba
The Galleries at Pasadena City College, CA
Hampton University Museum, VA
Kemper Art Museum, Kansas City, MO
La Salle University Art Museum, Philadelphia
Library of Congress, Washington, DC
The Metropolitan Museum of Art, New York
Musée d'Art Moderne de la Ville de Paris
The Museum of Modern Art, New York
Nasher Museum of Art, Duke University, Durham, NC
National Collections of France, Ministry of Culture, Paris
National Museum of African American History and Culture, Smithsonian Institution, Washington, DC
Newark Museum, NJ
New Orleans Museum of Art
New-York Historical Society Museum & Library
Pennsylvania Academy of the Fine Arts, Philadelphia
Philadelphia Art Alliance
Philadelphia Board of Education
Philadelphia Museum of Art
Ruth Chandler Williamson Gallery, Scripps College, Claremont Colleges, CA

Schomburg Center for Research in Black Culture, New York Public Library
Smithsonian American Art Museum, Washington, DC
The State Museum of Pennsylvania, Harrisburg
St. John's University, Queens, NY
Stuart A. Rose Manuscript, Archives, and Rare Book Library, Emory University, Atlanta
Studio Museum, New York
US General Services Administration
Yale University Art Gallery, New Haven, CT

CONTRIBUTORS

Christophe Cherix is the Robert Lehman Foundation Chief Curator of Drawings and Prints at the Museum of Modern Art. At MoMA, he has organized, among other exhibitions, *Betye Saar: Legends of "Black Girl's Window"* (with Esther Adler, 2019); *Adrian Piper: A Synthesis of Institutions, 1965–2016* (with Connie Butler and David Platzker, 2018); *Marcel Broodthaers: A Retrospective* (with Manuel Borja-Villel, 2016); *Yoko Ono: One Woman Show, 1960–1971* (with Klaus Biesenbach, 2015); and *Jasper Johns: Regrets* (with Ann Temkin, 2014).

Erin Jenoa Gilbert is a New York–based curator and director of exhibitions, publications, and acquisitions for Barbara Chase-Riboud. She was previously curator of African American manuscripts at the Archives of American Art, and has held positions at The Studio Museum in Harlem and the Art Institute of Chicago. She holds BA degrees in political science and African and African American studies from the University of Michigan, and a MA in postwar contemporary art from the University of Manchester.

Reginald Jackson is associate professor of premodern Japanese literature and performance at the University of Michigan. His research interests include medieval calligraphy, illustrated handscrolls, Noh dance-drama, contemporary Japanese choreography, African American literature, and queer studies. He holds a PhD from Princeton University in East Asian Studies and is the author of *Textures of Mourning: Calligraphy, Mortality, and* The Tale of Genji Scrolls (2018) and *A Proximate Remove: Queering Intimacy and Loss in* The Tale of Genji (2021).

Courtney J. Martin is the Paul Mellon Director at the Yale Center for British Art. Prior to her current appointment, Martin served as deputy director and chief curator of the New York–based Dia Art Foundation. She holds a PhD from Yale University, and has taught at Brown University and the Ford Foundation.

Akili Tommasino is associate curator of modern and contemporary art at the Metropolitan Museum of Art. He has held curatorial positions at the Museum of Fine Arts, Boston, and the Museum of Modern Art, New York, and was a Fulbright Fellow at the Centre Pompidou in Paris. A scholar of the twentieth-century avant-garde, he is completing his PhD at Harvard University, where he earned his MA and BA.

Stephanie Weissberg is curator at the Pulitzer Arts Foundation in St. Louis, Missouri, where she has organized *Lola Alvarez Bravo: Picturing Mexico* (2018); *Striking Power: Iconoclasm in Ancient Egypt* (2019); *Susan Philipsz: Seven Tears* (2019); *Terry Adkins: Resounding* (2020); and *Assembly Required* (2022), among other exhibitions. She has also held positions at the Brooklyn Museum, the Guggenheim, and Creative Time. She received her MA from New York University and BA from the University of California, Berkeley.

LENDERS TO THE EXHIBITION

Beth Rudin DeWoody
Nigel and Ayodele Hart
Stella Jones
Kemper Museum of Contemporary Art, Kansas City
The Museum of Modern Art, New York
Philadelphia Museum of Art
Private collection
Gardy St. Fleur Collection
Shah Garg Collection
The Studio Museum in Harlem
Yale University Art Gallery

BOARD OF DIRECTORS

This book is published on the occasion of the exhibition *Barbara Chase-Riboud Monumentale: The Bronzes*, organized by Stephanie Weissberg, Curator, Pulitzer Arts Foundation

Pulitzer Arts Foundation
September 16, 2022–February 5, 2023

Published by
Pulitzer Arts Foundation
3716 Washington Boulevard
St. Louis, MO 63108
pulitzerarts.org

Published in association with
Princeton University Press
Princeton and Oxford
41 William Street
Princeton, NJ 08540
USA

99 Banbury Road
Oxford OX2 6JX
UK
press.princeton.edu

Library of Congress Cataloging-in-Publication Data

Names: Weissberg, Stephanie, editor. | Martin, Courtney J., writer of preface. | Pulitzer Arts Foundation, organizer, host institution.
Title: Barbara Chase-Riboud, Monumentale : the bronzes / edited by Stephanie Weissberg.
Other titles: Monumentale : the bronzes
Description: St. Louis, MO : Pulitzer Arts Foundation ; Princeton : in association with Princeton University Press, [2023] | Includes bibliographical references.
Identifiers: LCCN 2022046392 | ISBN 9780691244648 (hardcover)
Subjects: LCSH: Chase-Riboud, Barbara—Exhibitions. | BISAC: ART / Individual Artists / General | ART / Sculpture & Installation
Classification: LCC NX512.C483 A4 2023 | DDC 730.92—dc23/eng/20221108
LC record available at https://lccn.loc.gov/2022046392

British Library Cataloging-in-Publication Data is available

Front cover: *La Musica Red Parkway, Josephine*, 2007 (detail). Bronze with red patina and silk. 72⅞ × 49 × 19 inches (480.1 × 91.8 × 61.6 cm). Private collection

All unidentified installation views are from the exhibition *Barbara Chase-Riboud Monumentale: The Bronzes*, Pulitzer Arts Foundation, St. Louis, September 16, 2022–February 5, 2023

10 9 8 7 6 5 4 3 2 1

Produced by Marquand Books, Seattle
marquandbooks.com
Editor: Donna Wingate
Copyeditor: Susan Higman Larsen
Publication Coordinator: Brittny Koskela
Proofreader: Jane Hyun
Designer: Ryan Polich
Typesetter: Tina Henderson
Color management: I/O Color, Seattle
Printed and bound in China by Artron Art Group

Image Credits

Frontispiece: Photo by Virginia Harold
Pg. 15, fig. 1: Photo by Robert Bayer. © Succession Alberto Giacometti / Artists Rights Society (ARS), NY
Pg. 16, fig. 2: Courtesy Fondation Giacometti, Paris
Pg. 17, fig. 4: © René Burri / Magnum Photos
Pg. 18: Courtesy Fondation Giacometti, Paris
Pg. 20, fig. 9: Courtesy The Newark Museum of Art
Pg. 20, fig. 10: Courtesy Philadelphia Museum of Art
Pg. 21, fig. 11: Courtesy Minneapolis Institute of Art
Pg. 22, fig. 13: Courtesy University of California, Berkeley Art Museum and Pacific Film Archive
Pg. 23, fig. 14: © Copyright Lee Bontecou, 2023.
Pg. 23, fig. 15: Courtesy Smithsonian American Art Museum, Washington, DC / Art Resource, NY
Pg. 24, fig. 16: Courtesy Nanjing Museum, Jiangsu
Pg. 27: Photo by Carol M. Highsmith Photography
Pgs. 34, 37, 38: Digital Images © The Museum of Modern Art / Licensed by SCALA / Art Resource, NY
Pg. 44: Courtesy Fondation Giacometti, Paris
Pg. 45, fig. 3: © René Burri / Magnum Photos
Pgs. 56, 61, 62: © The Museum of Modern Art / Licensed by SCALA / Art Resource, NY
Pg. 120, left: Philadelphia Museum of Art / Art Resource, NY; right: Image copyright © The Metropolitan Museum of Art. Image source: Art Resource, NY
Pg. 148: © René Burri / Magnum Photos
Pg. 150: © Martine Franck / Magnum Photos
Pgs. 159–61: Photos by Virginia Harold
Object Photography by Alise O'Brien: Pgs. 4, 12, 40, 50, 57, 58, 60, 65–97, 101–19, 121, 123–43, and cover photo.